# Freeing the World to Death

## Essays on the American Empire

### William Blum

Common Courage Press          Monroe, Maine

ISBN 1-56751-306-9 paper
ISBN 1-56751- 307-7 cloth

**Library of Congress Cataloging-in-Publication Data is
available on request from the publisher**

Common Courage Press
121 Red Barn Road
Monroe, ME  04951
800-497-3207

FAX (207) 525-3068
orders-info@commoncouragepress.com

www.commoncouragepress.com

Printed in Canada
**First Printing**

Do American leaders understand that terrorism against their country and its citizens is largely in reaction to their aggressive and violent foreign policy, or do they genuinely not know why the United States is so hated? Here are two answers:

Former president Jimmy Carter:

> We sent Marines into Lebanon and you only have to go to Lebanon, to Syria or to Jordan to witness first-hand the intense hatred among many people for the United States because we bombed and shelled and unmercifully killed totally innocent villagers—women and children and farmers and housewives—in those villages around Beirut....As a result of that...we became kind of a Satan in the minds of those who are deeply resentful. That is what precipitated the taking of our hostages and that is what has precipitated some of the terrorist attacks.[1]

Secretary of State Colin Powell, writing of what preceded the 1983 attack on the US Marine barracks in Lebanon:

> The USS New Jersey started hurling 16-inch shells into the mountains above Beirut, in World War II style, as if we were softening up the beaches on some Pacific atoll prior to an invasion. What we tend to overlook in such situations is that other people will react much as we would.[2]

The ensuing terrorist attack against US Marine barracks in Lebanon took the lives of 241 American military personnel.

# Contents

## The Cold War

## The Empire at Home

# Introduction

Question: What does American foreign policy have in common with Mae West?

There's the story told about the Hollywood sexpot showing off her luxurious home to someone. "My goodness, what a gorgeous home you have," exclaimed the visitor. And Mae West replied: "Goodness had nothing to do with it."

Which is what I try to make people understand about American foreign policy. The greatest myth concerning those policies, the conviction that most often makes it a formidable task for people like myself to get Americans to accept certain ideas, is the deeply-held belief that no matter what the United States does abroad, no matter how bad it may look, no matter what horror may result, the American government means well. American leaders may make mistakes, they may blunder, they may even on the odd occasion cause more harm than good, but *they do mean well.* Their intentions are always honorable. Of that Americans are certain. They genuinely wonder why the rest of the world can't see how kind and generous and self-sacrificing America has been. Even many people who take part in the anti-war movement have a hard time shaking off some of this mindset; they think, or would like to think, that the government just needs to be prodded back to its normal benevolent self.

Frances Fitzgerald, in her study of American history textbooks, observed that "According to these books, the United States had been a kind of Salvation Army to the rest of the world: throughout history, it had done little but dispense benefits to poor, ignorant, and diseased countries....the United States always acted in a disinterested fashion, always from the highest of motives; it gave, never took."[1]

Amongst developed nations, the United States is easily the most religious, more so even than most Third World countries, and many American citizens look upon their country in an almost sacred manner...chosen people, divine purpose, Manifest Destiny, missionaries; while its enemies dwell in the other realm, of the devil, "evil empire", "axis of evil". Rudy Giuliani, mayor of New York at the time of the September 11, 2001 attack, delivered his farewell speech in a church close to the site of Ground Zero, declaring: "Abraham Lincoln used to say that...The test of your Americanism was how much you believed in America. Because we're like a religion really—secular religion."[2]

A question that continually intrigues and perplexes those who long for the world to make sense and have feelings is this: Do American leaders really believe the utterances that emanate from their mouths? When the words "god" and "prayer" are regularly invoked in their talks, while American Hellfire missiles are sent screaming into a city center or a village marketplace teeming with life...when they carry on endlessly about democracy and freedom, while American soldiers are smashing down doors, dragging off the men, humiliating the women, traumatizing the children...when they proclaim the liberation of a people and the bringing forth of a better life, while vast quantities of American depleted uranium are exploding into a fine vapor which will poison the air, the soil, the blood, and the genes forever...

Do American leaders personally dwell on these contradictions? Do they even see them as contradictions? What emotional mechanism allows them to make peace with what they do so as to be able to live with themselves?

We'll never know for sure what their moral intuition whispers when they're sitting alone at midnight, but whatever it is, for them to have reached their high positions they had to resolve any ethical dilemmas long before, learning to summon up some comfortable dogma about "the greater good" or, as Theodore Roosevelt put it:

It is indeed a warped, perverse, and silly morality which would forbid a course of conquest that has turned whole continents into the seats of mighty and flourishing civilized nations. All men of sane and wholesome thought must dismiss with impatient contempt the plea that these continents should be reserved for the use of scattered savage tribes, whose life was but a few degrees less meaningless, squalid, and ferocious than that of the wild beasts with whom they hold joint ownership.[3]

If American leaders sincerely believe what they tell the world about the purity of America's motives, it can be justly maintained that they are as fanatic and as fundamentalist as Osama Bin Laden and his ilk. Can you argue with an Islamic fundamentalist about the morality of what he advocates? He'll insist that Allah is on his side, you're Satan, and you hate Islam. Can you argue with George Bush, Dick Cheney, Donald Rumsfeld or their acolytes about the morality of their policies? They'll insist that the Lord is on their side, you're soft on terrorism, and you hate America. We can say that the United States runs the world like the Taliban ran Afghanistan. Cuba is dealt with like a woman caught outside not wearing her *burkha*. Horrific sanctions are imposed on Iraq in the manner of banning music, dancing, and kite-flying in Kabul. Jean-Bertrand Aristide is banished from Haiti like the religious police whipping a man whose beard is not the right length.

For some Americans, belief in the nobility of US foreign policy may have taken a kick in the stomach by the release of the photos in the spring of 2004 showing abuse and torture of Iraqi prisoners, but for most a lifetime of inculcated loyalty, faith, and conviction does not crumble without a great deal of resistance. Such people should be asked this question: "What would the United States have to do in its foreign policy that would cause you to forsake your basic belief and support of it? In other words, what for you would be *too much?*" Most likely, whatever dreadfulness they might think of, the United States has already done it. More than once. Probably in their own lifetime. And well documented in an easily available publication.

As hateful as the acts depicted in the photos were, the publicizing of them was to be welcomed if it could rally world opinion against United States behavior; if there is no military force capable of beating back the American behemoth, moral condemnation does at least slow it down from time to time. Let the hooded, wired, and faceless man of Abu Ghraib, with arms outstretched like Christ on the cross, become a symbol of, and inspiration for, resistance to American imperialism.

Bush administration officials, like George W. and War Secretary Donald Rumsfeld, looked the American people squarely in the eye and in their most heartfelt-sounding voice told them that the abuse of the detainees in Iraq was completely inappropriate, un-American, and would not be tolerated. But the abuses had been going on for more than a year, complained about regularly by the International Red Cross, Amnesty International, and other human rights groups, and nothing had been done except, after ten months, an investigation, not for public consumption;[4] and when the military learned that CBS had photos of the abuses and was preparing to show them on TV, the chairman of the Joint Chiefs of Staff personally asked the station to hold off, which CBS did until, faced with being scooped, they presented the photos to a shocked America. Thus, for over a year, the imperial mafia could engage in their usual rationalizations, whatever they may be, before they were forced to go public with the appropriate platitudes.

This is written in June 2004, in the midst of the United States presidential election campaign. Millions of Americans, regardless of what they think of the Democratic Party candidate, are determined to vote for Anyone But Bush, so loathsome and repellent have the man and his policies become for them. They are convinced that the Bush administration is virtually unique in the manner in which it relates to the world; that no previous American government has ever exhibited such hubris, deceit, and secrecy; such murderous destruction, violation of international law, and disregard of world opinion.

They are mistaken. All this wickedness has been exhibited before, regularly; if not packed quite as densely in one administration as under Bush, then certainly abundant enough to reap the abhorrence of millions at home and abroad. From Truman's atom bomb and manipulation of the UN that spawned bloody American warfare in Korea, to Clinton's war crimes in Yugoslavia and vicious assaults upon the people of Somalia; from Kennedy's attempts to strangle the Cuban revolution and his abandonment of democracy in the Dominican Republic, to Ford's giving the okay to Indonesia's genocide against East Timor and his support of the instigation of the horrific Angola civil war; from Eisenhower's overthrow of democratically elected governments in Iran, Guatemala and the Congo and his unprincipled policies which led to the disaster known as Vietnam, to Reagan's tragic Afghanistan venture and unprovoked invasion of Grenada.

When the United Nations overwhelmingly voted its disapproval of the Grenada invasion, President Reagan responded: "One hundred nations in the UN have not agreed with us on just about everything that's come before them where we're involved, and it didn't upset my breakfast at all."[5] George W. couldn't have said it better.

For those who think the United States has been unconscionably brutal to detainees in Iraq, here's how the US handled them during Vietnam: "Two Vietcong prisoners were interrogated on an airplane flying toward Saigon. The first refused to answer questions and was thrown out of the airplane at 3,000 feet. The second immediately answered all the questions. But he, too, was thrown out."[6]

It would be difficult to find a remark made today by an American official about Iraq—illogical, arrogant, stupid, lying,

Orwellian, overblown, just plain wrong—which doesn't have any number of precedents during the Vietnam War period, that constantly had those opposed to that war shaking their heads or rolling their eyes.

Here is President Lyndon B. Johnson, 1966: "The exercise of power in this century has meant for all of us in the United States not arrogance but agony. We have used our power not willingly and recklessly ever, but always reluctantly and with restraint."[7]

Richard Nixon, waiting in the wings, 1965: "Victory for the Vietcong...would mean ultimately the destruction of freedom of speech for all men for all time not only in Asia but in the United States as well."[8]

Walt Rostow, State Department, Chairman, Policy Planning Council, 1965: "The other side is near collapse. In my opinion, victory is very near....You've got to see the latest charts. I've got them right here. The charts are very good....Victory is very near."[9]

Vice President Hubert Humphrey, 1967: "I believe that Vietnam will be marked as the place where the family of man has gained the time it needed to finally break through to a new era of hope and human development and justice. This is the chance we have. This is our great adventure—and a wonderful one it is."[10]

And on a day in July 1965, Arthur Sylvester, Assistant Secretary of Defense for Public Affairs, told American journalists that they had a patriotic duty to disseminate only information that made the United States look good. When one of the newsmen exclaimed, "Surely, Arthur, you don't expect the American press to be handmaidens of government," Sylvester responded, "That's exactly what I expect." Sylvester then replied to another question with: "Look, if you think any American official is going to tell you the truth, then you're stupid. Did you hear that?—stupid."[11]

This last of course does at least have the virtue of honesty.

Does anything done by the Bush administration compare to Operation Gladio? From 1947 until 1990, when it was publicly exposed, Gladio was essentially a CIA/NATO/MI6 operation in conjunction with other intelligence agencies and an assortment of the vilest of right-wing thugs and terrorists. It ran wild in virtually every country of Western Europe, kidnapping and/or assassinating political leaders, exploding bombs in trains and public squares with many hundreds of dead and wounded, shooting up supermarkets with many casualties, trying to overthrow governments...all with impunity, protected by the most powerful military and political forces in the world. Even today, the beast may still be breathing. Since the inception of the Freedom of Information Act in the 1970s, the CIA has regularly refused requests concerning the US/NATO role in Gladio, refusing not only individual researchers and the National Security Archive—the private research organization in Washington with a remarkable record of obtaining US government documents—but some of the governments involved, including Italy and Austria. Gladio is one of the CIA's family jewels, to be guarded as such.

The rationale behind it was your standard cold-war paranoia/propaganda: There's a good chance the Russians will launch an unprovoked invasion of Western Europe. And if they defeated the Western armies and forced them to flee, certain people had to remain behind to harass the Russians with guerrilla warfare and sabotage, and act as liaisons with those abroad. The "stay-behinds" would be provided with funds, weapons, communication equipment and training exercises.

As matters turned out, in the complete absence of any Russian invasion, the operation was used almost exclusively to inflict political and lethal damage upon the European Left, be it individuals, movements or governments, and heighten the public's fear of "communism". To that end, violent actions like those referred to above were made to appear to be the work of the Left.[12]

Neither did the Bush administration invent the American Empire and its schoolyard-bully behavior. An Empire can be defined as a state that has overwhelming superiority in military, economic and political power, and uses those powers to influence the internal and external behavior of other states to accommodate the empire's needs. This imperial power intrinsically includes the ability to overthrow or otherwise punish those governments which seek to thwart the empire's desires.

Does this not aptly describe the power and policies of American foreign policy for many decades, for a century, before the Bush administration came to be? It was long said in Latin America that the United States could instigate or discourage a coup with "a frown". In 1965 it was reported that the military coup ousting Dominican Republic President Juan Bosch went into action "as soon as they got a wink from the U.S. Pentagon."[13] As long ago as 1902, Colombia's Ambassador to the US, José Vicente Concha, writing about the pressure put on him by the United States regarding the building of the Panama Canal, said: "This uncle of ours can settle it all with a single crunch of his jaws."[14]

Frown, wink, crunch of jaws...and if facial actions didn't do the job, then a carefully chosen word or two, or money without end, or weapons of the chemical dust would. The reader is directed to chapter 15 for a list of 35 governments overthrown by the United States following World War II but prior to the Bush administration, in addition to 19 other serious attempts at regime change in the same period which didn't succeed.

Here are the words of former US Senator William Fulbright:

> The causes of the malady are not entirely clear but its recurrence is one of the uniformities of history: power tends to confuse itself with virtue and a great nation is peculiarly susceptible to the idea that its power is a sign of God's favor, conferring upon it a special responsibility for

other nations—to make them richer and happier and wiser, to remake them, that is, in its own shining image.[15]

Fulbright wrote those words about the Lyndon B. Johnson administration in 1966, not the George W. Bush administration in 2004.

Since the early 19th century, when the first European settlers began arriving in what was to become the western states of the United States of America, this has been an imperial nation, a conquering nation; annihilation of natives, acquisition, expansion, a society made safe for the freest of enterprise; belief in American "exceptionalism", a people providentially exempted from the dark side of human nature; all this in the American blood, the nation's myths, its songs, its national character.

The Monroe Doctrine of 1823 gave fair warning: "The American continents...are henceforth not to be considered as subjects for future colonization by any European powers....we should consider an attempt on their part to extend their system to any portion of this hemisphere as dangerous to our peace and safety." Add a word about "terrorists" and it could have been penned by Condoleezza Rice. The door was of course left open to hemispheric colonization or neo-colonization by the United States.

In the war with Mexico, beginning in 1846, the US went yet further; not simply colonization, but the wholesale incorporation of half of Mexico into the new Yankee land; a war that excited Congress, which approved it overwhelmingly with minimal discussion, and the American people, who rallied and rushed to volunteer for the splendid expedition. In December 1845, the editor of a New York daily had written of "our manifest destiny to overspread and to possess the whole of the continent which Providence has given us for the development of the great experiment of liberty and federated self-government entrusted to us."[16]

By the end of the century, when grandiose North American growth opportunities were thinning and new markets were needed, Washington heeded the siren's call to become a player in the global scene. Using the pretext that Spain was responsible for the blowing up of the USS *Maine*, it went to war and replaced the Spanish as the colonial power in the Philippines, Guam and Puerto Rico, and devised a special status for Cuba.

In the summer of 1898, a vigorous struggle began in the United States between imperialists and anti-imperialists concerning the Philippines and its people who were fighting against the American plan to subjugate them. Talk of empire, of the United States assuming a leading role in world politics, was a heady intoxicant that few could resist. The future liberal Supreme Court justice, Oliver Wendell Holmes, Jr., declared "I confess to pleasure in hearing some rattling jingo talk after the self-righteous and preaching discourse" of the anti-imperialists.[17]

The stage was now set for what *Time* magazine publisher Henry Lucewas later to call The American Century. Looking at it from the perspective of the consequences of American foreign policy, it was a century of wide-ranging domination and cruelty. A study by the Congressional Research Service of the Library of Congress, "Instances of Use of United States Armed Forces Abroad, 1798-1945", shows 65 such instances from 1900 to 1945, to which books by this author add, for the period 1945 to 2000, about eighty other very serious US interventions—military, economic, and/or diplomatic—into the affairs of foreign countries.[18]

What most of the countries on the receiving end of 20th century American imperialism had in common was their attempt to establish a society that offered an alternative to the capitalist model. In the eyes of Washington, this was the ultimate heresy, as it remains today. Such an endeavor had to be crushed, by any means necessary, lest it wind up serving as an example for others. Other targeted countries, while retaining free enterprise to one degree or another, were reluctant to allow the needs of American corporations to dictate their society's priorities; i.e., they were unwilling to permit the WTO/IMF/World Bank/free-trade beast to stomp in and privatize and sell the country's social assets to multinationals, to deregulate, erase their border, drive local industries and farmers into destitution, trash social services and safety nets, develop a cheap labor force, cheap raw materials, and a market for corporate goods, and put people in prison so prices could be free[19]...by now a painfully familiar syndrome known as "globalization", merely the latest transmutation of imperialism, the natural extension of capitalist growth and control; for some years ago, while we were all busy leading our little daily lives, a handful of corporations came along, and step by step, unannounced, purchased the world, then hung a sign out saying "Open for business", and have since then, understandably, insisted on exercising the rights of ownership. Globalization is nothing less than the recolonization of the underdeveloped world.

One of the problems in dealing with fanatics is their fanaticism.

It may be that George W. Bush's being held in such low esteem and producing visceral disgust in countless people owes as much to his character defects as to his policies, for the man comes off as woefully crass, uninformed, incurious, and inarticulate; as well as programmed, insufferably religious, dishonest, and remarkably insensitive—in the very midst of the burgeoning scandal about US military torture and sexual abuse of prisoners in Iraq, for example, Bush could bring himself to tell an audience: "The world is better off without Saddam Hussein in power....Because we acted, torture rooms are closed, rape rooms no longer exist."[20]

What has distinguished the Bush administration's foreign

policy from that of its predecessors has been its unabashed and conspicuously overt expressions of its imperial ambitions. They flaunt it, publicly and proudly declaring their intention—nay, their God-inspired *right and obligation*—to remake the world and dominate space; "full-spectrum dominance", a term coined by the military shortly before Bush came to office, well captures the Bush administration's style and ambition. The neo-conservatives who form the ideological backbone of the administration have not hesitated to put their dominance master plans into print on a regular basis, beginning with their now-famous 1992 Defense Planning Guidance draft: "we must maintain the mechanisms for deterring potential competitors from even *aspiring* to a larger regional or global role,"[21] and continuing through the National Security Strategy of 2002: "To forestall or prevent...hostile acts by our adversaries, the United States will, if necessary, act preemptively."

"Preemptive" military action is an example of what the post-World War II International Military Tribunal at Nuremberg, Germany called "a war of aggression"; the invasion of Poland was a case in point.

> We must make clear to the Germans that the wrong for which their fallen leaders are on trial is not that they lost the war, but that they started it. And we must not allow ourselves to be drawn into a trial of the causes of the war, for our position is that no grievances or policies will justify resort to aggressive war. It is utterly renounced and condemned as an instrument of policy.

Thus spoke Supreme Court Justice Robert L. Jackson, Chief US Prosecutor at the Tribunal, on August 12, 1945.[22]

On October 1 of the following year, the Tribunal handed down its judgment: "To initiate a war of aggression, therefore, is not only an international crime, it is the supreme international crime, differing only from other war crimes in that it contains within itself the accumulated evil of the whole."

The bombing and invasion of Afghanistan and Iraq by the Bush administration are wars of aggression and international crimes, but legally and morally no worse than many other US bombings and invasions, such as against Vietnam, Laos, Cambodia, Cuba, Grenada, Panama, and Yugoslavia.

"In politics, as on the sickbed, people toss from one side to the other, thinking they will be more comfortable." Johann Wolfgang von Goethe.

> An Amtrak train on its way to Washington was stopped in Cumberland, Md., for several hours and searched yesterday after passengers reported that two men of 'Middle Eastern descent' were acting suspiciously, the FBI said.[23]

We've been reading similar stories for three years now, involving trains, planes, buses, anywhere, anytime. In between we have Alerts Orange and Red, scary bioterrorism exercises, security precautions for major events reaching the outlandish proportions of a Hollywood thriller, and a host of other gross disruptions, inconveniences, and absurdities. We take our shoes off, empty our pockets, drop our pants, show our picture ID, show it again 20 feet away, whatever some bored hired hand gets a kick out of demanding, don't even think about making a joke. Much worse than any of this of course happens regularly to people all over the country, many of whom are imprisoned, without charges, without hope.

How long will this indignity to persons and the Constitution go on? Why, as long as the War on Terrorism goes on. And how long will the War on Terrorism go on? As long as there are anti-American terrorists out there of course. And how long will there be anti-American terrorists out there? Well, as long as the War on Terrorism and the rest of US foreign policy continue serving as factories for mass producing anti-American terrorists and laboratories for cultivating the terrorism virus. (See chapter 2 for a discussion of this paradigm.)

This book, dear reader, is a collection of essays written in recent years, some of which were published in various magazines (print and online) or in anthologies; some appeared in my occasional Internet newsletters (mostly under the name "The Anti-Empire Report"); some appeared only on my website, while others were written or modified explicitly for this book. My apologies that the varying times and locations of the essays have made some repetition of bits and pieces unavoidable.

## CHAPTER ONE

# The Anti-Empire Report

## Some Things You Need to Know Before the World Ends

### July 14, 2004

### How can we leave Iraq?

Those of us who call for the withdrawal of American troops from Iraq are usually met with some variation on the theme of "But we can't just leave!" Or "How can we just leave?" Which is what protesters were asked repeatedly during the Vietnam War, and to which we replied: "Well, you put some of the troops on ships and sail away, others you put into planes and *fly* away. What could be simpler?"...until American troops finally did leave, several years and hundreds of thousands of deaths, American and Vietnamese, later.

Theodore H. White, in his book, *In Search of History*, expressed his belief that President Kennedy would have pulled all American armed forces out of Vietnam after the 1964 election. He quotes a Kennedy aide who asked the president how he would do that. "Easy," quipped JFK. "Put in a government that will ask us to leave."

It appears that the Bush administration has now installed a government in Iraq to ask the United States to *stay*. Last month Iraq's new interim prime minister and former CIA asset, Ayad Allawi, formally invited US troops to remain in Iraq. Secretary of State Colin Powell then announced that Allawi had sent a letter outlining the terms under which he would agree to the presence of US-led coalition forces in Iraq. (He was of course in no position to drive any kind of hard bargain.) Powell said he would respond in a letter "in a positive vein" to Allawi's proposal.

Boy, that was a cliff-hanger.

Powell added that it was planned that Allawi's letter and Powell's response to it would form annexes to the UN resolution endorsing the transfer of sovereignty in Iraq.[1] They make it all sound so neat, so nice and legal, so open and spontaneous.

In the same vein, we have Hamid Karzai, the Washington-appointed president of Afghanistan. The conservative *Washington Times*, in a large page-one headline on June 16, treated the world to this bit of astounding news: "Karzai lauds US war on terrorism."

## I thought it was all Greek to him

Maybe Georgie W. is not as unlettered as he appears to be. Or perhaps it's one of his speech writers who has read Thucydides' *The History of the Poleponnesian War*, and the words of the Corinthians: "Do not delay, fellow-allies, but convinced of the necessity of the crisis, and the wisdom of our advice, vote for the war, undeterred by its immediate terrors, but looking beyond to the lasting peace by which it will be succeeded. War makes peace more secure." That was four centuries before Christ, the war lasting 27 years. Imagine how the ancient defense contractors must have cleaned up, like old Halliburtonakis led by Cheneyopoulos.

## Ronnie forgot all this, but we shouldn't

It's not too late is it, to pay a few more respects to Ronald Reagan? Here are a few items dug out from my files.

Reagan's excuses during L'affaire Contragate, also known as L'affaire Irangate, a paraphrased summary:

I didn't know what was happening.

If I did know, I didn't know enough.

If I knew enough, I didn't know it in time.

If I knew it in time, it wasn't illegal.

It it was illegal, the law didn't apply to me.

If the law applied to me, I didn't know what was happening.

Margaret Thatcher had this to say about her supposed great friend Ronnie: "Poor dear, there's nothing between his ears."[2]

In 1984, Reagan spoke to a group of American newspaper editors about possibly limiting a nuclear war to Europe, without a single one of them regarding it as newsworthy. The fuss about his remarks only came after a European reporter had read the transcript. This of course says as much about American newspaper editors as it does about Reagan.[3]

## Tradition ain't what it used to be

"This is a terrible thing," said Ali Hashim, 33, a shoe salesman in downtown Baghdad. "Hostage-taking, beheading ... it's not our tradition. We have a tradition of hospitality. This hurts the image of the Iraqi people."[4]

Imagine an American saying: "This is a terrible thing. Bombings, invasions, overthrowing governments, torture ... it's not our tradition. We have a tradition of peaceful solutions to conflicts with other countries and respect for international law. This hurts the image of the American people."

## Our bodies, ourselves

The upcoming Olympics has put the testing of athletes for drugs in the spotlight once again. And once again it raises this question in my mind: Presumably "drugs" are banned because they give an athlete an unfair advantage over athletes who are "clean." But of all the things that athletes, and other people, put into their bodies to improve their health, fitness and perform-

ance, why are drugs singled out? Doesn't taking vitamins give an
athlete an unfair advantage over athletes who don't take them?
Shouldn't vitamins be banned from sport competition? How
about various food supplements, for the same reason? Vitamins
and food supplements are often not any more "natural" than
drugs. Why not ban those who follow a healthy diet because of
the advantage this may give them? My questions are serious and
I'd welcome some feedback.

## And one on militarism?

The US State Department issues annual reports on the
countries of the world rating their performance in various cate-
gories. There are separate reports dealing with religious freedom, the war on terrorism, human rights, the war on drugs, and
trafficking in persons. What I'd like to see now is some government in the world issue a report rating countries on self-right-
eousness and arrogance.

## Something to keep in mind
## for a future US bombing

In April 1986, during the US bombing of Libya, the
French Embassy, located in a residential district, was destroyed.
This, after the French had refused to grant flyover rights to
American planes on their way to Libya.

In May 1999, during the US bombing of Belgrade, the
Chinese Embassy was hit, causing considerable damage and the
death of three people inside the embassy. An investigation by
*The Observer* of London revealed that the bombing was deliberate.[5]

In April 2003, US bombs dropped on Iraq found their way
to the Soviet embassy in Baghdad several times. The Russians
were suspicious enough to summon the US ambassador to the
Foreign Ministry. The Soviet embassy was also located in a residential district.[6]

May 12, 2004

# God, country and torture

On October 21, 1994, the United States became a State Party
to the "Convention Against Torture and Other Cruel, Inhuman
or Degrading Treatment or Punishment". Article 2, section 2 of
the Convention states: "No exceptional circumstances whatso-
ever, whether a state of war or a threat of war, internal political
instability or any other public emergency, may be invoked as a
justification for torture."

"If you open the window [of torture], even just a crack, the
cold air of the middle ages will fill the whole room."[7]

"The thing with the soldiers there, they think because
we're Americans, you can do whatever you want," said Spc.
Ramon Leal, an MP who served at Abu Ghraib prison in Iraq.

"You get a burning in your stomach, a rush, a feeling of hot
lead running through your veins, and you get a sense of power,"
said another soldier. "Imagine wearing point-blank body armor,
an M-16 and all the power in the world, and the authority of
God. That power is very addictive."[8]

America and God...Bush, Cheney, Rice, and other emi-
nences of the imperial mafia know well how to invoke these
feelings; with the help of the rest of flag-wavin' and bible-
wavin' America the proper emotions can be easily imparted
down to the ranks. The American part—the mystique of
"America"—can also be exported, and has been for decades.
Here's Chief Inspector Basil Lambrou, one of Athens' well-
known torturers under the infamous Greek junta of 1967-74.
Hundreds of prisoners listened to this little speech given by the
Inspector, who sat behind his desk which displayed the red,
white, and blue clasped-hand symbol of American aid. He tried
to show the prisoners the absolute futility of resistance: "You
make yourself ridiculous by thinking you can do anything. The
world is divided in two. There are the communists on that side

and on this side the free world. The Russians and the Americans, no one else. What are we? Americans. Behind me there is the government, behind the government is NATO, behind NATO is the U.S. You can't fight us, we are Americans."[9]

And here's Colin Powell at the 1996 Republican Convention: America is "a country where the best is always yet to come, a country that exists by divine providence." He then punched his fist into the air and shouted out, "America!"[10]

Defenders of the American soldiers accused of abusing the prisoners in Iraq have been insisting that the soldiers were only following orders. At the end of the Second World War, however, we read moral lectures to the German people on the inadmissibility of pleading that their participation in the Holocaust was in obedience to their legitimate government. To prove that we were serious, we hanged the leading examples of such patriotic loyalty and imprisoned many of the rest.

Said the International Military Tribunal: "The very essence of the Charter is that individuals have international duties which transcend the national obligations of obedience imposed by the individual state. He who violates the laws of war cannot obtain immunity while acting in pursuance of the authority of the state if the state in authorising action moves outside its competence under international law....The fact that the Defendant acted pursuant to order of his Government or of a superior shall not free him from responsibility, but may be considered in mitigation of punishment."[11]

## Cold War Redux

On May 11, the Senate Armed Services Committee held a hearing on Iraqi prisoner abuse, during which Senator James Inhofe (R.-OK) stated the following: "I have to say when we talk about the treatment of these prisoners that I would guess that these prisoners wake up every morning thanking Allah that Saddam Hussein is not in charge of these prisons. When he was in charge, they would take electric drills and drill holes through hands, they would cut their tongues out, they would cut their ears off. We've seen accounts of lowering their bodies into vats of acid....and lining up 312 little kids under 12 years old and executing them."

What does that remind you of? Right, the October 1990 testimony before a congressional committee by a young Kuwaiti woman who claimed she had witnessed Iraqi soldiers taking babies from incubators in Kuwait after Iraq had invaded and "leaving them on the floor to die". The story was quickly used by the Bush I administration in its push for war. The president on a number of occasions cited the infants' deaths as an example of what he said was Iraq's brutal treatment of innocent Kuwaitis. It turned out to be a hoax, unmitigated war propaganda, and the young woman turned out to be the daughter of the Kuwaiti ambassador to the United States. And the number of babies supposedly left to die? 312.[12]

The same day as the hearing a letter was printed in *The Washington Post* which spoke of "applying electric shocks, pulling out fingernails, crushing feet, or raping a loved one's wife, daughter or mother while forcing him to watch—all of which were practices employed by Saddam Hussein's henchmen."

And a while ago I received an email from one of my non-admirers who added to the list with "Children's eyes gouged out to elicit confessions from a parent; people having their tongues cut out and then left to bleed to death on streets; live bodies thrown into large mince machines."

What do we have here? A campaign highly reminiscent of the many anti-communist horror stories—torture and otherwise—that during the Cold War days of the 1950s-60s were passed around the anti-communist circuit, each person quoting from the same initial source, or the previous source. At some point a member of congress would read the horror story on the floor of congress and his remarks would thus appear in the *Congressional Record*; thereafter, those passing the story around could quote the *Congressional Record* as the source, as Senator Inhofe's statement can now be quoted citing a Senate hearing.[13]

I wrote to the non-admirer asking her what evidence she could offer to substantiate her claims. We then exchanged a few more emails but she had nothing at all to offer, quoting at one point something from a report of Amnesty International which made no mention of the subject at hand.

At the hearing, Sen. Inhofe added that if we're going to show pictures of American soldiers abusing prisoners at Abu Ghraib, we should also show pictures of the brutalities of Saddam Hussein, including those of "children being executed". It will be interesting to see if the good senator can produce such photos; perhaps of all 312?

## Brainwashed commies

George W. Bush, speaking in October 2003 after many resistance attacks in Iraq: "The more successful we are on the ground, the more these killers will react."[14]

Gen. Richard B. Myers, chairman of the Joint Chiefs of Staff, speaking in April 2004, depicted the insurrection and fighting that had risen over nearly a two-week period in an equally positive light. "'I would characterize what we're seeing right now as a—as more a symptom of the success that we're having here in Iraq,' he said...explaining that the violence indicated there was something to fight against—American progress in building up Iraq."[15]

Imagine that in the 1980s Russian leaders had used identical logic and language about how their war against Afghanistan insurgents was going for them. The American media would have had a field day of snide remarks about those poor brainwashed, Orwellian commies.

## Ungrateful Iraqis, befuddled Americans

"Another Marine, his face flushed with anger, approached an interpreter on the base and said: 'I just want to know why my friends are being hurt. Don't the Iraqis know we are here to help them build something new and better now that Saddam is gone?'"[16]

Yes, they know that. They just don't believe it.

Apropos of this, Hans Blix, the former UN weapons inspector in Iraq, recently claimed that Iraq was now worse off than under Saddam Hussein. "Saddam and his bloody regime has gone, but when figuring out the score the negatives weigh more," he said.[17]

## What songs are the Iraqis singing?

On February 17, 2003, a month before the US bombing began, I posted to the Internet an essay entitled "What Do the Imperial Mafia Really Want?" [see chapter 4], concerning the expected war against Iraq. Included in this were the words of Michael Ledeen, former Reagan official, then at the American Enterprise Institute, one of the leading drum-beaters for attacking Iraq: "If we just let our own vision of the world go forth, and we embrace it entirely, and we don't try to be clever and piece together clever diplomatic solutions to this thing, but just wage a total war against these tyrants, I think we will do very well, and our children will sing great songs about us years from now."

I could not resist. I recently sent Mr. Ledeen an email reminding him of his words and saying simply: "I'd like to ask you what songs your children are singing these days."

I received no reply.

Has there ever been an empire that didn't tell itself and the world that it was unlike all other empires, that its mission was not to plunder and control but to enlighten and liberate?

## More feet of clay

Former counter-terrorism official Richard Clarke was the fair- haired boy in March and April as a result of his testimony before the independent September 11 committee. To a multitude of Americans starved for inspirational and credible leadership he appeared to be the only official in the foreign policy establishment who took the pre-September 11 warnings seriously, who was open and honest, and who had the decency to say he was "sorry" to the families of the victims.

But in this sad day and age can such an image hold up once we look over a person's record? In 1999 the *Washington Post* reported that "Current and former administration foreign policy officials have identified Richard A. Clarke, the National Security Council's counter-terrorism coordinator, as the leading proponent for striking el Shifa."[18] This was a reference to the pharmaceutical plant in Sudan that the Clinton administration had deliberately destroyed the previous year in the stated belief that it was a plant for making chemical weapons for terrorists. In actuality, the plant in Khartoum produced about 90 percent of the drugs used to treat the most deadly illnesses in that desperately poor country; it was reportedly one of the biggest and best of its kind in Africa.

In his new book, *Against All Enemies*, Clarke discusses the Sudan bombing in several places, but in none does he give any indication of his role in the matter, nor does he make any mention at all that the plant was actually producing medicine. Instead he repeats many of the same fallacious arguments about how the plant was really producing chemical weapons, as if these arguments had not been totally discredited since 1998, so much so that when the plant's owner sued the US government, the United States did not even contest the suit, instead returning to him his bank account money that had been frozen. [See chapter 7]

## The Dems pull off another principled coup

On May 8, on his regular weekly radio broadcast, George W. commented about the Iraqi prisoner photos dominating the media at the time. Expecting this, the Democrats planned a counter commentary for that same day on their own radio broadcast. And who did the Democrats choose to discuss this issue of possible violations of the Geneva Conventions? Gen. Wesley Clark, an unindicted war criminal, who led the 1999 bombing of Yugoslavia which seriously violated those conventions amongst other international accords.[see chapter 23]

## Decadence and cruelty

At the peak of the international scandal about American abuse of Iraqi prisoners came the sale in New York of a painting by Picasso for a record $104.2 million. How, I wonder, will the proverbial history books deal with the level of cruelty and decadence of 21st century America?

### April 3, 2004

## A higher purpose

Saturday afternoon, March 6, a shuttle boat moving through Baltimore's Inner Harbor was hit by a sudden and ferocious gust of wind and capsized; 25 people were thrown overboard; some were trapped under the boat; disaster was imminent. But the scene was in sight of a group of sailors stationed at the Naval Reserve Center at Fort McHenry, about 1,000 feet away. They quickly sprung into action. Twenty-five Naval Reservists and career sailors in a combat landing craft arrived at the shuttle within minutes of the accident. The sailors lowered the craft's retractable landing ramp—designed to allow troops to exit the boat in a beach landing—and used it as a lever to lift the capsized vessel. It worked. The maneuver provided enough room to extract the people trapped beneath the boat. Other sailors dived into the water. Almost everyone was saved.[19]

And what thought came to me upon reading the story of this rescue? If only American military forces—who would really rather not study how best to kill—and their superb, costly equipment could be used for life-enhancing purposes all the time, in all corners of the world.

## So it always was, so it always will be

An article in *The Washington Post* of February 20, 1968 on the war in Vietnam included this: "It has never been clearer that the Marines are fighting for their own pride, from their own fear and for their buddies who have already died. No American in Hue is fighting for Vietnam, or against Communism."

Now do the obvious...replace Hue with Fallujah, Vietnam with Iraq, and Communism with terrorism.

## The Israeli lobby

Philip Zelikow is of the type of whom it is customarily said: "He has impeccable establishment credentials". He is currently executive director of the National Commission on Terrorist Attacks Upon the United States, a body created by Congress. Between 2001 and 2003 he served on the president's Foreign Intelligence Advisory Board, which reports directly to the president. Before his appointment to the FIAB he was part of the Bush transition team in January 2001. And in 1995 he co-authored a book with Condoleezza Rice.

It's recently been revealed that in 2002 he publicly stated that a prime motive for the upcoming invasion of Iraq was to eliminate a threat to Israel.

"Why would Iraq attack America or use nuclear weapons against us?" he asked a crowd at the University of Virginia on September 10, 2002. "I'll tell you what I think the real threat (is) and actually has been since 1990—it's the threat against

Israel. And this is the threat that dare not speak its name, because the Europeans don't care deeply about that threat, I will tell you frankly. And the American government doesn't want to lean too hard on it rhetorically, because it is not a popular sell."

And this seems to be the story that dare not speak its name. The story was revealed on March 29 by Inter Press Service, a major international news agency that is mainly published outside the United States. An extensive search of the Lexis-Nexis database revealed that only one English-language news source in the world picked up the story: another news agency, United Press International, on March 30. There thus appears to be no mainstream newspaper or broadcast medium that used it, though many subscribe to UPI. Can anything other than fear of the Israeli lobby account for this?

## I'll bet you never thought of that

On March 25, L. Paul Bremer, the American head of the occupation authority in Iraq, issued an executive order specifying that "All trained elements of the Iraqi armed forces shall at all times be under the operational control of the [American] commander of coalition forces for the purpose of conducting combined operations." The order was not referring simply to the present state of affairs; it was a command for the future, after the alleged return of sovereignty to the Iraqis on June 30.

In regard to the rather obvious and rather sensitive question of whether the Iraqis would stand for this continued American control, a US official in Baghdad had it all figured out: He declared that the Iraqis could hardly claim that Iraq's sovereignty was compromised by having its troops under American command when nations like Britain and Poland had placed military contingents in Iraq under an American general. "There's no sovereignty issue for them," he said.[20]

# Guinea pigs fighting for freedom and democracy

Jessica Horjus, a member of the US Air Force, refused to take the anthrax vaccine before deploying to a base in Kuwait, about 30 miles from Iraq, primarily because no anthrax has been found in Iraq; the vaccine, moreover, is a product that has accumulated thousands of reports of adverse reactions ranging from headaches and vomiting to severe autoimmune and neurological problems. Despite this and despite four years service and commendations and Good Conduct Medals, Horjus' commander demoted her and cut her pay in half.

In February, she declined a second and third order. In March, the young mother accepted the Air Force's offer of an other-than-honorable discharge. Some who have declined the vaccine have been imprisoned; others have been threatened with up to 10 years in prison, more than even rape or drug charges may bring in the military. Soldiers, citizen groups and members of Congress are increasingly calling upon defense officials to stop the vaccinations, which have been declined by numerous members of the armed services. All to no avail.[21]

What lies behind the military's obstinate refusal to bend and its desire to severely punish? Could it be that the Pentagon wants the vaccinations to continue so that statistics can be further compiled and refined about the effects of the vaccine? This would of course be using members of the armed forces as guinea pigs, but this is a practice which has a long tradition in the US military...GIs marched to nuclear explosion sites, subjected to chemical and biological weapons experiments, radiation experiments, behavior modification experiments that washed their brains with LSD, the list goes on...literally millions of experimental subjects, seldom given a choice or adequate information, often with disastrous effects to their physical and/or mental health, rarely with proper medical care or even monitoring.[22]

# What part of "no" don't they understand?

During a visit to the former Soviet republic of Kazakhstan on February 25, US Secretary of War Donald Rumsfeld was moved to declare: "It's interesting when one thinks about the problem of Iraq and their unwillingness to disarm that Kazakhstan stands as an impressive model of how a country can do it."

Rumsfeld's words inspire one to ask again the immortal question: Huh?

Hasn't the man heard yet that Iraq *did* disarm? And rather thoroughly it would appear.

Can we soon expect George W. to once again call upon Iraq to disarm?

"Had Iraq followed the Kazakhstan model after 17 U.N. resolutions and disarmed the way Kazakhstan did, there would not have been a war," Rumsfeld added.[23]

There's no reason to assume that anything short of the Second Coming would have dissuaded the neo-conservative troops from their long-held plans to conquer Iraq, but one still might ask, as supporters of the war have: Why didn't Iraq announce before the invasion that it had no weapons of mass destruction?

There are several answers to this question, the most important one being: They did. Iraqi Deputy Prime Minister Tariq Aziz announced it on at least two occasions on American television. In August 2002 he told Dan Rather: "We do not possess any nuclear or biological or chemical weapons."[24] In December he asserted to Ted Koppel: "The fact is that we don't have weapons of mass destruction. We don't have chemical, biological, or nuclear weaponry."[25]

But in any event, the Bush administration knew perfectly well that Iraq's military capability was nothing to be concerned about at all. Here's Colin Powell, speaking in February 2001 of US sanctions on Iraq: "And frankly they have worked. He

[Saddam Hussein] has not developed any significant capability with respect to weapons of mass destruction. He is unable to project conventional power against his neighbors."[26]

And here is Condoleezza Rice, in July of that year, speaking of Saddam Hussein: "We are able to keep arms from him. His military forces have not been rebuilt."[27]

## Personal responsibility à la America

"A compassionate society is one in which people respect one another, respect their religious views, respect their opinions. It's a society in which people take responsibility for the decisions they make." George W. Bush[28]

It's unclear what taking responsibility for one's decisions has to do with compassion, but the virtue that American society supposedly attaches to such behavior is legendary; many a Western film has revolved around the mystique of personal responsibility.

Thus it is that if people have problems caused by alcohol, owners of liquor stores and distilleries are not arrested.

If people have problems caused by smoking, cigarette vendors and manufacturers are not arrested.

If people have problems caused by obesity, food vendors and food manufacturers are not arrested.

Yet, if people have problems caused by recreational drugs, or even if they don't have problems but use or merely possess the drugs, those associated in any way with making such drugs available to the public are put away by the millions for godawful long times.

No sane person believes in the "war on drugs" any more. This implies of course that a major program of our nation is being directed by madmen. But you knew that.

## Love me, love me, love me, I'm a liberal

You've read about liberals starting their own radio network

to compete with the likes of Rush Limbaugh, Sean Hannity and Bill O'Reilly? When I first read about this I was only mildly enthused because, as I've mentioned before in this report, it's a fallacy to pose liberals as polar opposites to such conservatives. Will the new liberal network be ideologically challenging and tough enough, I wondered. But I was willing to keep an open mind and give them a chance. Then I read of the name of the new network—"Air America". A name intimately associated—indeed, virtually synonymous with—the CIA for more than 50 years, the Agency's principal airline.

It's not broadcast in my area, but I read a report of the station's first day on the air: Michael Moore apologizing to Al Gore for supporting Ralph Nader in 2000. A defense of Janet Reno's response to "terrorism" compared with that of John Ashcroft. (Did someone mention "Waco"?) Janeane Garofalo complaining about the "very vulgar things" said about Bill Clinton. Did they miss anyone in their valentine to the Democratic administration? Hillary Clinton was slated to appear on Day Two.[29]

Air America has the potential to do more harm to the progressive cause than Fox News Channel. Unsophisticated listeners, i.e., most Americans, will listen in and think that THIS is the alternative to what I've been hearing from the likes of Fox or neo-cons, and never imagine the world above and beyond; conservatives need not feel particularly threatened.


### March 10, 2004

## A quaint German custom the United States used to have

On March 4 a German appeals court ordered a new trial for the only person to be convicted for a role in the Sept. 11, 2001 attacks in the United States, saying the proceeding had been compromised by a US refusal to provide access to a key witness.

Defense attorneys for Mounir Motassadeq, a Moroccan citizen, had repeatedly asked for testimony from Ramzi Binalshibh, who is in secret US custody. US officials have called Binalshibh a central conspirator in the attacks but declined to produce him for the trial, citing national security concerns.

The appeals court found that the Hamburg court that had convicted Motassadeq had not adequately considered the implications of the absence of evidence from Binalshibh, resulting in a new trial.

Andreas Schulz, a German lawyer who has represented the families of September 11 victims, said many of his clients were very upset with the ruling. He said he had told them that the decision stemmed from the two countries' contrasting approaches to terrorism—the United States is waging war on it, while Germany is sticking with a courtroom approach.

The German system stresses "fair trial, presumption of innocence and all the values that were designed and generated after World War II," he said. "From the German point of view, it's absolutely [logical] to come up with a decision like the appeals court came up with today."[30]

## Neo-con(tradictions)

Colin Powell showed that he can be a neo-con hardliner just like the rest of the Bushgang. Speaking at the neo-conservative shrine, the Heritage Foundation, on March 2, Powell declared that Asian communism is "withering away." "The share of the economy owned by the government is smaller today in China than it is in France—always an interesting comparison to make."[31] What would be equally interesting would be to compare the standard of living, multiple benefits and labor rights of the average Chinese and French workers. An American worker would not fare too well either in comparison with a French worker. But at least the American and Chinese workers in the private sector have the deep satisfaction of knowing that their work is not tainted by any government ownership.

A new book, scheduled for release in late March, *At the Abyss: An Insider's History of the Cold War*, by Thomas Reed, a member of Ronald Reagan's National Security Council, reveals that Reagan approved a CIA plan to sabotage the economy of the Soviet Union through covert transfers of technology that contained hidden malfunctions, including software that later triggered a huge explosion in a Siberian natural gas pipeline. Reed writes that the pipeline explosion was carried out "in order to disrupt the Soviet gas supply, its hard currency earnings from the West, and the internal Russian economy." This was just one example of "cold-eyed economic warfare" against the Soviet Union that the CIA carried out during the Reagan administration, he writes.

Reagan was perhaps the leading neo-con of his day, often poking fun at the Soviet economic system and how it couldn't compare to the American system. Yet he apparently was not always willing to allow a wholly fair and honest competition between the two systems, preferring to rely on sabotage at times. This of course did not begin with the Reagan administration. The CIA was engaged in all kinds of economic dirty tricks against the Soviet Union and its satellites, particularly East Germany, for decades before Reagan.

## "Human kind cannot bear very much reality."
## —T.S. Eliot

Last year, Libya "accepted responsibility" for the bombing of PanAm flight 103 over Lockerbie, Scotland in 1988. Although a reading of the Libyan statements on the matter made it plain that they were NOT admitting to actually planting the deadly bomb, American and British officials pretended that it was such an admittance; ergo, case closed, the US and the UK had once again seen to it that justice triumphed, Libya will pay compensation to the victims' families, the US will consider lifting sanctions against Libya, everyone happy.

Then, on February 24, Libya's prime minister Shokri Ghanem insisted to the BBC that his government's statements were not an admission of actual guilt. "We thought it was easier for us to buy peace and this is why we agreed to compensation," he said. "Therefore we said: 'Let us buy peace, let us put the whole case behind us and let us look forward'."

Not fair! cried the White House and 10 Downing Street. Libya was not playing the game right. They were cheating. The Bush administration abruptly canceled plans to lift the travel ban and other restrictions on Libya that had been planned (in return for Libya scrapping its nuclear weapons program as well as the Lockerbie issue). "It's important for Libya to retract these statements," said the State Department, "and to make clear what their policy is as soon as possible."

The Libyan prime minister had of course made clear what he thought the truth was, but that was not what the State Department was asking for. They were asking to make the "policy" clear; i.e, Are you still playing the game or not?

The head of the UK families organization declared: "We don't understand the comments by prime minister Ghanem. Nobody knows why he has said this." The fact that Ghanem simply wanted to inject some truth into the matter and clear Libya's name apparently was not an option to be considered.

Then, Libya quickly returned to the game, saying it wanted "to set the record straight and be perfectly clear" about its position on the Lockerbie bombing. Its August 2003 statement of accepting responsibility for the plane bombing was still valid. "Recent statements contradicting or casting doubt on these positions are inaccurate and regrettable," said the Libyan government.

Just as quickly, the State Department, referring to the Libyan statement, announced: "They have done what they needed to do."[32]

## Make him an offer he can't refuse

Statement of Jean-Bertrand Aristide, President of Haiti, March 5, 2004, from exile in the Central African Republic:

"The 28th of February, at night, suddenly, American military personnel who were already all over Port-au-Prince descended on my house in Tabarre to tell me first that all the American security agents who have contracts with the Haitian government [to protect Aristide] only have two options. Either they leave immediately to go to the United States, or they fight to die. Secondly, they told me the remaining 25 of the American security agents hired by the Haitian government who were to come in on the 29th of February as reinforcements were under interdiction, prevented from coming. Thirdly, they told me the foreigners and Haitian terrorists alike, loaded with heavy weapons, were already in position to open fire on Port-au-Prince. And right then, the Americans precisely stated that they will kill thousands of people and it will be a bloodbath. That the attack is ready to start, and when the first bullet is fired nothing will stop them and nothing will make them wait until they take over, therefore the mission is to take me dead or alive....Faced with this tragedy, I decided to ask, 'What guarantee do I have that there will not be a bloodbath if I decided to leave?'

"In reality, all this diplomatic gymnastics did not mean anything because these military men responsible for the kidnapping operation had already assumed the success of their mission. What was said was done. This diplomacy, plus the forced signing of the letter of resignation, was not able to cover the face of the kidnapping."

A search of the Lexis-Nexis database on March 10 failed to turn up any article in an American newspaper or broadcast medium which discussed the contents of Aristide's statement; this despite news of it being carried by the Associated Press. Several papers in Canada and the UK did carry stories about the statement.

Thus it was that Aristide went into exile. And then Colin Powell, in the sincerest voice he could muster, told us that "He was not kidnapped. We did not force him onto the airplane. He went onto the airplane willingly. And that's the truth." Powell sounded as sincere as he had sounded a year earlier when he gave the UN a detailed inventory of the chemical, biological and nuclear weapons in Iraq. He did not explain why the United States did not protect Aristide from the rebels, which the US could have done with the greatest of ease, without so much as firing a single shot. Neither did Powell explain why Aristide would "willingly" give up his presidency.

Despite all the dishonesty surrounding Iraq, I'd guess that most Americans tend to believe Bush officials concerning Haiti because of a couple of reasons. One: Many of the media accounts of the past few months have mentioned that in 1994 the US military returned Aristide to power. That sounds pretty impressive; it indicates that concerning Haiti and Aristide the United States has its heart in the right place. But "the US military returned Aristide to power in 1994" is just the headline. If one reads the story below the headline the picture looks remarkably different. It's simply not the same story any longer. It can be read online.[33]

A second reason the public may support US policy in Haiti is that they've been fed one story after another about Aristide's government being brutal and corrupt and Aristide himself being mentally unstable and largely responsible for the current crisis. That's typical before the US moves to overthrow a foreign government. It's actually rather easy to plant such stories in the media, with or without their cooperation. In 1994, a similar story of Aristide being mentally unstable, a murderer and psychopath, was created and disseminated by a CIA official named Brian Latell, without any evidence to back up the charges.[34]

When a government or an individual becomes an ODE— Officially Designated Enemy—of the United States, one should take everything one hears about that government or person with a very large block of salt.

Of course to Washington officials it wouldn't matter if Aristide were a saint. He's on record as not being a great lover of globalization or capitalism. This is not the kind of man the imperial mafia wanted in charge of the assembly plant of the Western hemisphere. They wanted him out, and out he went.

So in the end, a democratically elected government was overthrown by the combined effort of the United States and France, with the help of Canada. Three of the big boys had something against one of the little boys...and we all know how such things wind up in this world; the way they always have, smooth as can be. And as usual, the rest of the big boys of the world said nothing, not a peep out of the European Union or NATO about this body blow to democracy, a subject they never tire of preaching about. France of course is a member of both.

## Is Cuba to blame?

A thought about another tiny country the world's only superpower just can't leave alone—Cuba. Cubans often complain about the many hardships imposed upon their life by the US blockade. Defenders of US policy reply that this is just an excuse for Cuba's own failings, that the hardships are the inevitable result of a socialist economic system. It makes me think of this analogy. Someone is constantly pounding your head with a hammer and you keep getting headaches. You complain to the wielder of the hammer and demand that he stop hitting you. The guy says to you: The headaches are due to the way you live; blaming me is just an excuse you make up to shirk your own responsibility. You then say to him: Well, why don't you stop hitting me on the head with your hammer so we can see if the headaches go away?

February 17, 2004

# Mushy-thinking liberals

The following is not simply a charge against humorist Al Franken. It's a charge against all mushy-thinking liberals. Franken tells us he is against the war in Iraq. But he was part of a tour that went to Iraq to entertain the troops, truly a feat of intellectual and moral gymnastics that enables him to oppose terrible military violence and crimes against humanity while honoring those who carry out the terrible military violence and crimes against humanity. Would he have condemned the oppression and torture inflicted by General Pinochet while expressing his support of the Chilean troops carrying out the oppression and torture?

The American troops in Iraq do not even have the defense of having been drafted.

Country singer Darryl Worley, who leans "a lot to the right," as he puts it, said he was far from pleased that Franken was coming along on the tour to Iraq. "You know, I just don't understand—why would somebody be on this tour if they're not supportive of the war?"

Franken says that the Bush administration "blew the diplomacy so we didn't have a real coalition." Presumably, if the United States had been more successful in bribing and threatening other countries to lend their name in support of the war Franken would have then seen the splendid beauty of the war effort himself. He also criticizes the administration because they "failed to send enough troops to do the job right", the *Washington Post* reported.[35] What "job" does the man think the troops were sent to do that has not been done up to his standards because of lack of manpower? Does he want them to be more efficient at killing Iraqis who resist the occupation?

Why does the military send performers to entertain the troops? To improve morale, to make the soldiers feel more appreciated. A happier soldier works at his "job" better.

And then we have the case of Michael Moore supporting unindicted war criminal General Wesley Clark for president. God help the American left.

## Why not just tell the truth?

On CNN's "Crossfire" program of January 5 co-host Paul Begala had this exchange with Ralph Nader:

BEGALA: Will you run for president in 2004?

NADER: I'm going to decide later this month. I'm in an exploratory stage, which, under the rules, means that you solicit any indication of advice, fund-raising, volunteers, support. Our Web site is NaderExplore04.organization, for anybody who wants to let us test the waters.

BEGALA: But you're not an indecisive man. And you're generally not thought of as sort of a typical politician, giving weasely answers. Why not just tell the truth? Why not just say, yes, I'm going to run or, no, I'm not? You—I just—frankly, I don't believe that you don't know. I think you have decided and you ought to just tell us.

So there we have it, the cat is out of the bag; mainstream media reporters really DO know that the members of congress and other mainstream politicians they typically interview typically do not give honest, complete, or enlightening answers. And the reporters typically go along with the charade even though they may be as fed up with the ritual as many of the listeners are. It's a tribute to Ralph Nader's integrity and candidness that Begala felt he could press him as he did.

## Son of the Cold War

During the Cold War the policy was called "containment"—surrounding the Soviet Union and its Eastern

European satellites with US military bases and concluding military/economic pacts with the surrounding countries. It made the Soviets highly nervous and paranoid about Washington's intentions, but what could they do about it? Start World War III?

Now, the Soviet Union and the Cold War are extinct, and what do we find? In the past few years, the United States has been setting up one military base after another in the former Soviet republics and satellite countries surrounding Russia, conducting military training and exercises with their new-found allies, setting up electronic communications interception stations, concluding all kinds of agreements with these governments, and prodding many of them to become members of NATO. The Russians have been complaining about this; at times vociferously. As have the Chinese as the US military presence draws closer.

"Look," said Russian president Vladimir Putin about NATO as far back as 2001, "this is a military organization. It's moving towards our border. Why?"[36]

"We are not trying to surround anyone," US Secretary of State Colin Powell told a Moscow radio station during a trip to Russia and Georgia in late January. "The Cold War is over. The Iron Curtain is down. Russia and the United States are now friends, not competitors or potential enemies, and we should not see things in old Cold War terms."

"Are we pointing a dagger in the soft underbelly of Russia?" Powell asked. "Of course not."

A State Department spokesman called the new bases "forward projection points."[37]

## Grandson of the Cold War

Imagine something like this happening in the Soviet Union or East Germany during the Cold War. Would we not have been preached to about the soullessness and mechanical nature of the communist system?

"For Myra Bronstein, the news that she had been laid off from the best job she ever had came on a Friday last May.

"The following week, she was back at work, having been told that if she wanted to receive her full severance package, she would have to train her replacements. They had flown in from India just for the occasion.

"In a tense meeting called by management at telecommunications firm WatchMark Corporation., the Indian workers sat across the table from the approximately 20 Seattle-area employees they would replace. The quality assurance manager stood up and in a very perky way said, 'This is my old staff, and this is my new staff,' said Bronstein, who spent three years at WatchMark testing software. 'The old staff was just trying not to cry'."[38]

## Whatsoever a man soweth ...

There are many ways to look at what the so-called War on Terror has reaped. Consider this:

Many Afghan and other prisoners being held by the United States in Afghanistan and Guantanamo Base, Cuba under conditions intolerable for humans have tried to kill themselves. The same is likely true for prisoners held in Iraq, although not yet reported.

Dozens of American soldiers in Afghanistan and Iraq have attempted suicide, presumably because of the horrible things they've seen and been forced to be part of.

Suicide bombers had not been an Iraqi custom before the American invasion and occupation.

An historical footnote: At least 20,000 Vietnam veterans took their own lives after the war.[39]

## Hmmm, What is the Man trying to tell us?

George W. Bush, November 19, 2002: "I do not need to explain why I say things. That's the interesting thing about being the president. Maybe somebody needs to explain to me why they say something, but I don't feel like I owe anybody an explanation."[40]

George W. Bush, February 7, 2004: "God serves his own purposes and does not owe us an explanation."[41]

## Why the absence of WMD should not be a big surprise

If George W. were actually into explanations, he might start with why his regime had us all believing that one could scarcely walk anywhere in Iraq without tripping over weapons of mass destruction, when over the course of several years in the 1990s the UN inspectors found and destroyed huge amounts of chemical, biological and nuclear weapons there. Scott Ritter, chief UN weapons inspector in Iraq, stated in September 2002:

> since 1998 Iraq has been fundamentally disarmed: 90-95% of Iraq's weapons of mass destruction capability has been verifiably eliminated. This includes all of the factories used to produce chemical, biological and nuclear weapons, and long-range ballistic missiles; the associated equipment of these factories; and the vast majority of the products coming out of these factories.[42]

And the following month, the director general of the International Atomic Energy Agency, Mohamed El Baradei wrote:

> Before being barred from Iraq in 1998 [by the United States], the International Atomic Energy Agency dismantled extensive nuclear weapons-related facilities." We neutralized Iraq's nuclear program. We confiscated its weapon-usable material. We destroyed, removed or rendered harmless all its facilities and equipment relevant to nuclear weapons production. And while we did not claim absolute certainty, we were confident that we had not missed any significant component of Iraq's nuclear program.[43]

## Getting to the nitty-gritty

Every election campaign, in addition to all the clichés, platitudes, and other repetitions *ad nauseam*, the question of "job experience" comes up. Here's my view of the matter: If my car needs repair it's important to have a mechanic who's experienced with the particular work involved. If I need an operation I want an experienced surgeon. But when it comes to a politician, all I care about is the person's politics, his stand on certain issues. Why should anyone be impressed because a candidate has held political office for decades if his views are diametrically opposed to theirs?

Military service is another irrelevancy they give me a headache with. What does being in the military, or seeing combat, or not being in the military, or even avoiding the draft, tell us about a candidate that his voting record and speeches don't tell us with much more clarity? I don't care if Bush was AWOL or a deserter, any more than I care if Kerry was a "hero", particularly in an unjust war.

Then there's this hangup about a candidate being "presidential" in his manner. I'd vote for Woody Allen at his most nebbish if he had the right politics.

### January 22, 2004

## The never-ending enemy invasion of America

"If we don't stop the Reds in South Vietnam, tomorrow they will be in Hawaii, and next week they will be in San Francisco." Lyndon B. Johnson, 1966[44]

A defeat in Congress for his war against the Sandinistas of Nicaragua, said President Reagan, would mean "consolidation of a privileged sanctuary for terrorists and subversives just two days' driving time from Harlingen, Texas." Ronald Reagan, 1986[45]

"Our military is confronting terrorists in Iraq and

Afghanistan and in other places so our people will not have to confront terrorist violence in New York or St. Louis or Los Angeles." George W. Bush, 2003[46]

## Supply and demand: a law written in heaven

"Unprecedented demand for the flu vaccine has caused its price to skyrocket across the United States, from $40 a vial two months ago to as high as $215 today, leading to charges that companies are price-gouging health agencies amid fears of an unusually harsh flu season....The [vaccine] companies say they are doing nothing wrong. It is a simple case of supply and demand, they say."[47]

The law of supply and demand...a law as necessary and as immutable as the law of gravity, or so they would have us all believe in the United States. But what does this so-called law mean? A manufacturer is selling a product for X dollars and presumably making a decent profit with X demand. Then, for whatever reason, the demand jumps, say it doubles, meaning that the manufacturer will make twice as much as before by continuing to sell the product for X dollars (probably even more than double because the cost per unit of manufacturing will likely decrease with higher output). That sounds pretty good. But according to the law of supply and demand, instead of counting their blessings, the manufacturer is inspired to raise the price to earn even more than double. In the case of the flu vaccine—like with any other "commodity"—what it comes down to is that the more people need it, the more businesses will make them suffer financially, punishing them for having human needs such as health care.

Is this not an odd way to organize a society of human beings? The kind of society the American Empire is determined to impose upon the entire known world.

## Preaching to the converted

"Preaching to the converted"..."Preaching to the choir"...That's what speakers and writers and other activists are repeatedly told they're doing; i.e., saying the same old thing to the same old people, just spinning their wheels. But long experience as speaker, writer and activist in the area of foreign policy tells me it just ain't so.

From the questions and comments I regularly get from my audiences, via email and in person, and from other people's audiences where I'm in attendance, I can plainly see that there are numerous significant gaps and misconceptions in the choir's thinking, often leaving them confused, unable to understand or see through the next government lie or shell game, unknowing or forgetful of what happened in the past that illuminates the present, or knowing the facts but unable to apply them at the appropriate moment, vulnerable to being led astray by the next person who offers a specious argument that opposes what they currently believe, or think they believe.

As cynical as others or themselves may think they are, they frequently are not cynical enough about the power elite's motivations, underestimating the government's capacity for perfidy, clinging to the belief that their government means well and doesn't lie directly in their face; while others of the choir are much *too* cynical, conspiracy theorists to a ridiculous degree—their inability to access my website at any time must be the work of the CIA, they inform me; hardly any political figure ever dies a natural death; any US policy toward any country is based on oil (or some similar manifestation of "vulgar Marxism").

In sum, with all of the above, their hearts may be in the right place, but their heads need working on. And in any event, very few people are actually born into the choir; they achieve choir membership only after being preached to, multiple times.

## Be alert! We need more lerts!

The recent Orange Alert of delayed and cancelled flights; fighter planes accompanying passenger planes; highly intrusive luggage and body searches and questioning of passengers; unschooled flunkies, relishing their new-found bully power, making decisions which can be appealed only to god; sealed manhole covers in Times Square New Year's Eve, mailboxes, trash cans and newspaper vending machines removed; and all the numerous other humiliating and discomforting aspects of an Ultra National Security State endowed with unbridled power—it all appears to have been inspired by the usual suspects: intercepted electronic communications and informers.

From my experience as an activist in the 1960s and 70s I know that informers, particularly those with the incentive of a cash payment, would take bits and pieces of real information—mundane details about legitimate political protest for example—and add some personal tidbits so they could perhaps lay claim to greater recompense. I can see where today's informers in the Arabic-speaking world would take bits and pieces of omnipresent anti-American-imperialism talk, perhaps throw a tablespoon of exaggeration into the mix, and wind up with a genuine "terrorist threat". They can cater any diet an American intelligence agency wants to eat. Some of them probably make their living in the information business, it's their most saleable commodity; at times they may even be motivated by the chance to harm a personal or political enemy.

In the 60s, I and friends in Washington would purposely engage in fanciful and radical conspiracy talk over the phone for the benefit and torment of supposed FBI eavesdroppers. We would speak in hushed conspiratorial tones, calling each other "comrade", using a coded-sounding language, and dropping heavy hints of secret meetings. Words like "Trotsky", "Lenin", "Do you have the tape?" and "Leave the documents in the usual spot" crossed our lips.

Without question, this game would be much more danger-ous to play today, but can all Middle-Easterners—who have much more reason to suspect that their communications are tapped than we had in the 60s—resist the temptation? If two or more of them mention the same air flight number or the same city the "intelligence" would be "confirmed".

## Why do people vote the way they do?

During the upcoming primary elections and presidential election in the United States if we could question each and every voter in depth, thoroughly probing their conscious and unconscious, to ascertain exactly why they voted for the candi-date they voted for, the resulting disclosure that most of the vot-ers acted on incorrect and/or wholly irrelevant beliefs might produce such a national embarrassment that it could lead to a call to scrap the whole tedious and exasperating process.

The old adage: "Never tell a child how they make sausages or laws" should be updated to include voting.

## The Bush Liebrary

The current tale that will eventually wind up in The Bush Liebrary is that the United States is busy preparing to turn over power—"governing power" they call it—to the people of Iraq by June 30. In deciding whether to suspend your customary mis-trust of the Bush regime you first have to remember that on sev-eral occasions in the past month or so high US officials have stated that a military force of at least 100,000 will remain in Iraq until at least 2006. The British have said the same. At the same time, Washington has announced that it will be building a huge embassy in Baghdad, which will house more than 3,000 employees.

Also keep in mind that a truly governing Iraqi govern-ment could demand that all foreign military forces leave, that privileges granted to foreign corporations be revoked, and that all assets given to these companies be returned because under the Geneva Convention an occupying power has no right to dispose of a country's assets.

The next time the Bush regime declares its determination to grant the Iraqi people self-rule, think "election in November". The Bushies are desperate to be able to present the Iraqi misadventure in some kind of positive light (even if it means allowing the much-maligned United Nations a more-than-token role), but it would all be subject to modification after the American election, no matter who wins.

## The stock market—raison d'être?

Associated Press headline, January 6, 2004: "Stocks sail on a raft of good news; Dow rises 134" *Washington Post* headline, January 21, 2004: "Dow Falls Despite Solid Earnings Reports"

One can find innumerable similar headlines over the years telling us that the stock market has risen or fallen for the very same reason in either case. Do the economic fundamentals change dramatically from day to day? We are told that the Dow or Nasdaq can rise or fall because of a war, an election, a scandal, a speech, the Fed raising the interest rate, the Fed lowering the interest rate, something called "profit taking"...or anything. There must be someone on Wall Street whose job it is each day to decide on the reason to be announced for the market's movement. Why do they even bother to make this daily announcement? Is it to show that the market is rational, that it has "meaning", and thus by implication that their work has meaning, that it's not just a glorified slot machine, a high-class regulated casino?

December 23, 2003

# ** CODE ORANGE ALERT ** NEWEST BULLETIN FROM WHITE HOUSE DON'T-THINK-TANK FLYING THROUGH THE AIR ** DUCK YOUR HEAD ** DON'T STEP IN IT **

Page one headlines in *The Washington Post*, *Los Angles Times* and *New York Times* of December 20 about Libya "vowing to give up its banned weapons!"...Bush and Blair—in a "choreographed sequence" as the *Post* called it—hailing Qaddafi's seeing the light!

What's that? You didn't know that Libya was stockpiling Weapons of Mass Destruction and was the newest Danger To The Civilized World? Think Iraq.

That's what Bush and Blair have been thinking—What can we do to regain our credibility as saviors, as the good guys? If only we could remove "another" imminent Weapons of Mass Destruction threat. Perhaps it might come out sounding believable this time.

Moammar Qaddafi is tailor-made to be used for the purpose. The habitually gullible Libyan leader has been dying for years to become "respectable" and end the American sanctions against his country. Or as Bush put it: "Leaders who abandon the pursuit of chemical, biological and nuclear weapons and the means to deliver them will find an open path to better relations with the United States and other free nations. Libya has begun the process of rejoining the community of nations."

Qaddafi, Tony Blair chimed in, made a "courageous decision." The British Prime Minister declared that "Libya's actions entitle it to rejoin the international community."

Will American and British voters be hearing about this "success" in their upcoming national elections *ad nauseam* in an attempt to spray over the awful odor of the Iraq misadventure?

We did not have to wait long to find out.

White House officials immediately said they "felt certain that the brewing military confrontation with Iraq influenced Qaddafi's decision to reach out". They "touted the Libyan move as vindication for the decision to go to war against Iraq...because of the message it sent."

Bush described Libya's announcement "as resulting from careful US strategy and diplomacy, including the decision to invade Iraq in March".

"I can't imagine that Iraq went unnoticed by the Libyan leadership," a senior US official added to the chorus.

And the *LA Times* opined that "Libya's announcement enables the Bush administration to claim a major foreign policy victory and deflect criticism that the war in Iraq had done little to decrease the broader threat of terrorism and proliferation of deadly weapons."

Yet it's unmistakable that Qaddafi has been "reaching out" to repair relations with the US and the UK long before their invasion of Iraq. Why else did he agree to turn over two Libyans for trial in 1999?

So how close were we to yet another Arab-terrorist-mad-man unleashing his vast arsenal of doomsday weapons upon an innocent and unsuspecting world? Here's what the leading three American newspapers reported (emphasis added):

"The Libyan foreign ministry issued a statement admitting that the country had SOUGHT to develop unconventional weapons."

US, UK, and UN "Experts met with [Libyan] scientists at research centers that COULD SUPPORT biological weapons research and also examined missile RESEARCH facilities."

"They also revealed "DUAL-USE" chemicals that can be used for peaceful purposes OR FOR WEAPONS."

"British officials said that experts were given access to RESEARCH projects, including uranium enrichment that COULD BE USED for nuclear weapons.

Finally, a US official said that "They found that the program was more advanced than had been previously confirmed...and that Libya possessed all the equipment and expertise NEEDED TO PRODUCE weapons-grade uranium." A petrified world hangs on the official's every word with bated breath...at last able to exhale when the official adds: "We did not see an enrichment facility. We saw the components that would make for an enrichment facility." He then adds that "the Libyans did not say they had produced any highly enriched uranium."

Washington spinmeisters may well try to make a mountain of uranium out of a molehill of sand, although other voices are already being heard. Ray Takeyh, a Libya expert at the Pentagon's National Defense University, declared that "Libya's program did not have a sophisticated enough infrastructure for a very viable program, and they haven't had it for years." And Joseph Cirincione at the Carnegie Endowment for International Peace said that "it made little sense for Libya to embark on a slow and costly nuclear weapons program and wondered how much of the nuclear research was new or simply left over from earlier, now discarded programs."

Summing it all up, "One senior Bush administration official, in a recent interview, said Libya's bumbling attempts at mastering the science of advanced weapons earned it a reputation as the 'clown prince of weapons of mass destruction'."

Is Libya's abandonment of any kind of WMD program a good thing no matter how primitive a stage it might have been at? Yes, and it would be even much better if all nations abandoned such programs whether primitive or advanced. George W. declared: "Those weapons do not bring influence or prestige. They bring isolation and otherwise unwelcome consequences...I hope that other leaders will find an example in Libya's announcement today."

This tired, sad old world can only wish that one of those leaders would be the president of the United States.

Oh, almost forgot, something called "oil" may also be a factor. US oil companies have long been eager to return to Libya, but have been stopped by the sanctions. This whole scenario is the kind of thing political leaders employ to sell a change of policy to the public, so that in this case if the US ends the sanctions it won't be seen as "rewarding an evildoer", but done because the evildoer has mended his ways.

## Mad dogs and Iraqimen

In any event, we must remember that even if Libya had a full complement of WMD, absent an irresistible desire for mass national suicide, they would not have been a threat to the United States.

The same of course applies to Iraq. Oh, people argue, Saddam Hussein is so crazy who knows what he might have done? But when it became obvious late last year that the US was intent upon invading Iraq, Hussein opened up the country to the UN weapons inspectors like he never had before. This was not the behavior of a crazy person; this was the behavior of a survivalist. He didn't even use those weapons when he was invaded in 1991 when he certainly had some of them. And we've now learned of the peace feelers which Iraq had put out to prevent the current war; they were not crazy at all.

President Reagan once referred to Qaddafi as the "mad dog of the Middle East".[48] As mentioned earlier, with any ODE (Officially Designated Enemy) of Washington, one should take everything one hears about that person with a very large block of salt.

## The spineless democrats, again

After the capture of Saddam Hussein, Democratic Party presidential candidate Howard Dean stated that this "has not made America safer." He was immediately punished for his outbreak of honesty and perception, being lambasted by other candidates and the media. He and his team have apparently learned their lesson. Commenting about the Libyan announcement about abandoning WMD programs, Dean advisor Ashton Carter stated: "We should hope that our resolve over Iraq's WMD had something to do with convincing the Libyan leadership to take this course."

The White House couldn't have said it better. Democrats once again refuse to challenge the basic contradictions and disinformation underlying the administration's foreign policy proclamations. They're usually afraid that they'll appear "unpatriotic".

## The PanAm 103 myth, again

Some of the current stories about Libya predictably contain references to that country's role in the bombing of PanAm flight 103 in 1988. This belief is etched in marble and will probably remain that way forever. But the fact remains that there's no proof or any good evidence of Libya's role in that tragedy despite a Libyan man sitting in prison for the crime after being convicted by a court in The Hague. (See chapter 10)

## Proper thinking about American foreign policy

You may have noticed that after many of the attacks against American forces in Iraq we've been told that it was "planned", or it showed all the indications of being planned. As opposed to what, we might ask—Unplanned? Spontaneous? An accident? Some guy was just walking along in Iraq, and he came upon an American military installation and suddenly he says to himself: Hey, I think I'll kill myself. Luckily I happen to have a large quantity of powerful explosives wrapped around my waist, with just the right detonator.

Why do they tell us this nonsense? Because a "planned" attack sounds more ominous, ruthless, sounds like an organization is behind it, and you know what kind of organization that might be. So it's another way of saying that the attacks are not being carried out by Iraqi people who are simply angry about what the Americans have done to their country and their lives.

You're not supposed to think in such terms, just like during the Cold War we were never supposed to think of the countless people in the Third World labeled "communist" as people fighting for their rights against US-supported repressive regimes, so now we're not supposed to think of anti-American resistance fighters as human beings with human motivations.

The word "communist" was used remarkably loosely during the Cold War, just as the word "terrorist" is used these days; or "al Qaeda"—almost every individual or group that Washington wants to stigmatize is charged with being a member of al Qaeda, as if there's a precise and meaningful distinction between fighting against American imperialism while being a member of al Qaeda and fighting against American imperialism while *not* being a member of al Qaeda; as if al Qaeda gives out membership cards to fit into your wallet, and each chapter of al Qaeda puts out a weekly newsletter and holds a potluck on the first Monday of each month.

## Oh come all ye (marketplace) faithful

On December 19, in announcing a major grant to the District of Columbia to help the homeless, the US Department of Housing and Urban Development (HUD) said the criteria for such grants "have been adjusted to promote the Bush administration's goal of ending chronic homelessness by focusing on permanent housing." This is certainly a noble aspiration, but do our noble leaders realize that it runs head-on into an even more cherished tenet of theirs?—Our salvation cometh from the market economy.

The two main causes for homelessness in the United States are clearly low wages and high rents; many of the homeless actually have jobs but don't earn enough to meet the exorbitant cost of renting an apartment. But what can a government with such a fundamentalist ideology do about such a state of affairs when wages and rents are dictated by "the magic of the marketplace", the wise "hidden hand" of free enterprise?

December 1, 2003

# He's still fumbling around for a reason

After failing to convince the world about any of his many reasons for starting a war, George W., on November 6, devoted almost all of a speech to the new improved reason—we invaded to install democracy; something that he had touched upon before, but in his endearingly simple manner he's now promoting it as the primary reason for the invasion and occupation, at least on Mondays and Thursdays.

In this speech, he waxed eloquent about democracy. If you're not sure whether this new reason deserves any more regard than any of the previous reasons, consider this: In the speech, he likened the battle against Iraqi insurgents to fighting against communism, "as in the defense of Greece in 1947."

Do you know what happened in Greece in 1947? There was a civil war. One side had amongst its prominent leaders people who had supported the Nazis in the world war, including those that actually fought with them. On the other side were people who had fought against the Nazis, and had actually forced them to leave Greece. Guess which side the United States supported back then? The fascists, of course. And this is what George Bush tells us is an inspiration for fighting the Iraqi resistance.

Greece was but one example of many after the war of the United States taking the side of its supposed former enemies, working closely with governments, movements and individuals who had taken part in the Nazi or Japanese war effort or had collaborated with German or Japanese occupation forces. Those who had opposed the likes of these were viewed by Washington as "communists" and treated accordingly.

## Ideology for all seasons

When a recent poll found that most Europeans believe that Israel is the greatest threat to world peace, Israeli government minister Natan Sharansky stated: "Behind the 'political' criticism of Israel lies nothing more than pure anti-Semitism."[49] What, I wonder, can "pure anti-Semitism" mean other than something like a belief that Jews are inherently inferior creatures, less human than other people, evil. Does the man really believe that that's what motivates critics of Israeli policies?

Sharansky was a leading dissident in his native Soviet Union before finally being released from prison and permitted to emigrate to Israel in 1986. What would he have thought in his dissident days if the Soviet leaders had declared that he and his fellow dissidents opposed the communist system purely because they believed that communists were some sort of subspecies, or because they hated Russians, or were self-hating Russians, or perhaps because they were Nazis (the German version of whom were in fact very anti-communist); anything to avoid having to deal with the questions raised by the dissidents about the actual policies of the communist government.

It may be that Natan Sharansky was able to see through and escape one kind of brainwashing only to fall victim to another kind.

## The mystique of America

We now know that Iraq tried to negotiate a peace deal with the United States to avoid the American invasion in March. Iraqi officials, including the chief of the Iraqi Intelligence Service, wanted Washington to know that Iraq no longer had weapons of mass destruction and offered to allow American troops and experts to conduct a search; they also offered full support for any US plan in the Arab-Israeli peace process and handing over a man accused of being involved in the World Trade Center bombing in 1993. If this is about oil, they said, they would also talk about US oil concessions.[50]

What is most surprising about this is not the offers per se, but the naiveté—undoubtedly fueled by desperation—on the part of the Iraqis that apparently led them to believe that the Americans were open to negotiation, to discussion, to being *reasonable*. The Iraqis apparently were sufficiently innocent about the fanaticism of the Bush administration that at one point they pledged to hold UN-supervised free elections; surely free elections is something the United States believes in, the Iraqis reasoned, and will be moved by.

Other countries have harbored similar illusions about American leaders. Over the years, a number of Third World leaders, under imminent military and/or political threat by the United States, have made appeals to Washington officials, even to the president in person, under the apparently hopeful belief that it was all a misunderstanding, that America was not really intent upon crushing them and their movements for social change.

The Guatemalan foreign minister in 1954, Cheddi Jagan of British Guiana in 1961, and Maurice Bishop of Grenada in 1983 all made their appeals to Washington to be left in peace.[51] All were crushed. In 1961, Che Guevara offered a Kennedy aide several important Cuban concessions if Washington would call off the dogs of war. To no avail.[52] In 1994, it was reported that the leader of the Zapatista rebels in Mexico, Subcommander Marcos, said that "he expects the United States to support the Zapatistas once US intelligence agencies are convinced the movement is not influenced by Cubans or Russians." "Finally," Marcos said, "they are going to conclude that this is a Mexican problem, with just and true causes."[53] Yet for many years, the United States has been providing the Mexican military with all the training and tools needed to kill Marcos' followers and, most likely, before long, Marcos himself.

And in 2002, before the coup in Venezuela that ousted Hugo Chavez, some of the plotters went to Washington to get

a green light from the Bush administration. Chavez learned of
this visit and was so distressed by it that he sent officials from
his government to plead his own case in Washington. The success of this endeavor can be judged by the fact that the coup
took place shortly thereafter.[54]

In a similar vein, in 1945 and 1946, Vietnamese leader Ho
Chi Minh, a genuine admirer of America, wrote at least eight
letters to President Truman and the State Department asking
for America's help in winning Vietnamese independence from
the French. He wrote that world peace was being endangered by
French efforts to reconquer Indochina and he requested that
"the four powers" (US, USSR, China, and Great Britain) intervene in order to mediate a fair settlement and bring the
Indochinese issue before the United Nations.[55] He received no
reply, for he was some sort of communist.

Syria today appears to be the latest example of this belief
that somewhere in Washington, somehow, there is a vestige of
human-like reasonableness that can be tapped. The Syrians
turn over suspected terrorists to the United States and other
countries and accept prisoners delivered to them by the US for
the clear purpose of them being tortured to elicit information.
The Syrians make it clear that they do these things in the hope
of appeasing the American beast; this while the United States
continues speaking openly of overthrowing the Syrian government and imposes strict sanctions against the country.

Was there anything Czechoslovakia could have done to
prevent a Nazi invasion in 1938? Or Poland in 1939?

## Those scary communists

On November 25 *The Washington Post* ran an obituary of
Sylvia Bernstein, the mother of former Post reporter Carl
Bernstein of Watergate fame. The obit recounted how both of
Carl's parents had been Communist Party members and had
endured long persecution by the government for their political

beliefs. Mrs. Bernstein had invoked her Fifth Amendment rights against self-incrimination when asked by congressional panels about her party involvement.

Then we learn that during the Clinton administration, she was a White House volunteer and answered the correspondence of first lady Hillary Rodham Clinton.

Since the 1960s, I have met numerous Communist Party members in the US, Europe and Latin America. In my experience, it has been very typical for these people to bear scarcely any resemblance to the stereotype of the "commie" of the "red menace" we were all raised to fear: a shadowy fiend out to subvert God, family, capitalism, and all else that was virtuous. In actuality, the commie fiends were usually no more radical than a liberal, a more consistent liberal than the non-party type perhaps, but a liberal nonetheless.

It's not a question of radicals being purists. It's a question of radicals being radicals.

### November 7, 2003

# The irony about Jewish influence

When Prime Minister Mahathir Mohamed of Malaysia recently declared that "Jews rule the world by proxy" and urged Muslim nations to unite to avoid being "defeated by a few million Jews,"[56] he was heavily criticized throughout the Western world for anti-Semitism. Largely obscured was the fact that in the same address, Mahathir had been much more harsh with his fellow Muslims, calling them a backward people, crippled by religious superstition and enfeebled by infighting. But no one in the West accused him of being anti-Muslim. And when the US Senate voted—without dissent—to restrict military aid to Malaysia in retaliation (for his remarks about Jews, not about Muslims), who amongst Mahathir's critics conceded that this lent some credence to his statement about Jewish influence?

## Nuking the State Department

The Most Reverend Pat Robertson recently called for the nuking of the State Department. "If I could just get a nuclear device inside of Foggy Bottom [nickname for the State Department]," he said over the radio. "I think that's the answer."[57]

Imagine that a Muslim minister—or any Muslim—had said the same on the radio, or even in a private conversation. Imagine *anyone* who wasn't an influential conservative Christian or Jew saying the same in this day and age. Imagine the consequences.

## Interventionism revisionism

George W. recently designated Otto Reich, his Special Envoy for Western Hemisphere Initiatives, to lead a delegation to attend the commemoration ceremony of the 20th Anniversary of "the restoration of democracy to Grenada". Bad enough that Reich has on his resumé abetting anti-Castro Cuban terrorists who bombed a plane out of the air killing 73 people, bad enough that what actually happened in October 1983 in Grenada was the US overthrowing another government which was not a threat to anyone and covering it up with a campaign of lies that stood unmatched until the present-day Iraq fiasco, but here's what "the restoration of democracy to Grenada" looked like at the time:

In 1984, former Premier Herbert Blaize was elected prime minister, his party capturing 14 of the 15 parliamentary seats. Blaize, who in the wake of the invasion had proclaimed to the United States: "We say thank you from the bottom of our hearts," had been favored by the Reagan administration. The candidate who won the sole opposition seat announced that he would not occupy it because of what he called "vote rigging and interference in the election by outside forces."

One year later, the Washington-based Council on

Hemispheric Affairs reported on Grenada as part of its annual survey of human rights abuses:

> Reliable accounts are circulating of prisoners being beaten, denied medical attention and confined for long periods without being able to see lawyers. The country's new US-trained police force has acquired a reputation for brutality, arbitrary arrest and abuse of authority.

The report added that an offending all-music radio station had been closed and that US-trained counter-insurgency forces were eroding civil rights.

By the late 1980s, the government began confiscating many books arriving from abroad, including Graham Greene's *Our Man in Havana* and *Nelson Mandela Speaks*. In April 1989, it issued a list of more than 80 books which were prohibited from being imported.

Four months later, Prime Minister Blaize suspended Parliament to forestall a threatened no-confidence vote resulting from what his critics called "an increasingly authoritarian style".[58]

## It's our own money, stupid!

A seemingly odd dispute broke out recently between the White House and a majority of the members of Congress, including many Republicans, over the nature of the Iraq reconstruction funds. Congress insisted that a significant portion of the money be in the form of loans, while the Bush administration wanted it all to be grants, even threatening a veto of the spending bill if it required Iraq to repay any of the money. In the end, the White House got its way. But what was it all about? Could it be that the Bushgang wanted to be more generous to the people of Iraq? That's hardly in keeping with its bombing, invasion and occupation of the same people. Rather, it may be another indication that the Bush Administration has no intention of leaving Iraq. A loan which has to be repaid would be money owed by the US occupation authorities, providing them with less funds for the likes of Halliburton, Bechtel and other friends of George and Dick.

## Differing objectives in Iraq and Vietnam

Comparisons between the current Iraq quagmire and the infamous Vietnam quagmire are being raised more and more these days. But one vital difference is never pointed out; namely, that in Vietnam the US had a temporary objective, while in Iraq it's permanent. In Vietnam, the object was to destroy the possibility of a state arising there that could serve as a good example of an alternative to the capitalist development model for other Asian countries. Ideally, this could be achieved by putting in power a government that would not pursue such a model. Although this proved beyond Washington's means, once Vietnam had been bombed, napalmed, and Agent-Oranged into a basket case, which would not inspire anyone, the US was free to leave, with mission accomplished. In Iraq, the object is to colonize the place for a host of ongoing imperial needs, so there's no plan to leave in the foreseeable future.

## Liberals: Conservatives
## How meaningful the distinction?

Clinton's former chief of staff, John Podesta, has formed a new think tank, the Center for American Progress. This was characterized by the *Washington Post* as "the liberal's answer to the conservative Heritage Foundation".[59] This is a very common misunderstanding in the mainstream media and among the public—the idea that neo-conservatives (far to the right on the political spectrum) and liberals (ever so slightly to the left of center) are ideological polar opposites. Thus, a radio or TV show with a neo-con and a liberal thinks of itself as "balanced". However, the opposite of a conservative—particularly the new breed that prominently advise the White House and Pentagon, and often occupy positions there—is a left-wing radical, progressive or socialist. Liberals are often closer to conservatives, particularly in foreign policy, than they are to these groupings on the far left. In this light, the never-ending debate about whether the media has a conservative or a liberal bias takes on much less significance.

## Opening of my talk delivered in Bologna, Italy, August 29

Good evening, it's very nice to be here.

It's a pleasure to get away from a country ruled by a man who's a fascist and very corrupt and has no compassion for the poor, and come to a country ruled by a man who's a fascist and very corrupt and has no compassion for the poor.

Is it better to live under *il Duce* or under *il Dope*? Well, *il Duce* at least has not killed thousands of people in Afghanistan and Iraq, but *il Dope* has done just that, with an empire much more powerful than Rome ever had.

### July 7, 2003

## A tale of two Georges: Bush and Orwell

The words and actions of the Bush administration have so often been labeled "Orwellian" that it's become virtually a cliché. But it's difficult to resist adding to the list.

At a July 1 White House press briefing, a reporter asked spokesman Ari Fleischer: "Ari, the United States just declared about 50 countries, including Colombia and six prospective NATO members, ineligible for military aid because they won't exempt Americans from the International Criminal Court. My question is, why is this priority more important than fighting the drug wars, integrating Eastern Europe?"

Fleischer replied: "Well, number one, because the

President is following the law. This is a law that Congress passed that the President signed, dealing with what's called Article 98 actions that would make certain that American military personnel and other personnel who are stationed abroad would not be subject to a court which has international sovereignty that's in dispute."

So what do we have here? The Bush administration drafts a law to serve its imperial needs, pushes it through Congress, and then, when the press expresses some skepticism about the law's effect, the same Bush administration justifies it by saying: "Well, the President is only following the law."

As to the court's sovereignty being in dispute, this is of course entirely centered in a city called Washington, DC.

Just a few days earlier, the Bush administration applied similar Orwellian logic to its decision to award more than a billion dollars for construction contracts in Iraq to seven American companies. When foreign governments became concerned that the United States would deny their companies access to the Iraqi market, American officials countered that US law requires that US companies be given preferable treatment.[60]

## You mean sanctions are really harmful after all?

For a dozen years, international groups supporting the Iraqi people campaigned to have the UN (read US) sanctions removed, sanctions which Clinton's National Security Advisor, Sandy Berger, called "the most pervasive sanctions every imposed on a nation in the history of mankind".[61] The United States, meanwhile, insisted that the suffering of the population was not due to the sanctions, but was the result of Saddam's lavish lifestyle. ("Soldiers of Iraq...Every night, children go to sleep hungry in Iraq...The amount of money Saddam spends on himself in one day would be more than enough to feed a family for a year," said a Pentagon radio program broadcast into Iraq.[62]) So then Saddam and his regime were overthrown. But the suffering continued anyhow in much the same ways. And then, with their usual lack of embarrassment, Washington officials declared that the sanctions are actually harmful and that they would have to be removed in order to provide humanitarian aid and rebuild the country. (It should be noted that neither had the Pentagon been embarrassed to be speaking about Iraqi children going to sleep hungry. The Iraqis who heard that message would likely find it absolutely incomprehensible to be told that the same occurs with numerous children in the United States.)

## Tribes, East and West

Reading about a horribly bloody suicide attack upon a Shiite Muslim mosque in Pakistan on July 4 that killed dozens, and which is blamed on members of the Sunni Muslims, I imagined what many Americans would think about this: "That's good, they should all just kill each other with their uncivilized tribal violence if they can't learn how to get along any better than that."

Then I thought about the American tribe which recently killed thousands of the Afghan tribe and then thousands more of the Iraqi tribe, for no discernible good reason or purpose, cheered on by the many other members of the American tribe at home waving their tribal flags and singing their tribal songs.

## Diamonds are a dictator's best friend

The Bush administration is agreeing that Charles Taylor, president of Liberia, can and should step down from office and safely leave the country even though Taylor was recently indicted by a UN-sponsored court in neighboring Sierra Leone for "bearing the greatest responsibility for war crimes, crimes against humanity and serious violations of international humanitarian law" during Sierra Leone's civil war. This is in

marked contrast to consistent US government demands of
recent years that all Serbian officials indicted for similar crimes
by the UN court in the Hague be turned over to the court, or
turn themselves in, with no exceptions, no going into exile, no
mercy. To show how serious Washington was about this, they
pressured the Yugoslav government to kidnap President
Slobodan Milosevic and hustle him off to the Hague. But that's
because the US had globalization and imperialist designs on
Yugoslavia's considerable assets and required that Milosevic and
his team be replaced with others who would be more amenable
to such objectives.

In 1998, President Clinton sent Jesse Jackson as his special
envoy to Liberia and Sierra Leone, the latter being in the midst
of one of the great horrors of the 20th century—You may
remember the army of mostly young boys, the Revolutionary
United Front (RUF), who went around raping and chopping off
people's arms and legs. African and world opinion was enraged
against the RUF, which was committed to protecting the diamond mines they controlled. Taylor was an indispensable ally
and supporter of the RUF and Jackson was a friend of his. Jesse
was not sent to the region to hound Taylor about his widespread
human rights violations, but instead, in June 1999, Jackson and
other American officials drafted entire sections of an accord
that made RUF leader, Foday Sankoh, Sierra Leone's vice president, and gave him official control over the diamond mines,
the country's major source of wealth.[63]

And what was the Clinton administration's interest in all
this? It's been speculated that the answer lies with certain individuals with ties to the diamond industry and to Clinton, while
he was president or while governor of Arkansas; for example,
Maurice Tempelsman, generous contributor to the Democratic
Party and escort of Secretary of State Madeleine Albright
around this time, whose Antwerp, Amsterdam and Tel Aviv
diamond marts arranged for Sierra Leone diamond sales to
Tiffany and Cartier.[64]

## Saddam's other side

Take the children out of the room. What follows is a kind word about Saddam Hussein. During his reign—except at times when war, US bombings and sanctions may have necessitated restrictions—the Iraqi people had free education all the way through university and medical school, free medical care, regular food packages for those in need, women's rights superior to anything in the Arab world, religious toleration for Christians and other non-Muslims, and even multi-candidate parliamentary elections, albeit all members of the Baath Party.

## Cuba and human rights

Cuba has recently been heavily criticized, by various shadings of leftists as well as by those to the right, for its sentencing a number of dissidents to prison because of their very close political and financial connections to American officials. Critics say that Cuba should not have over-reacted so, that these people were not really guilty of anything criminal.

While I personally think that the sentences were too long, we have to keep in mind that before the United States invaded Iraq there was extensive CIA and US military liaison on the ground with Iraqi dissidents and lots of propaganda to soften up the population beamed into Iraq with the indispensable help of other Iraqi dissidents. Can Cuba be expected to ignore something like this in the case of its own dissidents?

The United States has been on a ferocious rampage of bombing, invasion, taking over countries and threatening the same to others. The US ambassador to the Dominican Republic declared: "I think what is happening in Iraq is going to send a very positive signal, and it is a very good example for Cuba."[65] An advisor to Florida Governor Jeb Bush, speaking of Fidel Castro, said: "The administration has taken care of one tyrant already. I don't think they would vacillate about taking care of another one."[66]

Can Cuba be expected to ignore such threats as well? Is Washington's work with Cuban dissidents to be seen as a purely harmless undertaking? Not done for a purpose? How can Cuba not feel extremely threatened, even more than the usual threat of the past 44 years? How can they not take precautionary measures?

The United States is to the Cubans like al Qaeda is to Washington. Would the US ignore a group of American dissidents receiving funds from al Qaeda and engaging in repeated meetings with known leaders of that organization in the United States? In the past two years, the American government has arrested a great many people in the US and abroad on the basis of alleged ties to terrorism, with a lot less to go on than Cuba had.

## Great Powers

On several occasions I have been confronted with the argument that powerful countries have always acted like the United States, so why condemn the US so much? I respond that since one can find anti-Semitism in every country, why do we condemn Nazi Germany so much? It's a question of magnitude, is it not? The magnitude of US aggression puts it into a league all by itself.

### April 14, 2003

## The Warmongers' need for a justification for the devastation

When you wage a war that is strongly opposed by the great majority of those on the planet who think about such things, when your own people are becoming increasingly militant against your unilateral waging of that war, when you know well that your war is palpably and embarrassingly illegal, immoral, illogical and unjust, when you can't admit the real reasons for the war...then you have a consuming need to find a moral-sounding and credible selling point—"Regime change", to remove the evil Saddam, the Iraqi people will welcome us with flowers and music!

Thus was it mortifying for the warmongers that for more than the first two weeks of the war the Iraqi images shown to the world were largely of the dead, the wounded, the grief-stricken, the immense piles of rubble, the bombing-produced homeless, those bitterly angry at the United States. How could it be otherwise? What kind of people like their loved ones torn apart by missiles, their children without a limb, their homes, hospitals, schools and jobs destroyed?

The US military told its hapless soldiers and its embedded media that any negative reaction, or lack of a positive one, was all because the people were afraid of Saddam, as if one of his agents was standing behind each Iraqi citizen, gun at the ready. Why did at least hundreds of thousands of people fight and resist, many to the death, instead of surrendering, defecting, anything to show their gratitude for their "liberation"?

Now, any teenager flashing a victory sign, anyone climbing upon a toppled statue of Saddam or smiling for a camera is an American media star and evidence of the nobility of the war. But what portion of the Iraqi people are happy about the invasion—happy about *all* its effects? What are they happy about other than the removal of Saddam? And many Iraqis supported him. Of those "celebrating", how many have been touched by the death and destruction? How many even *know* about it? The US bombed Iraqi and Arabic TV off the air fairly early on for most of the country. Much of the telephone system was another early victim. When the Iraqis who were kept in the dark discover the horror will the American media be there to record the disappeared smiles?

As an American, I would also celebrate if the cruel and ignorant tyrant calling himself my leader were overthrown. But not if my city were bombed and my house demolished. No changes in Iraq justify the American onslaught. What kind of world would we have if any country could invade any other country because it didn't like the leader of that country?

In any event, the United States was not motivated at all by Saddam Hussein, or his evilness, or his alleged weapons of mass destruction, or his alleged threat to the United States. American officials made it explicitly clear before the invasion that the US intervention would take place even if Saddam resigned or chose to go into exile.[67]

## The myth of Soviet expansionism

One still often comes across references in the mainstream media to "the Soviet empire" and Russian "expansionism", in addition to that old favorite "the evil empire". These terms stem largely from erstwhile Soviet control of Eastern European states. But was the creation of these satellites following World War II an act of imperialism or expansionism? Or did the decisive impetus lie elsewhere?

Within the space of less than 25 years, Western powers had invaded Russia three times—the two world wars and the "intervention" of 1918-20—inflicting some 40 million casualties in the two world wars alone. To carry out these invasions, the West had used Eastern Europe as a highway. Should it be any cause for wonder that after World War II the Soviets wanted to close this highway down? In almost any other context, Americans would have no problem in seeing this as an act of self defense. But in the context of the Cold War such thinking could not find a home in mainstream discourse.

The Baltic states of the Soviet Union—Estonia, Latvia, and Lithuania—were not part of the highway and were frequently in the news because of their demands for more autonomy from Moscow, a story "natural" for the American media. These articles invariably reminded the reader that the "once_independent" Baltic states were invaded in 1939 by the

Soviet Union, incorporated as republics of the USSR, and have been "occupied" ever since. Another case of brutal Russian imperialism. Period. History etched in stone.

The three countries, it happens, were part of the Russian empire from 1721 up to the Russian Revolution of 1917, in the midst of World War I. When the war ended in November 1918, and the Germans had been defeated, the victorious Allied nations (US, Great Britain, France, *et al.*) permitted/encouraged the German forces to remain in the Baltics for a full year to crush the spread of Bolshevism there; this, with ample military assistance from the Allied nations. In each of the three republics, the Germans installed collaborators in power who declared their independence from the Bolshevik state which, by this time, was so devastated by the World War, the revolution, and the civil war prolonged by the Allies' intervention, that it had no choice but to accept the *fait accompli*. The rest of the fledgling Soviet Union had to be saved.

To at least win some propaganda points from this unfortunate state of affairs, the Soviets announced that they were relinquishing the Baltic republics "voluntarily" in line with their principles of anti-imperialism and self-determination. But is should not be surprising that the Soviets continued to regard the Baltics as a rightful part of their nation or that they waited until they were powerful enough to reclaim the territory.

Then we have Afghanistan. Surely this was an imperialist grab. But the Soviet Union lived next door to Afghanistan for more than 60 years without gobbling it up. And when the Russians invaded in 1979, the key motivation was the United States involvement in a movement to topple the Afghan government, which was friendly to Moscow. The Soviets could not have been expected to tolerate a pro-US, anti-communist government on its border any more than the United States could have been expected to tolerate a pro-Soviet, communist government in Mexico.

Moreover, if the rebel movement took power it would

have set up a fundamentalist Islamic government, which would have been positioned to proselytize the numerous Muslims in the Soviet border republics.

### April 1, 2003

## Orwell redux

Perhaps the most Orwellian quote to come out of the Vietnam war, now a classic, was "We had to destroy the village in order to save it." Now comes Mr. Rumsfeld, speaking in the heat of the new war against Iraq, of US "precision bombing": "It looks like it's a bombing of a city, but it isn't."[68]

We should say the "so-called" war against Iraq because it was really a thousand pound gorilla fighting a 90-year-old woman in a wheel chair. And we call our gorilla a "hero" for beating up the old woman and smashing her wheel chair.

In the play, *Galileo*, by Bertolt Brecht, one character says to another: "Unhappy the land that has no heroes."

And the other character replies: "No. Unhappy the land that *needs* heroes."

## The 100 percent solution for Iraq

The US decision to not continue its military campaign in 1991 and overthrow Saddam Hussein was likely due in large measure to the uncertainty of who or what would replace him. Washington didn't want a Shiite government, which might join forces with neighboring Iran; nor a Kurd government, which would upset ally Turkey; nor any kind of even-nominally democratic government, which would upset Saudi Arabia and Kuwait; nor any kind of truly progressive government, which would upset Washington. But for the current war this problem has been solved, with a remarkably simple solution— Washington itself will replace Hussein.

## And that's the way it should be

"A man who allegedly wanted to harm people of Middle Eastern descent because of his anger over the World Trade Center attack has been arrested in a string of New York workplace shootings that left four people dead."[69]

How does this differ from US armed forces killing people in Iraq and Afghanistan? The American servicemen will not be arrested.

## Do unto others before others do unto you

Here's one of the empire's arrogances which may have escaped your attention. First we have Robert Kagan, a leading light of the American foreign-policy establishment and an intellectual architect of an interventionism that seeks to impose a neo-conservative agenda upon the world, by force if necessary. Kagan declares that the United States must refuse to abide by certain international conventions, like the international criminal court and the Kyoto accord on global warming. The US, he says, "must support arms control, but not always for itself. It must live by a double standard."[70]

Now we have Robert Cooper, a senior British diplomat and key foreign policy advisor to Prime Minister Tony Blair. Cooper writes: "The challenge to the postmodern world is to get used to the idea of double standards....When dealing with more old- fashioned kinds of states outside the postmodern continent of Europe, we need to revert to the rougher methods of an earlier era—force, pre-emptive attack, deception, whatever is necessary to deal with those who still live in the nineteenth century world of every state for itself."[71]

His expression, "every state for itself", can be better understood as simply that some state, somewhere, is not doing what the American Empire and its junior partner in London wish. So there we have it. The double standard is in. The golden rule of do unto others as you would have others do unto you is out.

Noam Chomsky has spoken of "the principle of universality: if an action is right (or wrong) for others, it is right (or wrong) for us. Those who do not rise to the minimal moral level of applying to themselves the standards they apply to others plainly cannot be taken seriously when they speak of appropriateness of response; or of right and wrong, good and evil."

Robert Kagan and Robert Cooper and their ilk of course know this. A 7-year-old child, with his or her acute sense of unfairness, knows it very well. It's usually called hypocrisy. So why do the empire's intellectuals peddle this double-standard silliness? I'd put it this way: They, like most people, have a vision for the kind of world they'd like to live in; let's call it a laissez-faire, globalized, Judeo-Christian, law and order, white-man's-burden, ridding the planet of all governments not subservient to Washington, world. Now most of the world's people have experienced this stuff quite enough already, thank you. The imperial mafia thus have a very difficult time selling or defending their utopia on the basis of legal, moral, ethical or fairness standards. So what to do? Aha! They decide that they're not bound by such standards. But the rest of the world is.

## Christopher Hitchens

Presented here is a brief email exchange about Iraq with author and journalist Christopher Hitchens before the American invasion in March 2003. I hadn't planned on publicizing the exchange I had with the erstwhile man of the left, but inasmuch as he reneged on his promise and continues to write the same dribble, I am submitting it to the world's judgment.

```
October 20, 2002
Dear Mr. Hitchens,
    I've followed your support for the
American Empire's newest bombing hysteria,
```

but I have failed to hear from you any kind of response to the most important question: Do you support, once again, the dropping of large quantities of highly lethal explosives upon the heads of countless innocent men, women and children, destroying their homes, their schools, their hospitals, their lives, their futures?

If you can't deal with this question, but instead continue to content yourself with snapping at the heels of the left with irrelevant, esoteric, and (hopefully) droll side issues, then I would say that you are guilty of serious character failure and are engaging in nothing less than intellectual masturbation.

Sincerely,
Bill Blum

October 21, 2002
If you consider that a properly phrased question, or would publish it as such under your own name, then I am willing to reply to it. But I will, for now and for your sake, consider it confidential. Do you feel like having another try?
CH

October 21, 2002
If you can get it published and reply to it, that would suit me fine.
Bill Blum

That was the last I heard from Hitchens. My analysis is this: He was unable to respond in substance to the question I challenged him with and so he thought that he'd try intimidation instead, on the premise, apparently, that I would be embarrassed to see my email publicized. Why would he have thought I'd be embarrassed? Because I used the word "masturbation"? If not that, I can't imagine.

## Clinton as CIA informer?

One thing Hitchens and I do agree on is that well-known, but rarely mentioned, secret that Bill Clinton appears to have been a CIA asset around 1969-70 while a Rhodes Scholar at Oxford. Hitchens was a student there at the same time. "I think he was a double," Hitchens now says. "Somebody was giving information to [the CIA] about the anti-war draft resisters, and I think it was probably him. We had a girlfriend in common—I didn't know then—who's since become a very famous radical lesbian."[72]

In his book on the Clintons, Roger Morris, a former member of Nixon's National Security Council, writes of Clinton spying on anti-war activists and others in the UK and Sweden. He cites three former CIA sources and another government official in support of this thesis; two of the four claim to have seen documents to this effect.[73]

There is also Clinton's connection to Richard Stearns, former officer of the National Student Association in the 1960s. In an explosive exposé in 1967, the NSA was revealed to have had a long and close relationship with the CIA on international Cold-War activities, trying to counter Soviet influence among foreign students. As international vice president of the NSA, Stearns in all likelihood would have been witting of this. Clinton and Stearns met at Oxford, where Stearns was also a Rhodes Scholar. In 1970 the two young men traveled together in Europe. It may well be that Stearns handled Clinton's CIA recruitment.[74]

# Washington Post damage control for US foreign policy

Here we have Don Quixote Blum tilting at the *Washington Post* windmill as he has on numerous occasions over the years. His tilt here, via email, is with Michael Getler, the Post's Ombudsman. Getler did not tilt back. [words in brackets were added later]

March 5, 2003
Dear Mr. Getler,

I wonder if you're aware of how the Post sometimes deals with stories embarrassing to the US foreign policy establishment. Yesterday, March 4, the Post ran the story of US spying on Security Council members [during an ongoing crucial debate re attacking Iraq] a day after it broke all over the world; i.e., a day late. Why the wait? Apparently to locate a UN diplomat or two to make light of the whole matter. In fact, what finally appeared on page 17 (sic) was not a news story, but a story playing down the real news story. [The Post story was headlined: "Spying Report No Shock To U.N."]

The Post did the exact same thing a few days ago with the story by the Iraqi defector (Saddam's son-in-law), who, it turns out, had informed the UN inspectors in 1995 that Iraq had destroyed the vast majority of its WMD. The paper delayed publishing the story until it could find someone to cast doubt upon the significance of it.

Again, in the 1990s, with the famous exposure by Garry Webb of the San Jose Mercury about CIA funding drug traffickers in California, which helped to spawn the crack epidemic. The Post refrained from any report for about three weeks, until it ran a brief mention of the story as part of a larger story that cast doubt upon it.

Undoubtedly there have been many other examples of this practice.

Sincerely, William Blum


March 10, 2003
Dear Mr. Lynch and Mr. Getler,

Your coverup/downplaying of the US spying at the UN continues; not a word about the UN launching its own inquiry into the matter. (see below) You probably figure that only a few kooks like me notice such things so you can just ignore me, and the great majority of Post readers will be none the wiser. You're probably right. And there's no need for you to change such a policy, unless of course you feel any obligation toward making your readers wiser.
Bill Blum
[This is an excerpt from the article in *The Observer* (London) that accompanied the above email.]

UN launches inquiry into American spying
Martin Bright, Ed Vulliamy in New York and Peter Beaumont
Sunday March 9, 2003
The Observer
The United Nations has begun a top-level investigation

into the bugging of its delegations by the United States, first revealed in The Observer last week.

Sources in the office of UN Secretary General Kofi Annan confirmed last night that the spying operation had already been discussed at the UN's counter-terrorism committee and will be further investigated....

While the bugging of foreign diplomats at the UN is permissible under the US Foreign Intelligence Services Act, it is a breach of the Vienna Convention on Diplomatic Relations, according to one of America's leading experts on international law, Professor John Quigley of Ohio University.

He says the convention stipulates that: 'The receiving state shall permit and protect free communication on the part of the mission for all official purposes... The official correspondence of the mission shall be inviolable.'

On March 16, the Post published an op-ed by an outsider, David Greenberg, contrasting the British and American media reaction to the UN spying story. He wrote:

Back in the United States, journalists didn't ignore the story, but they steered clear of phrases such as "dirty tricks." Headlines soberly stated that "some say it's nothing to get worked up about"(the Los Angeles Times) or "No Shock to the U.N." (The Washington Post). Articles reminded readers that the United States has been secretly monitoring other countries' U.N. missions since the body's inception. Most commentators and kitchen-table kibitzers greeted the news with a yawn.

So...a violation of international law on a highly important issue of war and peace and a slap in the face of the United Nations and several foreign diplomatic missions are nothing to get worked up about or be shocked about because...the United States has been doing similar stuff for many years.

Just think of all the other things in this sad world that can be excused on the grounds that they've been going on for a long time.

*Some excerpts from earlier newsletters*

November 3, 2001

# Unleashing the CIA?

The old joke goes that in the waning days of the Second World War, when Hitler was told of yet another defeat on the battlefield, he slammed his fist into his desk and declared: "That does it! No more Mr. Nice Guy!"

We've been treated in the past couple of weeks to one press story after another about how the Bush administration seeks to "unleash" the CIA from its restrictions concerning things like political assassination and working with "unsavory" characters. The nature of the September 11 attack was such, we are told, that we have to remove our kid gloves and put on depleted-uranium- tipped brass knuckles.

The policies whose "revisions" are being discussed and leaked are principally a 25-year ban on the CIA and other agencies of the government from engaging in assassination, and a policy of the past five years or so of barring the CIA from employing real nasty killers and torturers abroad, or at least not without express approval from high up.

Why are they telling us these tales at this time? Is it to comfort the American public into believing that the government is holding nothing back in its campaign of making us more secure? Or can they actually believe that such announcements will put the fear of Allah in the Taliban leadership?

The fact is that since Gerald Ford signed a presidential order in 1976, which stated that "No employee of the United States shall engage in, or conspire to engage in, political assassination", the United States has attempted or plotted, on more than a dozen occasions, to administer what the CIA at one time called "suicide involuntarily administered".

In 1984, President Reagan issued an executive order which was actually referred to by the press as a "license to kill"—a license to kill anyone deemed a "terrorist". But this was cancelled the following year after the CIA arranged for a car bomb to kill one sheikh Fadlallah in Beirut; the bomb killed 80 people, the sheikh not being among their number. However, the license to kill was reinstated a few months later following a hijacking of a TWA plane.[75]

President Bush, the elder, added a new twist in 1989. He issued a "memorandum of law" that would allow "accidental" killing if it was a byproduct of legal action: "A decision by the President to employ overt military force...would not constitute assassination if US forces were employed against the combatant forces of another nation, a guerrilla force, or a terrorist or other organization whose actions pose a threat to the security of the United States." In other words, assassination was okay as long as we could say "oops!"

The last known assassination attempt was the firing of missiles into the home of Slobodan Milosevic in 1999.

It can thus be seen that all this talk we are being fed of late about giving the CIA "new" powers to engage in "targeted killings" is little more than spin, the native language of politicians.

The same can be said for the public now being told that because of the terrorist crisis, the CIA is going to be allowed to revert to the good ol' days when they could cozy up to the most despicable human rights violators without getting permission from headquarters. It's hard to imagine that in recent years that even if an Agency officer felt moved to ask for such permission that it would have been denied.

A CIA officer could not have set foot in Colombia, Peru, Mexico, Indonesia, Turkey, Kosovo or Croatia without tripping over an unindicted war criminal-cum-US ally. As I write this, the Agency is sleeping with the Northern Alliance of Afghanistan, a band of torturers, kidnappers and rapists so depraved that the people of Afghanistan at first welcomed the Taliban as heroes for conquering these worthies.

To top it all off, we are told that the finest legal minds of the Justice Department, State Department and Pentagon have put their fine minds together and have decided that the new marching orders are—will wonders never cease?—LEGAL!

All these announcements are designed not only to make Americans feel safer, but to give us a nice, warm, fuzzy feeling that our leaders are so honorable that they engage in protracted debates and soul searching before endorsing any policies not fit for our children's schoolbooks.

### May 19, 2001

## "It is dangerous to be right when the government is wrong." —Voltaire

An email letter sent to Senators Joseph Lieberman and Jessie Helms, May 19, 2001:

Dear Senators Lieberman and Helms,

I've just read about your proposal to give $100 million to support Cuban dissidents. I think that's just marvelous. But why stop there? Why not offer some support to American dissidents, of which I'm one? We can certainly use support of many kinds. For example at major protests in Seattle, Washington, Philadelphia and Los Angeles in the past 1 1/2 years we've suffered in the following ways:

- Police closed down protest headquarters, confiscating personal property, puppets, signs, banners, costumes, food, literature, medical supplies, etc.

- Protesters were teargassed, peppersprayed, watercannon-blasted, arrested en masse for no cause at all, with outlandish charges made up for the occasion.

- Those jailed had their heads smashed into concrete walls; were deprived of water, food and toilet for extended periods of time, forced to urinate on themselves; handcuffed from one wrist to the opposite calf, making sleep virtually impossible. (Sleep deprivation is regarded as a form of torture by Amnesty International.)

- Women prisoners were sexually molested and strip searched in front of male guards.

- Police infiltrated protest organizations and intercepted their email, fax and phone communications.

- Police pressured institutions like universities to not put up protesters and forced print copy shops to close to prevent protest material from being duplicated.

- Police smashed cameras and beat up people.

This list is a very partial one, but I'm sure you get the idea. Inasmuch as the government needs so much money now to give the rich a tax cut, we won't expect a matching $100 million, but rest assured that whatever amount you see in you heart to provide us with will be put to good democratic use.

In solidarity,
William Blum

## 2000

# Americans exempt from war crimes

The new International Criminal Court is the culmination of a campaign for a permanent war crimes tribunal that began with the Nuremberg trials after World War II. But the US government has refused to join, claiming that they're afraid of it being used "frivolously" to charge US soldiers with war crimes for actions during an American intervention. But I think their real concern is not that it will be used *frivolously*, but that it will be used *seriously*; and not against soldiers, but against leaders in Washington, and there are quite a few who would qualify.

The new court will not have any powers to judge past behavior, but based on the past, on the recent past, one can see why the powers that be in the United States would be uneasy. Of those that are still living, you have people like Reagan and Bush and Clinton and Colin Powell and Caspar Weinberger and Elliot Abrams and a whole bunch of other people who can easily have a case made against them for war crimes or crimes against humanity.

In any event, a reading of the court's charter makes it clear that "frivolous prosecutions" was a danger thought of in advance and enough safeguards are provided to prevent such from happening.

## 1999

# Dealing with the Mass American Mind

On December 26, 1998, *The Washington Post* published the results of a poll dealing with homosexuality. The results, in part, were as follows:

Question: "Do you think homosexual relations between consenting adults should be legal or illegal?"

Result:

Legal 55%

Illegal 34%
No opinion 11%
Question asked of those who thought it should be illegal: "Should homosexual relations be illegal even if this means that consenting adults who engage in these activities in their own homes could be prosecuted for a crime?"
Result:
Should still be illegal 33%
Changed mind: should be legal 56%
No opinion 11 %

Notice that the difference between the first and second questions is simply the addition of "in their own homes" and "prosecuted for a crime". Yet, 56% CHANGED THEIR MIND. What did they think when answering the first question—that homosexuals do their nasty stuff lying in the street? Or that "being illegal" carries no threat of prosecution for a crime?

With many polls, particularly those dealing with very sensitive or controversial issues, you can get markedly different results by a relatively minor change in the question, probably because most people are not in the habit of thinking through the consequences of an idea, and have to be made aware of the consequences; and they often tend to answer what they think they think, or what they think their milieu thinks they should think, so they have to be prodded outside of that milieu.

What if a poll were taken of Americans which asked: "Do you support the government's bombing of [Iraq, Yugoslavia, et al]?" While the bombing was going on, and for some time afterward, there would likely be a significant majority in favor of the bombing; many would think it unpatriotic to answer otherwise.

But what if those who expressed support of the bombing were then asked: "Do you support the bombing even if this means that hundreds or thousands of innocent people are being killed, many homes, schools, factories and jobs are being destroyed, and water, power and sanitation facilities are being crippled?"

1999

## Is this oversight of the CIA or is it oversight?

Rep. Porter J. Goss, (R.-FL), chairman of the House Intelligence Committee, which ostensibly oversees the CIA, is a former CIA clandestine service officer.

The Director of the CIA, George Tenet, is a former Senate Intelligence Committee staff director.

Britt Snider, Inspector-General of the CIA, is not only a former counsel to the Senate intelligence committee, he was the principal drafter of the legislation that established the position of Inspector-General in 1990.

Keith Hall, Director of the multibillion-dollar National Reconnaissance Office, a supersecretive Pentagon arm whose very existence wasn't publicly revealed until 1992, is a former Senate staffer.

# INTERVENTIONS ARE US

## CHAPTER TWO

# Myth and Denial in the War Against Terrorism
## Just Why Do Terrorists Terrorize?

I t dies hard. It dies very hard. The notion that terrorist acts against the United States can be explained by envy and irrational hatred, and not by what the United States does to the world—i.e., US foreign policy—is alive and well.

The fires were still burning intensely at Ground Zero when Colin Powell declared: "Once again, we see terrorism, we see terrorists, people who don't believe in democracy ..."[1]

George W. picked up on that theme and ran with it. He's been its leading proponent ever since September 11 with his repeated insistence, in one wording or another, that terrorists are people who hate America and all that it stands for, its democracy, its freedom, its wealth, its secular government." (Ironically, the president and Attorney General John Ashcroft probably hate our secular government as much as anyone.)

Here he is more than a year after September 11: "The threats we face are global terrorist attacks. That's the threat. And the more you love freedom, the more likely it is you'll be attacked."[2]

The American Council of Trustees and Alumni, a conservative watchdog group founded by Lynne Cheney, wife of the vice-president, announced in November 2001 the formation of the Defense of Civilization Fund, declaring that "It was not only America that was attacked on September 11, but civilization. We were attacked not for our vices, but for our virtues."[3]

In September 2002, the White House released the "National Security Strategy", purported to be chiefly the handiwork of Condoleezza Rice, which speaks of the "rogue states" which "sponsor terrorism around the globe; and reject basic human values and hate the United States and everything for which it stands."

In July of the following year, we could hear the spokesman for Homeland Security, Brian Roehrkasse, declare: "Terrorists hate our freedoms. They want to change our ways."[4]

Thomas Friedman the renowned foreign policy analyst of the *New York Times* would say amen. Terrorists, he wrote in 1998 after two US embassies in Africa had been attacked, "have no specific ideological program or demands. Rather, they are driven by a generalized hatred of the US, Israel and other supposed enemies of Islam."[5]

This *idée fixe*—that the rise of anti-American terrorism owes nothing to American policies—in effect postulates an America that is always the aggrieved innocent in a treacherous world, a benign United States government peacefully going about its business but being "provoked" into taking extreme measures to defend its people, its freedom and its democracy. There consequently is no good reason to modify US foreign policy, and many people who might otherwise know better are scared into supporting the empire's wars out of the belief that there's no choice but to crush without mercy—or even without evidence—this irrational international force out there that hates the United States with an abiding passion.

Thus it was that Afghanistan and Iraq were bombed and invaded with seemingly little concern in Washington that this could well create many new anti-American terrorists. And indeed, since the first strike on Afghanistan in October 2001 there have been literally scores of terrorist attacks against American institutions in the Middle East, South Asia and the Pacific, more than a dozen in Pakistan alone: military, civilian, Christian, and other targets associated with the United States, including the October 2002 bombings in Bali, Indonesia, which destroyed two nightclubs and killed more than 200 people, almost all of them Americans and their Australian and British allies. The following year brought the heavy bombing of the US-managed Marriott Hotel in Jakarta, Indonesia, the site of diplomatic receptions and 4th of July celebrations held by the American Embassy.

Even when a terrorist attack is not aimed directly at Americans, the reason the target has been chosen can be because the country it takes place in has been cooperating with the United States in its so-called "War on Terrorism". Witness the horrendous attacks of recent years in Madrid, Turkey and Saudi Arabia.

A US State Department report on worldwide terrorist attacks showed that the year 2003 had more "significant terrorist incidents" than at any time since the department began issuing statistics in 1982; the 2003 figures do not include attacks on US troops by insurgents in Iraq.[6]

## Terrorists in their own words

The word "terrorism" has been so overused in recent years that it's now commonly used simply to stigmatize any individual or group one doesn't like, for almost any kind of behavior involving force. But the word's *raison d'être* has traditionally been to convey a political meaning, something along the lines of: the deliberate use of violence against civilians and property to intimidate or coerce a government or the population in furtherance of a political objective.

Terrorism is fundamentally propaganda, a very bloody form of propaganda.

It follows that if the perpetrators of a terrorist act declare what their objective was, their statement should carry credibility, no matter what one thinks of the objective or the method used to achieve it. Let us look at some of their actual declarations.

The terrorists responsible for the bombing of the World

Trade Center in 1993 sent a letter to the *New York Times* which stated, in part: "We declare our responsibility for the explosion on the mentioned building. This action was done in response for the American political, economical, and military support to Israel the state of terrorism and to the rest of the dictator countries in the region."[7]

Richard Reid, who tried to ignite a bomb in his shoe while aboard an American Airline flight to Miami in December 2001, told police that his planned suicide attack was an attempt to strike a blow against the US campaign in Afghanistan and the Western economy. In an e-mail sent to his mother, which he intended her to read after his death, Reid wrote that it was his duty "to help remove the oppressive American forces from the Muslims land."[8]

After the bombings in Bali, one of the leading suspects—later convicted—told police that the bombings were "revenge" for "what Americans have done to Muslims." He said that he wanted to "kill as many Americans as possible" because "America oppresses the Muslims."[9]

In November 2002, a taped message from Osama bin Laden began: "The road to safety begins by ending the aggression. Reciprocal treatment is part of justice. The [terrorist] incidents that have taken place...are only reactions and reciprocal actions."[10]

That same month, when Mir Aimal Kasi, who killed several people outside of CIA headquarters in 1993, was on death row, he declared: "What I did was a retaliation against the US government" for American policy in the Middle East and its support of Israel.[11]

It should be noted that the State Department warned at the time that the execution of Kasi could result in attacks against Americans around the world.[12] It did not warn that the attacks would result from foreigners hating or envying American democracy, freedom, wealth, or secular government.

Similarly, in the days following the start of US bombing of

Afghanistan there were numerous warnings from US government officials about being prepared for retaliatory acts, and during the war in Iraq, the State Department announced: "Tensions remaining from the recent events in Iraq may increase the potential threat to US citizens and interests abroad, including by terrorist groups."[13]

Another example of the difficulty the Bush administration has in consistently maintaining its simplistic *idée fixe*: In June 2002, after a car bomb exploded outside the US Consulate in Karachi, killing or injuring more than 60 people, the *Washington Post* reported that "US officials said the attack was likely the work of extremists angry at both the United States and Pakistan's president, Gen. Pervez Musharraf, for siding with the United States after September 11 and abandoning support for Afghanistan's ruling Taliban."[14]

George W. and others of his administration may or may not believe what they tell the world about the motivations behind anti-American terrorism, but, as in the examples just given, some officials have questioned the party line for years. A Department of Defense study in 1997 concluded: "Historical data show a strong correlation between US involvement in international situations and an increase in terrorist attacks against the United States."[15]

Former US president Jimmy Carter told the *New York Times* in a 1989 interview:

> We sent Marines into Lebanon and you only have to go to Lebanon, to Syria or to Jordan to witness first-hand the intense hatred among many people for the United States because we bombed and shelled and unmercifully killed totally innocent villagers—women and children and farmers and housewives—in those villages around Beirut....As a result of that...we became kind of a Satan in the minds of those who are deeply resentful. That is what precipitated the taking of our hostages and that is what has precipitated some of the terrorist attacks.[16]

Colin Powell has also revealed that he knows better. Writing of this same 1983 Lebanon debacle in his memoir, he forgoes clichés about terrorists hating democracy: "The U.S.S. *New Jersey* started hurling 16-inch shells into the mountains above Beirut, in World War II style, as if we were softening up the beaches on some Pacific atoll prior to an invasion. What we tend to overlook in such situations is that other people will react much as we would."[17]

The ensuing terrorist attack against US Marine barracks in Lebanon took the lives of 241 American military personnel.

The bombardment of Beirut in 1983 and 1984 is but one of many examples of American violence against the Middle East and/or Muslims since the 1980s. The record includes:

- the shooting down of two Libyan planes in 1981
- the bombing of Libya in 1986
- the bombing and sinking of an Iranian ship in 1987
- the shooting down of an Iranian passenger plane in 1988
- the shooting down of two more Libyan planes in 1989
- the massive bombing of the Iraqi people in 1991
- the continuing bombings and sanctions against Iraq for the next 12 years
- the bombing of Afghanistan and Sudan in 1998
- the habitual support of Israel despite the routine devastation and torture it inflicts upon the Palestinian people
- the habitual condemnation of Palestinian resistance to this
- the abduction of "suspected terrorists" from Muslim countries, such as Malaysia, Pakistan, Lebanon and Albania, who are then taken to places like Egypt and Saudi Arabia, where they are tortured
- the large military and hi-tech presence in Islam's holiest land, Saudi Arabia, and elsewhere in the Persian Gulf region

- the support of undemocratic, authoritarian Middle East governments from the Shah of Iran to the Saudis.

"How do I respond when I see that in some Islamic countries there is vitriolic hatred for America?" asked George W. "I'll tell you how I respond: I'm amazed. I'm amazed that there's such misunderstanding of what our country is about that people would hate us. I am—like most Americans, I just can't believe it because I know how good we are."[18]

It's not just people in the Middle East who have good reason for hating what the US government does. The United States has created huge numbers of potential terrorists all over Latin America during a half century of American actions far worse than what it's done in the Middle East. If Latin Americans shared the belief of radical Muslims that they will go directly to paradise for martyring themselves in the act of killing the great Satan enemy, by now we might have had decades of repeated terrorist horror coming from south of the border.

As it is, there have been many non-suicidal terrorist attacks against Americans and their buildings in Latin America over the years.

To what extent do Americans really believe the official disconnect between what the US does in the world and anti-American terrorism? One indication that the public is somewhat skeptical came in the days immediately following the commencement of the bombing of Iraq on March 20 of this year. The airlines later announced that there had been a sharp increase in cancellations of flights and a sharp decrease in future flight reservations in those few days.[19]

In June, the Pew Research Center released the results of polling in 20 Muslim countries and the Palestinian territories that brought into question another official thesis, that support for anti-American terrorism goes hand in hand with hatred of American society. The polling revealed that people interviewed had much more "confidence" in Osama bin Laden than in

George W. Bush. However, "the survey suggested little correlation between support for bin Laden and hostility to American ideas and cultural products. People who expressed a favorable opinion of bin Laden were just as likely to appreciate American technology and cultural products as people opposed to bin Laden. Pro- and anti-bin Laden respondents also differed little in their views on the workability of Western-style democracy in the Arab world."[20]

## The Iraqi resistance

The official Washington mentality about the motivations of individuals they call terrorists is also manifested in current US occupation policy in Iraq. Secretary of War Donald Rumsfeld has declared that there are five groups opposing US forces—looters, criminals, remnants of Saddam Hussein's government, foreign terrorists and those influenced by Iran.[21] An American official in Iraq maintains that many of the people shooting at US troops are "poor young Iraqis" who have been paid between $20 and $100 to stage hit-and-run attacks on US soldiers. "They're not dedicated fighters," he said. "They're people who wanted to take a few potshots."[22]

With such language do American officials avoid dealing with the idea that any part of the resistance is composed of Iraqi citizens who are simply demonstrating their resentment about being bombed, invaded, occupied, and subjected to daily humiliations.

Some officials convinced themselves that it was largely the most loyal followers of Saddam Hussein and his two sons who were behind the daily attacks on Americans, and that with the capture or killing of the evil family, resistance would die out; tens of millions of dollars were offered as reward for information leading to this joyful prospect. Thus it was that the killing of the sons elated military personnel. US Army trucks with loudspeakers drove through small towns and villages to broadcast a message about the death of Hussein's sons. "Coalition forces have won a great victory over the Baath Party and the Saddam Hussein regime by killing Uday and Qusay Hussein in Mosul," said the message broadcast in Arabic. "The Baath Party has no power in Iraq. Renounce the Baath Party or you are in great danger." It called on all officials of Hussein's government to turn themselves in.[23]

What followed was several days of some of the deadliest attacks against American personnel since the guerrilla war began. Unfazed, American officials in Washington and Iraq continue to suggest that the elimination of Saddam will write finis to anti-American actions.

Another way in which the political origins of terrorism are obscured is by the common practice of blaming poverty or repression by Middle Eastern governments (as opposed to US support for such governments) for the creation of terrorists. Defenders of US foreign policy cite this also as a way of showing how enlightened they are. Here's Condoleezza Rice:

> [The Middle East] is a region where hopelessness provides a fertile ground for ideologies that convince promising youths to aspire not to a university education, a career or family, but to blowing themselves up, taking as many innocent lives with them as possible. We need to address the source of the problem.[24]

Many on the left speak in a similar fashion, apparently unconscious of what they're obfuscating. This analysis confuses terrorism with revolution.

In light of the several instances mentioned above, among others which could be cited, of US officials giving the game away, in effect admitting that terrorists and guerrillas may be, or in fact are, reacting to actual hurts and injustices, it may be that George W. is the only true believer among them, if in fact *he is one*. The thought may visit leaders of the American Empire, at least occasionally, that all their expressed justifications for invading Iraq and Afghanistan and for their "War on Terrorism" are no more than fairy tales for young children and grown-up innocents. But officialdom doesn't make statements to represent reality. It constructs stories to legitimize the pursuit of interests. And the interests here are irresistibly compelling: creating the most powerful empire in all history, enriching their class comrades, remaking the world in their own ideological image.

Being the target of terrorism is just one of the prices you pay for such prizes, and terrorist attacks provide a great excuse for the next intervention, the next expansion of the empire, the next expansion of the military budget.

A while ago, I heard a union person on the radio proposing what he called "a radical solution to poverty—pay people enough to live on."

Well, I'd like to propose a radical solution to anti-American terrorism—stop giving terrorists the motivation to attack America. As long as the imperial mafia insist that anti-American terrorists have no good or rational reason for retaliation against the United States for anything the US has ever done to their countries, as long as US foreign policy continues with its bloody and oppressive interventions, the "War on Terrorism" is as doomed to failure as the war on drugs has been.

If I were the president, I could stop terrorist attacks against the United States in a few days. Permanently. I would first apologize—very publicly and very sincerely—to all the widows and orphans, the impoverished and the tortured, and all the many millions of other victims of American imperialism. Then I would announce to every corner of the world that America's global military interventions have come to an end. I would then inform Israel that it is no longer the 51st state of the union but—oddly enough—a foreign country. Then I would reduce the military budget by at least 90% and use the savings to pay reparations to the victims and repair the damage from the many American bombings, invasions and sanctions. There would be more than enough money. One year's military budget in the United States is equal to more than $20,000 per hour for every hour since Jesus Christ was born. That's one year.

That's what I'd do on my first three days in the White House. On the fourth day, I'd be assassinated.

## September 11 Commission

On June 16, 2004, the National Commission on Terrorist Attacks Upon the United States (investigating the events of September 11, 2001), issued a report which stated that Khalid Sheik Mohammed, regarded as the mastermind of the attacks, wanted to personally commandeer one aircraft and use it as a platform to denounce U.S. policies in the Middle East. Instead of crashing it in a suicide attack, the report says, Mohammed planned to kill every adult male passenger on the plane, contact the media while airborne, and land at a U.S. airport. There he would deliver his speech before releasing all the women and children.[25]

The question once again arises: Why was Mohammed planning on denouncing US policies in the Middle East? Why wasn't he instead planning to denounce America's democracy, freedom, wealth and secular government?

Two days later, Islamic militants in Saudi Arabia beheaded an employee of the leading US defense contractor, Lockheed Martin, maker of the Apache helicopter, on which the victim, Paul Johnson, Jr. had long worked. His kidnappers said he was singled out for that reason. "The infidel got his fair treatment....Let him taste something of what Muslims have long tasted from Apache helicopter fire and missiles."[26]

## Addendum: Terrorists as mentally retarded

The reluctance to ascribe rational human motivations to militant political opponents is not confined to American leaders. Documents disclosed in 2002 in Spain reveal that during the 1936-39 civil war, the Spanish fascists subjected their leftist prisoners to a battery of physical and psychological tests for the purpose finding some inherent deformity that would explain their bizarre ideology. Unsurprisingly, they concluded that amongst the captured members of the pro-republican International Brigades, almost a third of the British nationals were "mental retards". Another third were deemed to be suffering degenerative mental illnesses that were turning them into schizoids, paranoids or psychopaths. Their fall into Marxism was, in turn, exacerbated by the fact that 29% were also considered "social imbeciles". As *The Guardian* of London noted:

> For dictator General Francisco Franco's chief psychiatrist, Dr. Antonio Vallejo Nagera, it must have seemed obvious. If the generalissimo and his fellow right-wing rebels in the Spanish civil war were crusaders for justice, God and the truth, then their leftwing opponents had to be mad, psychotic or at least congenitally subnormal.

Dr. Vallejo concluded: "Once more we see confirmed that social resentment, frustrated aspirations and envy are the sources of Marxism.[27] Also in 2002, it was reported that:

> In an attempt to divine the terrorist impulse, German officials authorized the removal and study of the brains of four Red Army Faction leaders following their deaths in the 1970s, according to news reports in Germany, but scientists apparently came up with no physiological explanation for the leaders' political violence.[28]

Anything for officials to avoid facing up to social and political realities.

## CHAPTER THREE

# Reflections on September 11, 2001 and the Bombing of Afghanistan

[A version of this essay first appeared in *Shattered Illusions: Analyzing the War on Terrorism*, edited by Aftab Ahmad Malik (UK, 2002)]

Following the terrible, momentous events of September 11, 2001, the most pressing mission facing the United States, in addition to punishing the perpetrators who were still alive, was—or should have been—to not allow what happened to pass without deriving important lessons from it to prevent its recurrence. Clearly, the most meaningful of these lessons was the answer to the question: Why do terrorists hate America enough to give up their lives in order to deal the country such mortal blows?

Of course it's not America the terrorists hate; it's American foreign policy. It's what the United States has done to the world in the past half century—all the violence, the bombings, the depleted uranium, the cluster bombs, the assassinations, the promotion of torture, the overthrow of governments, and much more.

The terrorists—whatever else they might be—are also rational human beings; which is to say that in their own minds they have a rational justification for their actions. Most terrorists are people deeply concerned by what they see as social, political, or religious injustice and hypocrisy, and the immediate grounds for their terrorism is often retaliation for an action of the United States.

The magnitude of the September 11 attack was such that the American media—the serious or passably serious segment of it—were obliged to delve into areas they normally do not visit. A number of mainstream newspapers, magazines and radio stations, in their quest to understand "Why?", suddenly—or so it seemed—discovered that the United States had been engaged in actions such as those mentioned above and countless other interventions in foreign lands over decades that could indeed produce a great measure of anti-American feeling.

This was one positive outcome of the tragedy. This "revelation," however, appeared to escape the mass of the American people, the great majority of whom get their snatches of foreign news from tabloid newspapers, lowest-common-denominator radio programs, and laughably superficial TV newscasts.

Thus it was that instead of an outpouring of reflection upon what the United States does to the world to make it so hated, there was an outpouring of patriotism of the narrowest kind: Congress members stood on the steps of the Capitol and sang "God Bless America", stores quickly sold out their stocks of American flags, which fluttered high and low from whatever one's eyes fell upon, callers to radio shows spit out venom and bloodlust, at entertainment and sporting events it became *de rigueur* to begin with a military and/or patriotic ceremony, one could hardly pick up a newspaper or turn on the radio or TV without some tribute to American courage, and everyone and his cousin were made into "heroes".

And the serious American media soon returned to normal mode; i.e., one could regularly find more significant and revealing information concerning US foreign policy in the London papers, *The Guardian* and *The Independent*, than in the *New York Times* and *Washington Post*.

## The Perpetrators

For more than three months the most powerful nation in history rained down a daily storm of missiles upon one of the poorest and most backward people in the world. Eventually, this question pressed itself onto the world's stage: Who killed more innocent, defenseless people? The terrorists in the United States on September 11 with their flying bombs? Or the Americans in Afghanistan with their AGM-86D cruise missiles, their AGM-130 missiles, their 15,000 pound "daisy cutter" bombs, their depleted uranium, and their cluster bombs?

By year's end, the count of the terrorists' victims in New York, Washington and Pennsylvania stood at about 3,000. The total count of civilian dead in Afghanistan was essentially ignored by American officials and just about everyone else, but a painstaking compilation of numerous individual reports from the domestic and international media, aid agencies, and the United Nations, by an American professor—hunting down the many separate incidents of 100-plus counts of the dead, the scores of dead, the dozens, and the smaller numbers—arrived at considerably more than 3,500 through early December, and still counting.[1]

This latter figure does not include those who died later of bomb injuries, or those who died from cold and hunger due to the bombing's interruption of aid supplies and destruction of their homes, which turned them into refugees. Neither does it include the thousands of "military" deaths or the hundreds of prisoners who were murdered by Washington's new "freedom fighters" in conjunction with American military and intelligence operatives. In the final analysis, the body count will also be missing the inevitable victims of cluster bombs-turned landmines (tragically, amongst the first victims of the US bombing were four UN minesweepers) and those who perish slower deaths from depleted-uranium-caused sicknesses.

There will be no minutes of silence for the Afghan dead,

no memorial services attended by high American officials and entertainment celebrities, no messages of condolence sent by heads of state, no millions of dollars raised for the victims' families. Yet, all in all, it was a bloodbath that more than rivals that of September 11.

And of the thousands dead in Afghanistan, how many, can it be said with any certainty, had played a conscious role in the American catastrophe?

According to the video of Osama bin Laden presented to the world by the US government, he himself didn't find out the exact date of the terrorist act until five days before it took place, and most of the hijackers did not know they were part of a suicide mission until they prepared to board the planes. (The FBI reportedly came to the latter conclusion long before the video was made public.)[2] Given that, it appears eminently safe to say that exceedingly few other people in the world were knowingly in on the plot, perhaps a number that can be counted on the fingers of one hand. Consequently, if the American bombing campaign was designed to kill the actual perpetrators, it was a fool's mission; a violent fool.

If Timothy McVeigh, perpetrator of the terrible bombing of the federal building in Oklahoma City in 1995, had not been quickly caught, would the United States have bombed the state of Michigan or any of the other places he called home? No, they would have instituted a mammoth manhunt until they found him and punished him. But in Afghanistan, the United States proceeded virtually on the assumption that everyone who supported the Taliban government, native or foreigner, was 1) a "terrorist" and 2) morally, if not legally, stained with the blood of September 11—or perhaps one or another anti-US terrorist action of the past—and was thus fair game.

Whatever one thinks of the appalling society the Taliban created, they have not really been associated with terrorist acts, and the masses of Taliban supporters can't be held responsible if their leader, one person, allows foreign terrorists into the country, any more than I would want to be held responsible for all the anti-Castro terrorists in Miami. Most of the foreigners had probably come to Afghanistan to help the Taliban in their civil war, nothing the US government should be concerned about. Might some of them in the future be up to no good? Quite possibly. But which ones? Preventive execution is a questionable enough concept, but what the US carried out was *random* preventive execution, bombing whom it may concern.

However, when the shoe is on another foot, even American officials can perceive which is the honorable path to walk. Speaking of Russia's problem with Chechnya in 1999, the US State Department's second in command, Strobe Talbott, urged Moscow to show "restraint and wisdom". Restraint, he said, "means taking action against real terrorists, but not using indiscriminate force that endangers innocents."[3]

Suggesting a moral equivalency between the United States government and terrorists (or, during the cold war, with communists) never fails to inflame American anger. The terrorists purposely aimed to kill civilians we are told (actually, many of the victims were military or military employees), while any non-combatant victims of the American bombings were completely accidental.

Whenever the United States goes into one of its periodic bombing frenzies and its missiles take the lives of numerous civilians, this is called "collateral damage"—inflicted by the Fates of War; for the real targets, we are invariably told, were military.

But if day after day, in one country after another, the same scenario takes place—dropping prodigious quantities of powerfully lethal ordnance from very high altitudes with the full knowledge that large numbers of civilians will perish or be maimed, even without missiles going "astray"—what can one say about the intentions of the American military? The best, the most charitable, thing that can be said is that they simply don't care. They want to bomb and destroy for certain political ends and they don't particularly care if the civilian population suffers grievously. "Negligent homicide" might be suitable legal terminology.

In Afghanistan, when, on successive days in October, US gunships machine-gunned and cannoned the remote farming village of Chowkar-Karez killing as many as 93 civilians, a Pentagon official was moved to respond at one point: "the people there are dead because we wanted them dead", while US Defense Secretary Donald Rumsfeld commented: "I cannot deal with that particular village."[4]

On occasion, US bombing campaigns do have as part of their agenda the causing of suffering, hoping that it will lead the people under the falling bombs to turn against the government. This was a recurrent feature of the bombing of Yugoslavia in 1999. US/NATO officials, in their consummate arrogance, freely admitted this again and again.[5]

And in Afghanistan we have the example of the chief of the British Defense Staff, Adm. Sir Michael Boyce, declaring that the bombing will continue "until the people of the country themselves recognize that this is going to go on until they get the leadership changed."[6]

Such a policy fits very well into the FBI definition of terrorism, which speaks of the use of force or violence against persons or property "to intimidate or coerce a government, the civilian population, or any segment thereof, in furtherance of political or social objectives."

In any event, the September 11 terrorists could just as easily claim that their aim was not to kill civilians but to inflict great damage to the institutions that represent and carry out American imperialism: the World Trade Center—the economic arm; the Pentagon—the military arm, and the aborted plane attack may well have been intended for the political arm: the White House. After all, if killing civilians were their principal aim they could have flown one or more planes into a full football stadium—right into the stands—and killed many thousands more. It was, in fact, football season.

## The less Americans know, the better they feel

In reaction to a number of gruesome images of Afghan bombing victims, and expressed European and Middle-Eastern concern about civilian casualties, the American media strove to downplay the significance of such deaths. The chairman of Cable News Network (CNN) advised the news staff that it "seems perverse to focus too much on the casualties or hardship in Afghanistan."[7]

A Fox News Channel report on the war wondered why journalists should bother covering civilian deaths at all. "The question I have," said the host, "is civilian casualties are historically, by definition, a part of war, really. Should they be as big news as they've been?" His guest from National Public Radio replied: "No. Look, war is about killing people. Civilian casualties are unavoidable." Another guest, a columnist from the national magazine, U.S. News & World Report, had no argument: "Civilian casualties are not...news. The fact is that they accompany wars."[8]

But if in fact the September 11 attacks were an act of war, as the world has been told repeatedly by George W. Bush and his minions, then the casualties of the World Trade Center were clearly civilian war casualties. Why then has the media devoted so much time to their deaths?

These were the only kind of deaths Americans wanted to hear about and they could become furious when told of Afghan deaths. A memo circulated at the Panama City, Florida News Herald warned editors: "DO NOT USE photos on Page 1A showing civilian casualties from the U.S. war on Afghanistan. Our sister paper in Fort Walton Beach has done so and received hundreds and hundreds of threatening e-mails and the like."[9]

The American powers-that-be can indeed count on support for their wars from the American people and the corporate media. It would take an exemplary research effort to uncover a single American daily newspaper that unequivocally opposed the US bombing of Afghanistan.

Or a single American daily newspaper that unequivocally opposed the US-NATO bombing of Yugoslavia two years earlier.

Or a single American daily newspaper that unequivocally opposed the US bombing of Iraq in 1991.

Is this not remarkable? In a supposedly free society, with a supposedly free press, and almost 1,500 daily newspapers, the odds should be decidedly against this being the case.

In 1968, at the height of the Vietnam War, a survey by the *Boston Globe* of editorial positions of 39 leading US newspapers found that "none advocated a pull-out"[10]

They're sacrosanct, these foreign invasions. When "our boys are putting their lives on the line," the media holds its tongue; though it's reached the stage where "our boys" are seldom putting their lives on the line at all because they're bombing from fifteen thousand feet above the victims. Yet, the old expression still holds: "Once at war, to reason is treason."

There's the story from the Cold War about a group of Russian writers touring the United States. They were astonished to find, after reading the newspapers and watching television, that almost all the opinions on all the vital issues were the same. "In our country," said one of them, "to get that result we have a dictatorship. We imprison people. We torture them. Here you have none of that. How do you do it? What's the secret?"

## The Mecca of hypocrisy

After the terrorist attacks in the United States, Secretary of State Colin Powell condemned "people who believe with the destruction of buildings, with the murder of people, they can somehow achieve a political purpose."[11]

Does that not precisely describe what the United States was aiming for two years earlier with its relentless bombing of Yugoslavia? And is this not the same Colin Powell who directed the horrific bombings of Panama and Iraq? Do American leaders think that no one has any memory? Or do they simply not care what people think?

More hypocrisy of the breathtaking kind: President Bush and other officials have routinely and angrily declared that it's not only terrorists that the US is going to be waging war against, it's any nation which *harbors* terrorists. However, as I've documented elsewhere, the reader can see that there are few, if any, nations that harbor more terrorists than the United States.[12]

## Winning Afghan hearts and minds

Bombs were not all that fell from the sky from American airplanes. There were also food packages. Was it not something inordinately strange for the United States to be dropping both bombs and food on the people of Afghanistan on the same days?

If the Japanese had dropped some nice packages of teriyaki along with the bombs at Pearl Harbor, would Americans and the world have looked more kindly on the Japanese?

Perhaps if the September 11 terrorists had dropped some hot pastrami sandwiches on downtown Manhattan before their hijacked planes hit the World Trade Center ...

But these things work of course. Millions of Americans felt a rush of pride about their country's magnanimity. The United States, the inventor and perfecter of modern advertising and public relations, had done it again.

And in the same vein, there were the many flyers dropped upon the people of Afghanistan. Here's one dropped around Oct. 20:

Do you enjoy being ruled by the Taliban? Are you proud to live a life of fear? Are you happy to see the place your family has owned for generations a terrorist training site? Do you want a regime that is turning Afghanistan into the Stone Age and giving Islam a bad name? Are you proud to live under a government that harbors terrorists? Are you proud to live in a nation ruled by extreme fundamentalists? The Taliban have robbed your country of your culture and heritage. They have destroyed your national monuments, and cultural artifacts. They rule by force, violence, and fear based on the advice of foreigners. They insist that their form of Islam is the one and only form, the true form, the divine form. They see themselves as religious experts, even though they are ignorant. They kill, commit injustice, keep you in poverty and claim it is in the name of God.

In the same spirit, the following flyer might be dropped over the United States:

Do you enjoy being ruled by the Republican-Democratic Party? Are you proud to live a life of fear, insecurity and panic? Are you happy to see the place your family has owned for generations taken away by a bank? Do you want a regime that is turning the United States into a police state and giving Christianity a bad name? Are you proud to live under a government that harbors hundreds of terrorists in Miami? Are you proud to live in a nation ruled by extreme capitalists and religious conservatives? The capitalists have robbed your country of your equality and justice. They have destroyed your national parks and rivers and corrupted your media, your elections and your personal relations. They rule by threat of unemployment, hunger, and homelessness based on the advice of a god called the market. They insist that their form of organizing a society and remaking the world is the one and only form, the true form, the divine form. They see themselves as morality experts, even though they are ignorant. They bomb, invade, assassinate, torture, overthrow, commit injustice, keep you and the world in poverty and claim it is in the name of God.

## Rebuilding Afghanistan?

"U.S. Meeting Envisions Rebuilding Afghanistan" read the headline in the *Washington Post* of November 21. After a one-day meeting in Washington of leaders from two dozen nations and international organizations, US and Japanese officials said they had developed an "action program" for the long-term rebuilding of the war- ravaged country.

This should throw another log on the feel-good-about-America fire that's been warming the frazzled citizenry since September 11. But like much of that fuel, there's likely a lot more propaganda here than substance.

It's a remarkable pattern. The United States has a long record of bombing nations, reducing entire neighborhoods, and much of cities, to rubble, wrecking the infrastructure, ruining the lives of those the bombs didn't kill. And afterward doing nothing to repair the damage.

On January 27, 1973, in Paris, the United States signed the "Agreement on Ending the War and Restoring Peace in Vietnam". Among the principles to which the United States agreed was the one stated in Article 21: "In pursuance of its traditional [sic] policy, the United States will contribute to healing the wounds of war and to postwar reconstruction of the Democratic Republic of Vietnam [North Vietnam] and throughout Indochina."

Five days later, President Nixon sent a message to the Prime Minister of North Vietnam in which he stipulated the following:

(1)  The Government of the United States of America will contribute to postwar reconstruction in North Vietnam without any political conditions.

(2)  Preliminary United States studies indicate that the appropriate programs for the United States contribution to postwar reconstruction will fall in the range of $3.25 billion of grant aid over 5 years."

Nothing of the promised reconstruction aid was ever paid. Or ever will be.

During the same period, Laos and Cambodia were devastated by US bombing as unrelentlessly as was Vietnam. After the Indochina wars were over, these nations, too, qualified to become beneficiaries of America's "traditional policy" of zero reconstruction.

Then came the American bombings of Grenada and Panama in the 1980s. There goes our neighborhood. Hundreds of Panamanians petitioned the Washington-controlled Organization of American States as well as American courts, all the way up to the US Supreme Court, for "just compensation" for the damage caused by Operation Just Cause (this being the not-tongue-in-cheek name given to the American invasion and bombing). They got just nothing, the same amount the people of Grenada received.

It was Iraq's turn next, in 1991: 40 days and nights of relentless bombing; destruction of power, water and sanitation systems and everything else that goes into the making of a modern society. We all know how much the United States has done to help rebuild Iraq.

In 1998, Washington in its grand wisdom fired more than a dozen cruise missiles into a building in Sudan which it claimed was producing chemical and biological weapons. The completely destroyed building was actually a pharmaceutical plant. The United States effectively admitted its mistake by unfreezing the assets of the plant's owner it had frozen. Surely now it was compensation time. But as of October 2001, nothing had been paid to the owner, who had sued, the Sudanese government, or those injured in the bombing. [see chapter 7]

The following year we had the case of Yugoslavia; 78 days of round-the-clock bombing, transforming an advanced state into virtually a pre-industrial one; the reconstruction needs were breathtaking. Two years later, June 2001, after the Serbs had obediently followed Washington's wishes to oust Slobodan

Milosevic and turn him over to the kangaroo court in the Hague that the US had pushed through the Security Council, a "donor's conference" was convened by the European Commission and the World Bank, supposedly concerned with Yugoslavia's reconstruction. It turned out to be a conference concerned with Yugoslavia's debts more than anything else.

Serbian premier Zoran Djindjic, regarded as highly pro-Western, said, in a July interview with the German news-magazine *Der Spiegel*, that he felt betrayed by the West. "It would have been better if the donors-conference had not taken place and instead we had been given 50 million DM in cash....In August we should be getting the first installment, 300 million Euro. Suddenly we are being told, that 225 million Euro will be withheld for the repayment of old debts which in part were accumulated during Tito's time. Two thirds of that sum are fines and interests, accrued because Milosevic refused for ten years to pay back these credits. We shall get the remaining 75 million Euro in November at the earliest. Such are the princi-ples in the West, we are being told. This means: A seriously ill person is to be given medicine after he is dead. Our critical months will be July, August and September."

It's been 2 1/2 years since Yugoslavian bridges fell into the Danube, the country's factories and homes destroyed, its roads made unusable, transportation torn apart. As of yet, the coun-try has not received any funds for reconstruction from the archi-tect and leading perpetrator of the bombing campaign, the United States.

Whoever winds up ruling Afghanistan will be conspicu-ously unable to block the establishment of US military bases, electronic listening posts, oil and gas pipelines, or whatever else Washington would like to build there. As to the United States doing some building for the Afghan people, they may have a long wait.

In marked contrast to the *Washington Post* headline of November 21 noted above, was the report in the same newspaper five weeks later: "The Bush administration has made clear that because it has paid for most of the military campaign that made the new government possible, it expects other countries, especially Japan and European nations, to lead the way in rebuilding the country."[13]

As if the American bombing campaign had been carried out at the request of, or for the benefit of, Japan and Europe, and not for Washington's own interests.

Following their bombing of Iraq in 1991, the United States wound up with military bases in Saudi Arabia, Kuwait, Bahrain, Qatar, Oman and the United Arab Emirates.

Following their bombing of Yugoslavia in 1999, the United States wound up with military bases in Kosovo, Albania, Bulgaria, Macedonia, Hungary, Bosnia, and Croatia.

Following their bombing of Afghanistan, the United States appears on course to wind up with military bases in Afghanistan, Pakistan, Kazakhstan, Uzbekistan, Tajikistan, Kyrgyzstan, and elsewhere in the area.

The bombing, invasion and occupation of Afghanistan were conducted—apart from the primitive lashing out in blind revenge against...somebody—primarily for the purpose of insuring the installation of a new government that will be sufficiently amenable to Washington's international objectives, including the siting of bases and electronic communications intercept stations and the running of oil and gas pipelines through the country from the Caspian Sea region.

For years, the American oil barons have had their eyes on the vast oil and gas reserves of this area, ideally with an Afghanistan-Pakistan route to the Indian Ocean, thus keeping Russia out of the picture. The oilmen have been quite open about this, giving very frank testimony before Congress for example. For several years, State Department and oil company officials met with the Taliban to discuss this, in Afghanistan and in the United States. George W. has now appointed a special American envoy to Afghanistan. His name is Zalmay

Khalilzad and lo and behold the man is a former aide to the American oil company Unocal, which has been highly active in the region for years in pursuit of the Caspian oil and gas.

For a long time Khalilzad lobbied publicly for a more sympathetic US government policy towards the Taliban, defending the Taliban regime against the many accusations of human rights violations, until the 1998 bombings of the American embassies in Africa and the US bombing of Afghanistan in retaliation. Until then, overthrowing the Taliban had not been a goal of Washington, but now that they've done it they would like the world to believe that it's a victory for freedom, and women's rights.

But the welfare of the people of Afghanistan does not appear to count for much, considering that the elements put into power by US military might are largely those whose earlier rule, before the Taliban, was so oppressive that many Afghans welcomed the Taliban to power; the newest atrocities of these worthies, carried out under cover of American firepower, show that they haven't lost their touch. The prime minister of the interim government, Hamid Karzai, though himself not seeming too villainous, may have a credibility problem, given his long close contact with the US State Department, National Security Council, Congress, and other pillars of the American establishment.[14] And he's also a former employee of Unocal.

Despite these ties, when leaders of the interim government asked the United States to halt its bombing in December because of the frequent mass deaths of innocents, Washington refused, saying it had its own timeline. This does not bode well for the future Afghan government and society; neither does Karzai's appointment of General Rashid Dostum as deputy defense minister, a man amongst whose charms is the habit of punishing his soldiers by tying them to tank tracks and then driving the tanks around his barracks' square to turn them into mincemeat.[15]

## Is this any way to end terrorism?

The American scorched-earth bombing of Afghanistan may well turn out to be a political train wreck. Can it be doubted that thousands throughout the Muslim world were emotionally and spiritually recruited to the cause of the next Osama bin Laden by the awful ruination and perceived injustice? That is to say, the next generation of terrorists. Indeed, in December, while the American bombs were still falling on Afghanistan, a man—British citizen Richard Reid, who was a convert to Islam—tried to blow up an American Airlines plane en route to the United States with explosives hidden in his shoes.

At the London mosque that Reid had attended, the cleric in charge warned that extremists were enlisting other young men like Reid and that agents aligned with radical Muslim figures had stepped up recruiting efforts since September 11. The cleric said that he knew of "hundreds of Richard Reids" recruited in Britain. Reid, described in the press as a "drifter", reportedly traveled to Israel, Egypt, the Netherlands, and Belgium before arriving in Paris and boarding the American Airlines plane.[16] This raises the question of who was financing him. The freezing of numerous bank accounts of alleged terrorist groups throughout the world by the United States may have rather limited effect.

Americans do not feel any more secure in their places of work, in their places of leisure, or in their travels than they did a day before their government's bombings began.

Will the power elite pursue a path designed to douse hatred of the United States, or one bound to inflame it? Here's James Woolsey, former Director of the CIA, speaking in December in Washington, advocating an invasion of Iraq and unconcerned about the response of the Arab world: The silence of the Arab public in the wake of America's victories in Afghanistan, he said, proves that "only fear will re-establish respect for the U.S."[17]

## CHAPTER FOUR

# What Do the Imperial Mafia Really Want?

[written Feb. 17, 2003; the invasion of Iraq took place on March 20]

W hich is the more remarkable—that the United States can openly announce to the world its determination to invade a sovereign nation and overthrow its government in the absence of any attack or threat of attack from the intended target? Or that for an entire year the world has been striving to figure out what the superpower's real intentions are?

There are of course those who accept at face value Washington's stated motivations of "liberating" the people of Iraq from a dictatorship and bestowing upon them a full measure of democracy, freedom, prosperity and other eternal joys which are the stuff of American folklore. In light of a century of well-documented US foreign policy which reveals a virtually complete absence of such motivations, along with repeated opposite consequences resulting from such policies, we can dispense with this endeavor to appeal to the terminal gullibility of the American people; similarly with the government's attempt at humor by warning us that Iraq is an imminent military threat.

Presented here are some reflections about several of the causes that make the hearts of the imperial mafia beat faster in regard to Iraq, which may be helpful in arguing the anti-war point of view:

**Expansion of the American Empire:** adding more military bases and communications listening stations to the Pentagon's portfolio, setting up a command post from which to better monitor, control and intimidate the rest of the Middle East.

**Idealism:** the imperial mafia fundamentalists remaking the world in America's image, with free enterprise, belief in a political system straight out of an American high-school text-book, and Judeo-Christianity as core elements. They assume that US moral authority is as absolute and unchallengeable as its military power. Here is Michael Ledeen, former Reagan official, now at the American Enterprise Institute (one of the leading drum-beaters for attacking Iraq): "If we just let our own vision of the world go forth, and we embrace it entirely, and we don't try to be clever and piece together clever diplomatic solutions to this thing, but just wage a total war against these tyrants, I think we will do very well, and our children will sing great songs about us years from now."

**Oil:** to be in full control of Iraq's vast reserves, with Saudi oil and Iranian oil waiting defenselessly next door; OPEC will be stripped of its independence from Washington and will no longer think about replacing the dollar with the Euro as its official currency, as Iraq has already done; oil-dependent Europe may think twice next time about challenging Washington's policies; the emergence of the European Union as a competing superpower may be slowed down.

**Globalization:** Once relative security over the land, people and institutions has been established, the transnational corporations will march into Iraq ready to privatize everything at fire-sale prices, followed closely by the IMF, World Bank, World Trade Organization and the rest of the international financial extortionists.

**Arms industry:** As with each of America's endless wars, military manufacturers will rake in their exorbitant profits, then deliver their generous political contributions, inspiring Washington leaders to yet further warfare, each war also being the opportunity to test new weapons and hand out contracts for the rebuilding of the country just demolished. As an added bonus, Pentagon officers have jobs waiting for them with the same companies when they retire.

**Israel:** The men driving Bush to war include long-time militant supporters of Israel, such as Richard Perle, Paul Wolfowitz, and Douglas Feith, who, along with the rest of the powerful American- Israeli lobby, have advocated striking Iraq for years. Israel has been playing a key role in the American military buildup to the war. Besides getting rid of its arch enemy, Israel may have the opportunity after the war to carry out its final solution to the Palestinian question—transferring them to Jordan, ("liberated") Iraq, and anywhere else that expanded US hegemony in the Middle East will allow. At the same time, Iraq's abundant water could be diverted to relieve a parched Israel and an old Iraqi-to-Israel oil pipeline could be rejuvenated.

## CHAPTER FIVE

# Setting a High (Double) Standard

## Supplying Saddam Hussein with Weapons of Mass Destruction

[A version of this essay appeared in *The Progressive*, April 1998]

After her now-infamous 1996 remark that the "price" of American sanctions against Iraq—the death of half a million children—"is worth it", Secretary of State Madeleine Albright travels around the world to gather support for yet more punishment of a country where American bombings and seven years of sanctions have left about a million men, women andchildren dead and a previously well-off nation plunged intopoverty, disease, and malnutrition.

Their crime? They have a leader who refuses to cede all sovereignty to the United States (acting under its usual United Nations cover) which demands that every structure in Iraq, including the presidential palaces, be available for inspection for "weapons of mass destruction". After more than six years of these inspections, and significant destruction of stocks of forbidden chemical, biological, and nuclear weapon material, as well as weapons research and development programs, the UN team still refuses to certify that Iraq is clean enough.

Inasmuch as the country is larger than California, it's understandable that the inspectors cannot be certain that all prohibited weapons have been uncovered. It's equally understandable for Iraq to claim that the United States can, and will, continue to find some excuse not to give Iraq the certification needed to end the sanctions. Indeed, President Clinton has said more than once that the US will not allow sanctions to be lifted as long as Saddam Hussein remains in power.

It can be said that the United States has inflicted more vindictive punishment and ostracism upon Iraq than upon Germany or Japan after World War II.

The Saddam Hussein regime must wonder at the high (double) standard set by Washington. Less than a year ago, the US Senate passed an act to implement the "Convention on the Prohibition of the Development, Production, Stockpiling and Use of Chemical Weapons and on Their Destruction" (Short title: Chemical Weapons Convention), an international treaty which has been ratified by more than 100 nations in its five-year life.

The Senate act, Section 307, stipulates that "the President may deny a request to inspect any facility in the United States in cases where the President determines that the inspection may pose a threat to the national security interests of the United States." Saddam has asked for no more than that for Iraq. Presumably, under the Senate act, the White House, Pentagon, etc. would be off limits, as Saddam insists his presidential palaces should be, as well as the military unit responsible for his personal security, which an American colonel demanded to visit.

Moreover, Section 303 states that "Any objection by the President to an individual serving as an inspector...shall not be reviewable in any court." Again, this echoes a repeated complaint from the Iraqis—a recent team of 16 inspectors included 14 from the US and Britain, Saddam's two principal adversaries who are, at this very moment, busily planning new bombing raids on Iraq. The team was led by a US Marine Corps captain, a veteran of the Gulf War, who has been accused of spying by Iraq. But the Iraqis do not have a corresponding right of exclusion. The same section of the Senate act also provides that an FBI agent "accompanies each inspection team visit" in the United States.

The wishes of the Iraqi government to place certain sites off limits and to have less partisan inspectors have been dismissed out of hand by US government spokespersons and the American media. The prevailing attitude has been: "What do they have to hide?" (chuckle, chuckle).

The hypocrisy runs deeper yet. In his recent State of the Union address, President Clinton spoke of how we must "confront the new hazards of chemical and biological weapons and the outlaw states, terrorists and organized criminals seeking to acquire them." He castigated Saddam Hussein for "developing nuclear, chemical and biological weapons" and called for strengthening the Biological Weapons Convention. "You cannot defy the will of the world," the president proclaimed to Hussein. "You have used weapons of mass destruction before. We are determined to deny you the capacity to use them again."[1]

Who among the president's listeners knew, who among the media reported, that the United States had been the supplier to Iraq of much of the source biological and other materials and equipment Saddam's scientists required to create biological and chemical warfare programs?

According to a Senate Report of 1994[2]: From 1985, if not earlier, through 1989, a veritable witch's brew of biological materials was exported to Iraq by private American suppliers pursuant to application and licensing by the US Departmentof Commerce. Amongst these materials, which often produce slow and agonizing deaths, were:

- *Bacillus Anthracis*, cause of anthrax.

- *Clostridium Botulinum*, a source of botulinum toxin.

- *Histoplasma Capsulatam*, cause of a disease attacking lungs, brain, spinal cord and heart.

- Brucella Melitensis, a bacteria that can damage major organs.

- Clotsridium Perfringens, a highly toxic bacteria causing

systemic illness.

- Clostridium tetani, highly toxigenic.
- Also, Escherichia Coli (E.Coli); genetic materials; human and bacterial DNA.

Dozens of other pathogenic biological agents were shipped to Iraq during the 1980s. The Senate Report pointed out: "These biological materials were not attenuated or weakened and were capable of reproduction."[3]

"It was later learned," the committee stated, "that these microorganisms exported by the United States were identical to those the United Nations inspectors found and removed from the Iraqi biological warfare program."[4]

Additionally, United States exports to Iraq in this period included:

- Chemical warfare agent precursors.
- Chemical warfare agent production facility plans and technical drawings.
- Chemical warhead filling equipment.[5]

These exports continued to at least November 28, 1989 despite the fact that Iraq had been reported to be engaging in chemical warfare and possibly biological warfare against Iranians, Kurds, and Shiites since the early 1980s.

During the Iraq-Iran war of 1980-88, the United States gave military aid and intelligence information to both sides, hoping that each would inflict severe damage on the other, in line perhaps with what Noam Chomsky has postulated:

It's been a leading, driving doctrine of US foreign policy since the 1940s that the vast and unparalleled energy resources of the Gulf region will be effectively dominated by the United States and its clients, and, crucially, that no independent, indigenous force will be permitted to have a substantial influence on the administration of oil production and price.

This policy, as well as financial considerations, were likely the motivating forces behind selling Iraq the biological and chemical materials. (Iran was at that time regarded as the greater threat to the seemingly always threatened US national security.)

Indeed, there is evidence that Washington encouraged Iraq to attack Iran and ignite the war in the first place. A recently discovered Department of State document from Secretary of State Alexander Haig to President Reagan about Haig's trip to the Middle East in April 1981, said: "It was also interesting to confirm that President Carter gave the Iraqis a green light to launch the war against Iran through Fahd [Saudi Arabia's crown prince, later king]."[6]

As the American public and media are being prepared to accept and cheerlead the next bombing of the people of Iraq, the stated rationale, the official party line, is that Iraq is an "outlaw" state (or "rogue" state, or "pariah" state—the media obediently repeats all the White House and State Department buzz words), which is ignoring a United Nations Security Council resolution. Israel, however, has ignored many such resolutions without the US bombing Tel Aviv, imposing sanctions, or even cutting back military aid. But by some arcane ideological alchemy, Israel is not deemed an "outlaw" state by Washington.

Neither does the United States regard itself as such for turning its back on a ruling of the U.N.'s World Court in 1984 to cease its hostile military actions against Nicaragua, or for the numerous times the US has totally ignored overwhelming General Assembly resolutions, nor for its repeated use of chemical and biological agents against Cuba since the 1960s.

In any event, the weapons monitoring disagreement is between Iraq and the United Nations, not Iraq and the United

States. And the U.N. has not authorized any of its members to use force.

"What gives Britain and the United States the right to go it alone on this?" asked an unusually brave reporter at a February 6 Clinton/Blair press conference.

President Clinton offered no direct reply to the question. Prime Minister Blair gave no reply at all.[7]

The bombing looks to be inevitable; the boys are busy moving all their toys into position. Of course, no one knows what it will accomplish besides more death and destruction, and perhaps distracting the media from L'Affaire Clinton-Lewinsky. Saddam will remain in power. He'll be more stubborn than ever about the inspections. There may be one consolation for the Iraqi people. Discussing Secretary of Defense William Cohen's view of the matter, the press said: "U.S. officials remain wary—as he recalled they were during the 1991 war that evicted Iraqi forces from Kuwait—of doing so much military damage to Iraq as to weaken its regional role as a counterweight to Iran."[8]

## CHAPTER SIX

# Debate in Dublin: "America's foreign policy does more harm than good."

O n October 9, 2003 a debate was held at venerable Trinity College in Dublin. Organized by the University Philosophical Society, the proposition to be debated was: "America's foreign policy does more harm than good."

Supporting the proposition were: William Blum, American author; David Barsamian, American radio journalist and author; and Tom Hanahoe, Irish author.

Arguing against the proposition were: John Bruton, former Irish prime minister; Bill Rammell, British MP and minister in the Foreign Office; and Gideon Rose, Managing Editor of "Foreign Affairs", the journal of the Council on Foreign Relations, and former member of the Clinton National Security Council.

My opening presentation was as follows:

Let me take you back to the year 1975. There was a committee of the US congress called the Pike Committee, named after its chairman Otis Pike. This committee investigated the covert side of US foreign policy and discovered a number of scandalous secrets, some of which were leaked to the public, while others remained secret. In an interview Congressman Pike stated that any member of Congress could see the entire report if he agreed not to reveal anything that was in it. "But not many want to read it," he said.

The interviewer asked him "Why?"

And Pike replied: "Oh, they think it is better not to know. There are too many things that embarrass Americans in that report. You see, this country went through an awful trauma with Watergate. But even then, all they were asked to believe was that their president had been a bad person. In this new situation they are asked much more; they are asked to believe that their country has been evil. And nobody wants to believe that."

The word for that is of course "denial". The fact that we are here to discuss the question of whether American foreign policy does more harm than good is further proof of that denial, for the question has been answered many times over. I could fill up this entire room with books floor to ceiling and wall to wall documenting the great harm done to every corner of the world by American foreign policy.

Here is a short summary of what Washington has been engaged in from the end of World War II to the present:

- Attempting to overthrow more than 50 foreign governments.

- Unprovoked military invasion of some 20 sovereign nations.

- Working to crush more than 30 populist movements which were fighting against dictatorial regimes.

- Providing indispensable support to a small army of brutal dictatorships: Mobutu of Zaire, Pinochet of Chile, Duvalier of Haiti, Somoza of Nicaragua, the Greek junta, Marcos of the Philippines, Rhee of Korea, the Shah of Iran, 40 years of military dictators in Guatemala, Suharto of Indonesia, Hussein of Iraq, the Brazilian junta, Trujillo of the Dominican Republic, the Taliban of Afghanistan, and others.

- Dropping powerful bombs on the people of about 25 countries, including 40 consecutive days and nights in Iraq, 78 days and nights in Yugoslavia, and several months in

Afghanistan, all three of these countries having met the first requirement as an American bombing target—being completely defenseless. And not once ever has the United States come even close to repairing the great damage caused by its bombings. Afghanistan and Iraq are of course the latest examples.

- Increasing use of depleted uranium, one of the most despicable weapons ever designed by mankind, which produces grossly deformed babies amongst its many endearing qualities, and which, in a civilized world not intimidated by the United States, would be categorically banned.

- Repeated use of cluster bombs, another fiendish device designed by a mad scientist, which has robbed numerous young people of one or more limbs, and some of their eyesight, and continues to do so every day in many countries as the bombs remain on the ground.

- Assassination attempts on the lives of some 40 foreign political leaders.

- Crude interference in dozens of foreign democratic elections.

- Gross manipulation of labor movements.

- Shameless manufacture of "news", the disinformation effect of which is multiplied when CIA assets in other countries pick up the same stories.

- Providing handbooks, materials and encouragement for the practice of torture.

- Chemical or biological warfare or the testing of such weapons, and the use of powerful herbicides, all causing terrible effects to the people and environments of China, Korea, Vietnam, Laos, Panama, Cuba, Iraq, Afghanistan, Serbia and elsewhere.

- Encouragement of drug trafficking in various parts of the world when it served the CIA's purposes.

- Supporting death squads, particularly in Latin America.

- Causing grievous harm to the health and well-being of the

world's masses by turning the screws of the IMF, World Bank, WTO, and other international financial institutions, as well as by imposing unmerciful sanctions and embargoes.

Much of the above has led to millions of refugees wandering homeless over the earth.

And what do those who champion the mystique of "America" offer in defense of this record? Well, denial is the first line of defense. Well-known and respected foreign policy analysts in the United States write entire books on American foreign policy with little more than a hint of what I've just mentioned. When all else fails, they fall back on the argument that "The United States means well." American policies, they will concede, may sometimes be foolish or mistaken, Washington may sometimes blunder, even occasionally do a bit more harm than good as things turn out...but the intention is always benevolent.

Let us look at a recent example of what some people would say was evidence of US foreign policy being a force for good—Afghanistan, where the awful Taliban were overthrown. How can one argue against that? Well, in the past two years ...

- warlords have returned to extensive power

- opium cultivation is once again booming

- a man hand-picked by Washington is president; both the president and several of his ministers are actually Afghan-Americans

- countless homes and other buildings have been destroyed by US bombing

- thousands of innocent civilians have been killed as well as thousands of others engaged in combat who were only defending the country they lived in from a foreign invasion; not one of the many dead has been shown to have had any connection to the September 11 attack; most of the so-called "terrorists" at the training camps had come to Afghanistan to aid the Taliban in their civil war, a religious mission, none of Washington's concern

- crime and violence are once again a danger in the cities' neighborhoods, which had been made safer by the Taliban

- the country is occupied by foreign troops who often treat the population badly, including the use of torture; US forces seize Afghans and take them away without explanation and keep them incommunicado indefinitely; some are sent to the 21st century's Devils Island in Guantanamo Base, Cuba.

- in Kabul, the number of children suffering from malnutrition is almost double what it was before the American invasion[1]

- depleted uranium has begun to show its ugly face

- Afghanistan has become a protectorate of the US and NATO.

- the quality of women's lives has very slightly improved, but remember, the awful Taliban regime would never have come to power in the first place if the United States, in the 1980s and 90s, had not played an essential role in the overthrow of a secular and fairly progressive government, which allowed women much more freedom than they'll ever have under the current government.[2]

The problem, then as now, is that the consequences for the people of Afghanistan have been a matter of imperial indifference. On Washington's agenda in this case are secure oil and gas pipelines, military bases, and, if and when security can be instituted, the forces of globalization will march in.

Meanwhile in Iraq, what the US bombing, invasion and occupation have brought to the people there is every bit as appalling.

As to my opposition in the debate, I do not have access to the text of their talks, so all I can do is point out that John Bruton was critical of US foreign policy on so many points that he could have been mistaken for being part of the side I was on. Bill Rammell was also critical of US foreign policy, though considerably less so than Bruton was; near the conclusion of the debate he was reduced to calling David Barsamian "anti-American". And Gideon Rose, the most fervent of the opposing speakers, was reduced to asking the audience to please understand that the choice is "a world run by the United States or a world run by Osama bin Laden". I would place Rose in the category of "the best and the brightest", the type that brought us Vietnam and now brings us Iraq.

At the end of the evening, the large audience, by calling out "Aye" or "Nay", overwhelmingly declared those supporting the proposition to be the victors.

## CHAPTER SEVEN

# The 1998 Bombings of Afghanistan and Sudan's Medicine Supply

[written November 8, 1998]

If the United States can bomb the Afghanistan headquarters of Osama bin Laden, who allegedly had masterminded terrorist bombings of two US embassies in Africa on August 7, then can not Cuba do the same to the offices of Cuban exiles in Miami, guilty of hundreds of terrorist acts against the Castro government? Can not Cuba bomb CIA headquarters? Using the same argument of self-defense that Washington uses of course.

As a result of the US bombings of Afghanistan and Sudan on August 20, Americans are less safe now in much of the world.

The camp that the United States bombed in Afghanistan was originally set up by the CIA in the 1980s to train Afghan and other Muslim guerrillas in their war against the Soviet-supported government, which was trying to drag Afghanistan into the 20th century. At that time bin Laden and his men were regarded as "freedom fighters" rather than "terrorists". The veterans of that war have since used their training, experience and weaponry to carry out terrorist actions all over the world, including the World Trade Center in New York in 1993.

US Attorney General Janet Reno urged the White House to delay the air attacks in order to give the FBI time to assemble more evidence linking bin Laden to the embassy bombings. Justice Department officials said they understood that Reno warned the White House that it was not clear, based on the information thenavailable, that the United States had enough evidence against binLaden to meet the standards of international law. She also felt that the administration had not accumulated enough clear evidence of a link between bin Laden and the targets the United States planned to attack.[1] (Of course, even if there were clear evidence on these matters, that would not justify the unilateral bombing of sovereign nations with unpredictable consequences for the residents.)

The al Shifa plant in Khartoum, Sudan, bombed by the United States, produced a full range of antibiotics and medicines for malaria, rheumatism, tuberculosis, diabetes, and other ailments, in sum total about 90 percent of the drugs used to treat the most deadly illnesses in this desperately poor country. Reportedly one of the biggest and best of its kind in Africa, it was privately owned and had been partly financed by the Eastern and Southern African Preferential Trade Association, a thoroughly respectable regional trading body.[2] The White House, however, insisted that al Shifa was in fact a chemical weapons factory with political and financial links to the omnipresent Osama bin Laden.

After the plant bombing, evidence began to accumulate which put the White House thesis into question:

•Belfast independent film-maker Irwin Armstrong, who visited the plant last year while making a promotional video for the Sudanese ambassador in London, said: "The Americans have got this completely wrong. In other parts of the country I encountered heavy security but not here. I was allowed to wander about quite freely. This is a perfectly normal chemical factory with the things you would expect—stainless steel vats and technicians."[3]

•Tom Carnaffin of England worked as a technical manager from 1992 to 1996 for the family who owned the plant. He stated: "I have intimate knowledge of that factory and it just does not lend itself to the manufacture of chemical weapons. The Americans claimed that the weapons were being manufactured in the veterinary part of the factory. I have intimate knowledge of that part of the [plant] and unless there have been some radical changes in the last few months, it just isn't equipped to cope with the demands of chemical weapon manufacturing.

"You need things like air locks but this factory just has doors leading out onto the street....I have personal knowledge of the need for medicine in Sudan as I almost died while working out there. The loss of this factory is a tragedy for the rural communities who need those medicines."[4]

•"Al Shifa certainly did not try to hide its existence," wrote a journalist for The Observer of London. "Signs in plenty direct you to it long before you get there." After the bombing there was "no sign of anyone trying to hide anything either. Access is easy. Much of Khartoum seems to have come to take a look."[5]

•Henry Jobe, an American chemical engineer who designed the plant for a Sudanese businessman, said he was surprised when he saw the footage of the bombing on TV and the official statements that followed because he had designed the plant as a pharmaceuticals factory.

Asked whether his design could be used to make chemical weapons, he said: "No, we didn't intend a dual use for it. We didn't design anything extra in there. The design we made was for pharmaceuticals. It's possible it could have been changed. I don't know about it. We never discussed one second about any kind of chemical [weapons] operations."

However, one senior US intelligence source has stated: "We have no evidence or have seen no products, commercial products, that are sold out of this facility."

Jobe replied that he was surprised by the statement. "That is misinformation, because it was designed for it."[6]

A State Department spokesman conceded that the plant "very well may have been producing pharmaceuticals. But...the factory also was producing precursor elements."[7]

• In the Jordanian capital, Amman, an engineer involved in the construction of al Shifa also challenged Washington's claims. Ahmad Salem, who supervised the building of the plant between 1993 and 1997, said: "There is no chance that this factory could be used to produce chemical weapons, it was designed to produce medicine for people and animals."[8]

• Just hours after US missiles destroyed the plant, Germany's Ambassador to Sudan, Ambassador Werner Daum sent a letter to superiors in Bonn disputing the American justification for the attack. "One can't, even if one wants to, describe the Shifa firm as a chemical [weapons] factory."[9]

• The only proof provided so far by the United States to justify its attack is based on a soil sample allegedly collected from near the plant. American officials, who have refused to make the sample available to a wider body of international experts, say traces of a VX nerve gas precursor called Empta found in the soil amount to "irrefutable" evidence that the nerve agent was being manufactured there.

Sudan's Interior Minister has raised questions about the source of the soil sample. He said most of the area around al Shifa was paved with only a tiny amount of open land used for the cultivation of rose bushes.

"The American claim is totally unfounded," the Minister said. "If you look around, you will not see any soil in the immediate vicinity of our factory premises."

The US allegation has also been put into question by Western scientists who have pointed out that the same ingredients are used for chemical weapons and beer, that mustard gas is similar in make-up to the anti-clogging agent in ballpoint-pen ink, and that the cherry flavoring in sweets is one of the constituent parts of the gas used in combat.

Moreover, the Organization for the Prohibition of

Chemical Weapons (OPCW, in the Hague) has stated that Empta could be used for legitimate commercial purposes, including the manufacture of fungicides and microbial agents. Experts add that the chemical structure of Empta also closely resembles Fonofos, an insecticide on sale in Africa.[10]

•A senior inspector in the OPCW pointed out that Empta was unlikely to be found, unaltered, in the ground for the simple reason that it is highly reactive and, once in the earth, would react with other chemicals and begin to break down.[11]

•The United States, before the bombing, flew a reconnaissance mission over the plant to test for traces of gas and failed to find any.[12]

In light of all this uncertainty, why did the United States see fit to send more than a dozen Tomahawk cruise missiles screaming into the plant? At first, the US said that al Shifa was part of bin Laden's economic network. But in the face of denials from the plant's Sudanese owner, Saleh Idris, administration officials then stated that they were unsure of bin Laden's financial interest in the plant. There was as well the perceived political need for some kind of act of retaliation for the embassy bombings, and some kind of distraction from the escalating Monica Lewinsky scandal then enveloping the White House and the media.

But could this also have been a case of putting the "madman theory" into practice? An internal 1995 study, "Essentials of Post-Cold War Deterrence," by the Strategic Command, the headquarters responsible for the US strategic nuclear arsenal, said that the US may be able to deter its adversaries by presenting an "irrational and vindictive" demeanor. "Because of the value that comes from the ambiguity of what the US may do to an adversary if the acts we seek to deter are carried out, it hurts to portray ourselves as too fully rational and cool-headed....That the US may become irrational and vindictive if its vital interests are attacked should be a part of the national persona we project to all adversaries."

"Our target was terror," said President Clinton. But so was his solution.

At the United Nations, a few days after the bombing, Sudan requested an investigation, which was backed by other Arab states. But US Deputy Ambassador Peter Burleigh declared that it was unnecessary to send a technical team to examine US claims about the production of chemical agents because Washington already had the evidence.

"Putting together a technical team to confirm something that we already know, based on our own information, doesn't seem to have any point to us," Burleigh said.

White House spokesman Mike McCurry added: "Our confidence that that facility was manufacturing chemical weapons precursors is quite high."[13]

## Postscript

After destroying Saleh Idris's plant, Washington froze $24 million in his London bank accounts. But the US was never able to prove any of its assertions about him or al Shifa. As the case fell apart completely, Idris sued to recover his money as well as compensation for his pulverized plant.

Finally, in May 1999, the United States unfroze Idris's accounts rather than contest his suit because they knew they had no case. But as of the end of that year, the US had yet to apologize to Sudan or to Idris for the plant's destruction, or for the serious harm done to his reputation, and had yet to compensate him for the loss of the plant and the loss of business; nor the plant's employees for the loss of their jobs and income, or the ten people who were injured.

"Never before," observed former CIA official Milt Bearden, "has a single soil sample prompted an act of war against a sovereign state."[14]

## CHAPTER EIGHT

# Peru: Their Terrorists, Our Freedom Fighters

[This essay first appeared in *I.F. Magazine**, July-August 1997]

Imagine that what happened in Peru were to take place in Cuba—14 Cuban dissidents taking over a large social gathering and holding a few hundred people hostage, including Fidel Castro's brother Raúl and other prominent officials, as well as foreign ambassadors and businessmen. Imagine that the Cuban rebels made demands similar to those of the MRTA in Peru—raising the standard of living of the masses, bettering prison conditions, freeing a number of political prisoners, and improving the state of civil liberties.

Imagine the reaction of the American media. The MRTA "terrorists", through an arcane ideological alchemy, would be transformed into anti-communist "freedom fighters". The Cuban dissidents' demands would be reported fully, seriously, and regularly. What had been seen before as an appalling, illegitimate way to achieve social change would give way effortlessly to a sincere appreciation that under intolerable conditions, desperate people can be reduced to reckless measures.

We now know that in Lima, on April 22 [1997], the Peruvian government did what it knows best, applying "brute military force as the final solution to social problems."[1] Peruvian commandos, under orders to take no prisoners, exe-

---

* *I.F. Magazine* was published by noted journalist Robert Parry. The title is explained by: "In the independent tradition of George Seldes' *In Fact* and I.F. Stone."

cuted all the rebels who survived the initial onslaught. Only
Peruvian President Alberto Fujimori still denies this. Two
teenage girls among the rebels were heard giving themselves up
as troops stormed the mansion. "We surrender! We surrender!"
the girls shouted, according to an intelligence agent who mon-
itored the raid through listening devices. They were both shot
dead.[2]

The Peruvian minister of agriculture, Rodolfo Munante,
one of the hostages, disclosed that "One rebel surrendered in
the room where the judges were...he told the judges he surrendered, but then a soldier entered and machine-gunned the
rebels in the room."[3]

Munante had a further story to tell. He said he could not
sleep for thinking about a young rebel who spared his life. "I've
hardly slept. I went to bed late and was thinking all the
time...I've remembered and remembered the attitude of that
youngster." Moments after the Peruvian troops burst into the
building to rescue the hostages, one of the teenage rebels came
into the room where high-ranking captives were held and
pointed his rifle straight at the agriculture minister.

"I don't know what happened," said Munante. "I don't
know if he doubted, but I saw sadness in his eyes, maybe because
of the order to kill us, or maybe because he saw his life slipping
away. Then, in a matter of seconds, he turned straight around
and closed the door."[4]

The young man, who was shot dead moments later, may
have had second thoughts due to the close ties that had formed
between captors and captives after 18 weeks inside the resi-
dence, said Munante. "After so many days of talking and talking an emotional bond had been established."

"I feel a lot for the youngsters, who were humble people
from the Peruvian jungle," Jorge Gumucio, the Bolivian ambassador, who was also a hostage, said. "But we knew from the start
that it was either us or them."[5]

It would have been a lot more of "us", but "them" released

more than 80 percent of the hostages within the first two weeks; then, as time went by, released others who had become, or claimed to be, ill; never killed a single hostage, never hurt any of them. They were rewarded by a complete refusal by Fujimori to make even the slightest concession, all the while planning their summary execution.

Imagine again that Cuba had been the stage for this tragedy. The halls of the US Congress would have been filled with operatic wails and forehead smiting over the cold-blooded execution of the freedom fighters, with Jesse Helms waving a sword and pleading to lead the invasion of Cuba. Ol' Bill, at his heartfelt best, would have assured the families of the slain rebels: "I feel your pain!". Flags would have flown at half-mast in Miami, and any one there who dared to question the prevailing wisdom or the prevailing emotion would risk premature death.

But inasmuch as these idealistic young people were not seeking to overthrow a socialist government, their lives have been accorded scant value in the American media. An editorial in *The Washington Post* remarked upon the "successful rescue in which there were amazingly small losses of life: One hostage and two attackers died." Then, quite parenthetically: "The guerrillas, who had claimed a revolutionary cause but found few takers among Peru's terrorism-weary population, lost all 14 of their own." Period.[6]

Social indoctrination is likely one reason for lack of support for the MRTA. One of the saddest sights to observe in the TV coverage of the events, was the scene of the many Peruvian soldiers celebrating their victory. These *indígena*-looking young men, finding in military service perhaps their only way to escape poverty, hunger and unemployment, shouting for joy, back- slapping, high-fiving, burning an MRTA flag, all because they had killed a number of other poverty-stricken young *indígenas* who were struggling to wrench a concession or two from the government to lighten the load of the poor and the imprisoned.

A "terrorist"—the Nazi's term for World War II resistance fighters—fights for what he believes in; a soldier fights for what someone else believes in—in this case the wealthy coercing the poor to kill the poor to keep the wealthy in power. So it always was.

As might be expected, the commandos received training and sophisticated technological help from the United States for their operation, including overflights of the RU-38A airplane, which can photograph a building and gauge the thickness of its walls, amongst other details crucial to planning the raid.[7]

Support of the Peruvian government in such circumstances would be regarded by Washington as the most natural and good thing in the world. In all certainty, however, if Cuba had assisted the MRTA members in any way, there would have been denunciation throughout the Americas, particularly in Washington.

And what is the nature of this Peruvian government that inspires the support of the United States? In April 1992, President Fujimori closed down the nation's Congress and dismissed much of the judiciary, giving himself dictatorial power. Following the standard script, the United States immediately protested, announcing the suspension of all foreign aid programs to Peru. It was not long before this aid was resumed, if, in fact, it was ever actually cut off, because Washington was interested in drug interdiction in Peru, and even more so in helping the Peruvian government combat leftist and populist rebellion (as in 1965, when a force of US Green Berets was sent to Peru and, in a military operation of some size, helped to wipe out the guerrilla movements of that period.)[8]

Indeed, the anti-drug campaign in Peru, as in Colombia, appears to have been used as a cover for the anti-guerrilla campaign. Fujimori's chief aide and personal lawyer, Vladimiro Montesinos, has had ties to drug cartels and been accused as well of setting up death squads and being a long-time CIA asset.

The Peruvian Congress has been reinstated, but this has

scarcely meant a reawakening of freedom and democracy in Peru. The latest State Department human rights report on Peru states: "Security forces were responsible for extrajudicial killings, disappearances, torture, and beatings." Yet the White House continued to offer its unqualified support and encouragement to the Fujimori government, for its opponents were of the notorious leftist persuasion. The Cold War is alive and well. If the Soviet Union still existed, the rebel action in Peru would have been branded as part of the International Communist Conspiracy. Which conspiracy do the anti-communists blame now? Could it be that the revolutionary and "terrorist" actions of the Cold War were home grown, springing from indigenous roots?

## Postscript

In May 2002, with Fujimori in exile, and a government Truth and Reconciliation Commission holding public hearings about the human rights violations of his government, arrest warrants were issued against 12 commandos who participated in the 1997 raid. The commandos were accused of executing several MRTA rebels who had surrendered. The military refused to turn over any of the commandos, saying the soldiers were only doing their duty by protecting Peru. In response to protests in support of the commandos and calls in Congress for a blanket amnesty, the warrants were revoked.[9]

## CHAPTER NINE

# Madeleine Albright, Ethically Challenged

[written 1998-1999]

1) "Asked if it is not hypocritical to punish Burma for human rights violations while refraining from sanctions on China for similar actions, Albright replied, 'We have consistent principles and flexible tactics'."[1]

The same "flexible tactics" (English translation: hypocrisy) are evident in the policies embraced by Albright toward Cuba, Libya, Iraq, et al, as opposed to the policies toward Turkey, Indonesia, Mexico, Peru, and Colombia.

2) At a "Town Hall" meeting, held in Columbus, Ohio, February 18, 1998, concerning impending American bombing strikes against Iraq, Albright was heckled and asked critical, and perhaps uncomfortable, questions. At one point, her mind and her integrity could come up with no better response than to make something up: "I really am surprised," she declared, "that people feel that it is necessary to defend the rights of Saddam Hussein."[2]

At another point, a besieged Albright was moved to yell: "We are the greatest country in the world and what we are doing is serving the role of the indispensable nation to see what we can do to make the world safer for our children and grand-children and for those people around the world who follow the rules."[3] On TV the next morning, she reiterated: "If we have to use force, it is because we are America! We are the indispensable nation. We stand tall, and we see further into the future."[4]

Patriotism is indeed the last refuge of a scoundrel, though her words didn't quite have the ring of "Deutschland über alles" or "Rule Britannia".

Finally, unable to provide answers that satisfied or quieted the questioners at the Town Hall, Albright stated that she would meet with some of them after the meeting to answer their questions. But as soon as the meeting ended, the Secretary of State was out of there, posthaste. Her offer, it would seem, had just been a tactic to try and pacify the hostile crowd.[5]

3) Television interview, "60 Minutes", May 12, 1996:

Lesley Stahl, speaking of US sanctions against Iraq: "We have heard that a half million children have died. I mean, that's more children than died in Hiroshima. And—and you know, is the price worth it?"

Madeleine Albright: "I think this is a very hard choice, but the price—we think the price is worth it."

Yet, at the Town Hall meeting referred to above, Albright was seemingly not embarrassed to declare: "I am willing to make a bet to anyone here that we care more about the Iraqi people than Saddam Hussein does. He does not care a fig."[6]

4) Albright in Guatemala, talking to a group of impoverished children: "Why would [I] and the United States care about what is happening here? The reason is we are all one family and when one part of our family is not happy or suffers, we all suffer."[7]

Thus spaketh the principal foreign policy officer of the country directly responsible for bringing more than 40 years of poverty, torture, death squads, massacres and disappeared people to Guatemala, all extremely well documented.

5) "To a student who asked [Albright] whether the United States was not spending too much of its resources on being the world's policeman and too little on more pressing domestic concerns, Albright asked him in return to estimate what share of the federal budget goes to foreign policy. When he guessed 15

or 20 percent, Albright pounced."

"It's 1 percent, 1 percent of the entire budget," Albright said.[8]

Her reply was conspicuously disingenuous. At best, she was referring to the budget of only the State Department, concealing what everyone knows, even the teenage student she browbeat—US foreign policy expenditures must include the Defense Department, the CIA, the National Security Agency, and a host of other government agencies. Together they consume more than 50 percent of the budget.

6) In February 1996, as UN ambassador, Albright reacted with righteous indignation against the Cuban pilots who expressed satisfaction after shooting down two planes of Cubans from Florida which were headed toward Cuba. "This one won't mess around any more," one of the attacking pilots is reported to have exclaimed.

"I was struck by the joy of these pilots in committing cold-blooded murder," Albright said, accusing the Cuban pilots of "cowardice."[9]

What, one may ask, did she think of the American pilots who, while bombing and strafing helpless retreating Iraqis in 1991, exclaimed: "we toasted him"..."we hit the jackpot"..."a turkey shoot"..."shooting fish in a barrel"..."basically just sitting ducks"..."There's just nothing like it. It's the biggest Fourth of July show you've ever seen, and to see those tanks just `boom', and more stuff just keeps spewing out of them...they just become white hot. It's wonderful."[10]

7) On October 8, 1997, in announcing the designation of 18 additional foreign political organizations as terrorist- supporting groups, Secretary of State Albright declared that she wanted to help make the United States a "no support for terrorism zone". It could be suggested that if the Secretary were truly committed to this goal, instead of offering her usual lip

service, she should begin at home—the anti-Castro community in Miami, collectively, is one of the longest-lasting and most prolific terrorist organizations in the world. Over the years they've carried out hundreds of bombings, arson attacks, shootings, and murders, blown up an airplane, killing 73 people, fired a bazooka at the United Nations, and much more. But Madame Albright will not lift a finger against them.

The State Department designates Cuba as one of the states which harbors terrorists.

8) As UN Ambassador, Albright informed the Security Council during a 1994 discussion about Iraq: "We recognize this area as vital to US national interests and we will behave, with others, multilaterally when we can and unilaterally when we must."[11]

Albright was thus stating that the United States recognizes no external constraints on its behavior, when it decides that a particular area of the world is "vital to US national interests". It would of course be difficult to locate a spot on the globe that Albright and the United States do not regard as "vital to US national interests."

9) On more than one occasion while UN ambassador, Albright has yelled at UN Secretary-General Boutros-Ghali that he must not publish the report about Israel's bombing of the UN-run refugee camp in Qana, Lebanon, in April 1996, which killed more than 100 refugees. The UN report said that the attack was not a mistake, as Israel claimed. Albright—who has surrounded herself with alumni of Israeli and Jewish lobbies—warned the Secretary- General that if the report came out, the US would veto him for his second term.

The report came out, and so did Boutros Boutros-Ghali.[12]

10) And here we have Madeleine the humanitarian: It is "not a good idea" to link human rights and trade issues.[13]

A philosophy that could have been used to justify trade with Nazi Germany...or anyone else...or with a country doing anything.

11) Albright To Colin Powell, who felt that the US should not commit military forces to Bosnia until there was a clear political objective: "What's the point of having this superb military that you're always talking about if we can't use it?"

"I thought I would have an aneurysm," Powell later wrote. "American GIs were not toy soldiers to be moved around on some sort of global game board."[14]

All of the above, however, may be regarded as mere peccadilloes of Madame Albright when compared to her roles in: (a)blocking UN reinforcements going to Rwanda during the infamous massacre of 1994; (b)getting the US involved in its bloody debacle in Somalia in 1993; (c)pushing hard for the bombing of Yugoslavia, 78 days of horrific death and destruction for the people of Serbia and Kosovo for no reason honorable enough to admit to.

## CHAPTER TEN

# The Bombing of PanAm Flight 103— Case Not Closed

[This essay appeared in *Everything You Know Is Wrong*, Russ Kick, editor, 2002]

The newspapers were filled with pictures of happy relatives of the victims of the 1988 PanAm bombing. A Libyan, Abdelbaset Ali Mohmed al Megrahi, had been found guilty of the crime the day before, January 31, 2001, by a Scottish court in the Hague, though his co-defendant, Al Amin Khalifa Fhimah, was acquitted. At long last there was going to be some kind of closure for the families.

But what was wrong with this picture?

What was wrong was that the evidence against Megrahi was thin to the point of transparency. Coming the month after the (s)election of George W. Bush, the Hague verdict could have been dubbed Supreme Court II, another instance of non-judicial factors fatally clouding judicial reasoning. The three Scottish judges could not have relished returning to the United Kingdom after finding both defendants innocent of the murder of 270 people, largely from the UK and the United States. Not to mention having to face dozens of hysterical family members of the victims in the courtroom. The three judges also well knew the fervent desires of the White House and Downing Street as to the outcome. If both men had been acquitted, the United States and Great Britain would have had to answer for a decade of sanctions and ill will directed toward Libya.

One has to read the entire 26,000-word "Opinion of the

Court", as well as being very familiar with the history of the case going back to 1988, to appreciate how questionable the judges' verdict was.

The key charge against Megrahi—the *sine qua non*—was that in Malta he had placed explosives in a suitcase and tagged it so it would lead the following charmed life: 1)loaded aboard an Air Malta flight to Frankfurt without an accompanying passenger; 2)transferred in Frankfurt to the PanAm 103A flight to London without an accompanying passenger; 3)transferred in London to the PanAm 103 flight to New York without an accompanying passenger.

To the magic bullet of the JFK assassination, can we now add the magic suitcase?

This scenario by itself would have been a major feat and so unlikely to succeed that any terrorist with any common sense would have found a better way. But aside from anything else, we have this—as to the first step, loading the suitcase at Malta: there was no witness, no video, no document, no fingerprints, nothing to tie Megrahi to the particular brown Samsonite suitcase, no past history of terrorism, no forensic evidence of any kind linking him or Fhimah to such an act.

And the court admitted it: "The absence of any explanation of the method by which the primary suitcase might have been placed on board KM180 [Air Malta] is a major difficulty for the Crown case."[1]

Moreover, under security requirements in 1988, unaccompanied baggage was subjected to special X-ray examinations, plus—because of recent arrests of suspected terrorists in Germany—the security personnel in Frankfurt were on the lookout specifically for a bomb secreted in a radio, which turned out to indeed be the method used with the PanAm 103 bomb.

Requiring some sort of direct and credible testimony linking Megrahi to the bombing, the Hague court placed great—nay, paramount—weight upon the supposed identification of the Libyan by a shopkeeper in Malta, as the purchaser of the clothing found in the bomb suitcase. But this shopkeeper had earlier identified several other people as the culprit, including one who was a CIA agent.[2] When he finally identified Megrahi from a photo, it was after Megrahi's photo had been in the world news for years. The court acknowledged the possible danger inherent in such a verification: "These identifications were criticised *inter alia* on the ground that photographs of the accused have featured many times over the years in the media and accordingly purported identifications more than 10 years after the event are of little if any value."[3]

There were also major discrepancies between the shopkeeper's original description of the clothes-buyer and Megrahi's actual appearance. The shopkeeper told police that the customer was "six feet or more in height" and "was about 50 years of age." Megrahi was 5'8" tall and was 36 in 1988. The judges again acknowledged the weakness of their argument by conceding that the initial description "would not in a number of respects fit the first accused [Megrahi]" and that "it has to be accepted that there was a substantial discrepancy."[4] Nevertheless, the judges went ahead and accepted the identification as accurate.

Before the indictment of the two Libyans in Washington in November 1991, the press had reported police findings that the clothing had been purchased on November 23, 1988.[5] But the indictment of Megrahi states that he made the purchase on December 7. Can this be because the investigators were able to document Megrahi being in Malta (where he worked for Libya Airlines) on that date but cannot do so for November 23?[6]

There is also this to be considered—If the bomber needed some clothing to wrap up an ultra-secret bomb in a suitcase, would he go to a clothing store in the city where he planned to carry out his dastardly deed, where he knew he'd likely be remembered as an obvious foreigner, and buy brand new, easily traceable items? Would an intelligence officer—which Megrahi was alleged to be—do this? Or even a common boob? Wouldn't it make more sense to use any old clothing, from anywhere, from some untraceable source?

Furthermore, after the world was repeatedly assured that these items of clothing were sold only on Malta, it was learned that at least one of the items was actually "sold at dozens of outlets throughout Europe, and it was impossible to trace the purchaser."[7]

The "Opinion of the Court" placed considerable weight on the suspicious behavior of Megrahi prior to the fatal day, making much of his comings and goings abroad, phone calls to unknown parties for unknown reasons, the use of a pseudonym, etc. The three judges tried to squeeze as much mileage out of these events as they could, as if they had no better case to make. But if Megrahi was indeed a member of Libyan intelligence, we must consider that intelligence agents have been known to act in mysterious ways, for whatever assignment they're on. The court, however, had no idea what assignment, if any, Megrahi was working on.

There is much more that is known about the case that makes the court verdict and written opinion questionable, although credit must be given the court for its frankness about what it was doing, even while it was doing it. "We are aware that in relation to certain aspects of the case there are a number of uncertainties and qualifications," the judges wrote. "We are also aware that there is a danger that by selecting parts of the evidence which seem to fit together and ignoring parts which might not fit, it is possible to read into a mass of conflicting evidence a pattern or conclusion which is not really justified."[8]

It is remarkable, given all that the judges conceded was questionable or uncertain in the trial—not to mention all that was questionable or uncertain that they *didn't* concede—that at the end of the day they could still declare to the world that "There is nothing in the evidence which leaves us with any reasonable doubt as to the guilt of [Megrahi]."[9]

*The Guardian* of London later wrote that two days before

the verdict "senior Foreign Office officials briefed a group of journalists in London. They painted a picture of a bright new chapter in Britain's relations with Colonel Gadafy's regime. They made it quite clear they assumed both the Libyans in the dock would be acquitted. The Foreign Office officials were not alone. Most independent observers believed it was impossible for the court to find the prosecution had proved its case against Megrahi beyond reasonable doubt."[10]

## Alternative scenario

There is, moreover, an alternative scenario, laying the blame on Palestinians, Iran and Syria, which is much better documented and makes a lot more sense, logistically and otherwise.

Indeed, this was the Original Official Version, delivered with Olympian rectitude by the United States government—guaranteed, sworn to, scout's honor, case closed—until the buildup to the Gulf War came along in 1990 and the support of Iran and Syria was needed.

Washington was anxious as well to achieve the release of American hostages held in Lebanon by groups close to Iran. Thus it was that the scurrying sound of backtracking became audible in the corridors of the White House.

Suddenly—or so it seemed—in October 1990, there was a New Official Version: It was Libya—the Arab state least supportive of the U.S. build-up to the Gulf War and the sanctions imposed against Iraq—that was behind the bombing after all, declared Washington.

The two Libyans were formally indicted in the US and Scotland on Nov. 14, 1991.

"This was a Libyan government operation from start to finish," declared the State Department spokesman.[11]

"The Syrians took a bum rap on this," said President George H.W. Bush.[12]

Within the next 20 days, the remaining four American hostages were released along with the most prominent British hostage, Terry Waite.

The Original Official Version accused the PFLP-GC, a 1968 breakaway from a component of the Palestine Liberation Organization, of making the bomb and somehow placing it aboard the flight in Frankfurt.

The PFLP-GC was led by Ahmed Jabril, one of the world's leading terrorists, and was headquartered in, financed by, and closely supported by, Syria. The bombing was allegedly done at the behest of Iran as revenge for the U.S. shooting down of an Iranian passenger plane over the Persian Gulf on July 3, 1988, which claimed 290 lives.

The support for this scenario was, and remains, impressive, as the following sample indicates:

In April 1989, the FBI—in response to criticism that it was bungling the investigation—leaked to CBS the news that it had tentatively identified the person who unwittingly carried the bomb aboard. His name was Khalid Jaafar, a 21-year-old Lebanese-American. The report said that the bomb had been planted in Jaafar's suitcase by a member of the PFLP-GC, whose name was not revealed.[13]

In May, the State Department stated that the CIA was "confident" of the Iran-Syria-PFLP-GC account of events.[14]

On Sept. 20, *The Times* of London reported that "security officials from Britain, the United States and West Germany are 'totally satisfied' that it was the PFLP-GC" behind the crime.

In December 1989, Scottish investigators announced that they had "hard evidence" of the involvement of the PFLP-GC in the bombing.[15]

A National Security Agency electronic intercept disclosed that Ali Akbar Mohtashemi, Iranian interior minister, had paid Palestinian terrorists $10 million to gain revenge for the downed Iranian airplane.[16] The intercept appears to have occurred in July 1988, shortly after the plane was shot down.

Israeli intelligence also intercepted a communication between Mohtashemi and the Iranian embassy in Beirut "indicating that Iran paid for the Lockerbie bombing."[17]

Even after the Libyans had been indicted, Israeli officials declared that their intelligence analysts remained convinced that the PFLP-GC bore primary responsibility for the bombing.[18]

In 1992, Abu Sharif, a political adviser to PLO chairman Yasser Arafat, stated that the PLO had compiled a secret report which concluded that the bombing of 103 was the work of a "Middle Eastern country" other than Libya.[19]

In February 1995, former Scottish Office minister, Alan Stewart, wrote to the British Foreign Secretary and the Lord Advocate, questioning the reliability of evidence which had led to the accusations against the two Libyans. This move, wrote *The Guardian*, reflected the concern of the Scottish legal profession, reaching into the Crown Office (Scotland's equivalent of the Attorney General's Office), that the bombing may not have been the work of Libya, but of Syrians, Palestinians and Iranians.[20]

We must also ask why Prime Minister Margaret Thatcher, writing in her 1993 memoirs about the US bombing of Libya in 1986, with which Britain had cooperated, stated: "But the much vaunted Libyan counter-attack did not and could not take place. Gaddafy had not been destroyed but he had been humbled. There was a marked decline in Libyan-sponsored terrorism in succeeding years."[21]

## Key Question

A key question in the PFLP-GC version has always been: How did the bomb get aboard the plane in Frankfurt, or at some other point? One widely disseminated explanation was in a report, completed during the summer of 1989 and leaked in the fall, which had been prepared by a New York investigating firm called Interfor. Headed by a former Israeli intelligence agent, Juval Aviv, Interfor—whose other clients included Fortune 500 companies, the FBI, IRS and Secret Service[22]—was hired by the law firm representing PanAm's insurance carrier.

The Interfor Report said that in the mid-1980s, a drug and arms smuggling operation was set up in various European cities, with Frankfurt airport as the site of one of the drug routes. The Frankfurt operation was run by Manzer Al-Kassar, a Syrian, the same man from whom Oliver North's shadowy network purchased large quantities of arms for the contras. At the airport, according to the report, a courier would board a flight with checked luggage containing innocent items; after the luggage had passed all security checks, one or another accomplice Turkish baggage handler for PanAm would substitute an identical suitcase containing contraband; the passenger then picked up this suitcase upon arrival at the destination.

The only courier named by Interfor was Khalid Jaafar, who, as noted above, had been named by the FBI a few months earlier as the person who unwittingly carried the bomb aboard.

The Interfor report spins a web much too lengthy and complex to go into here. The short version is that the CIA in Germany discovered the airport drug operation and learned also that Kassar had the contacts to gain the release of American hostages in Lebanon. He had already done the same for French hostages. Thus it was that the CIA and the German *Bundeskriminalamt* (BKA, Federal Criminal Office) allowed the drug operation to continue in hopes of effecting the release of American hostages.

According to the report, this same smuggling ring and its method of switching suitcases at the Frankfurt airport were used to smuggle the fatal bomb aboard flight 103, under the eyes of the CIA and BKA.

In January 1990, Interfor gave three of the baggage handlers polygraphs and two of them were judged as being deceitful when denying any involvement in baggage switching. However, neither the U.S., UK or German investigators showed any interest in the results, or in questioning the baggage handlers. Instead, the polygrapher, James Keefe, was hauled before a Washington grand jury, and, as he puts it, "They were bent on destroying my credibility—not theirs" [the baggage handlers]. To Interfor, the lack of interest in the polygraph results and the attempt at intimidation of Keefe was the strongest evidence of a cover-up by the various government authorities who did not want their permissive role in the baggage switching to be revealed.[23]

Critics claimed that the Interfor report had been inspired by PanAm's interest in proving that it was impossible for normal airline security to have prevented the loading of the bomb, thus removing the basis for accusing the airline of negligence.

The report was the principal reason PanAm's attorneys subpoenaed the FBI, CIA, DEA, State Department, National Security Council, and NSA, as well as, reportedly, the Defense Intelligence Agency and FAA, to turn over all documents relating to the crash of 103 or to a drug operation preceding the crash. The government moved to quash the subpoenas on grounds of "national security", and refused to turn over a single document in open court, although it gave some to a judge to view privately.

The judge later commented that he was "troubled about certain parts" of what he'd read, that he didn't "know quite what to do because I think some of the material may be significant."[24]

## Drugs Revelation

On October 30, 1990, NBC-TV News reported that "PanAm flights from Frankfurt, including 103, had been used a number of times by the DEA as part of its undercover operation to fly informants and suitcases of heroin into Detroit as part of a sting operation to catch dealers in Detroit."

The TV network reported that the DEA was looking into the possibility that a young man who lived in Michigan and regularly visited the Middle East may have unwittingly carried the bomb aboard flight 103. His name was Khalid Jaafar. "Unidentified law enforcement sources" were cited as saying that Jaafar had been a DEA informant and was involved in a drug-sting operation based out of Cyprus. The DEA was investigating whether the PFLP-GC had tricked Jaafar into carrying a suitcase containing the bomb instead of the drugs he usually carried.

The NBC report quoted an airline source as saying: "Informants would put [suit]cases of heroin on the PanAm flights apparently without the usual security checks, through an arrangement between the DEA and German authorities."[25]

These revelations were enough to inspire a congressional hearing, held in December, entitled, "Drug Enforcement Administration's Alleged Connection to the PanAm Flight 103 Disaster."

The chairman of the committee, Cong. Robert Wise (D-WV), began the hearing by lamenting the fact that the DEA and the Department of Justice had not made any of their field agents who were most knowledgeable about flight 103 available to testify; that they had not provided requested written information, including the results of the DEA's investigation into the air disaster; and that "the FBI to this date has been totally uncooperative."

The two DEA officials who did testify admitted that the agency had, in fact, run "controlled drug deliveries" through Frankfurt airport with the cooperation of German authorities, using U.S. airlines, but insisted that no such operation had been conducted in December 1988. (The drug agency had said nothing of its sting operation to the President's Commission on Aviation Security and Terrorism which had held hearings in the first months of 1990 in response to the 103 bombing.)

The officials denied that the DEA had had any "association with Mr. Jaafar in any way, shape, or form." However, to questions concerning Jaafar's background, family, and his frequent trips to Lebanon, they asked to respond only in closed session. They made the same request in response to several other questions.[26]

NBC News had reported on October 30 that the DEA had told law enforcement officers in Detroit not to talk to the media about Jaafar.

The hearing ended after but one day, even though Wise had promised a "full-scale" investigation and indicated during the hearing that there would be more to come. What was said in the closed sessions remains closed.[27]

One of the DEA officials who testified, Stephen Greene, had himself had a reservation on flight 103, but he canceled because of one or more of the several international warnings that had preceded the fateful day. He has described standing on the Heathrow tarmac, watching the doomed plane take off.[28]

There have been many reports of heroin being found in the field around the crash, from "traces" to "a substantial quantity" found in a suitcase.[29] Two days after the NBC report, however, the *New York Times* quoted a "federal official" saying that "no hard drugs were aboard the aircraft."[30]

## The film

In 1994, American filmmaker Allan Francovich completed a documentary, "The Maltese Double Cross", which presents Jaafar as an unwitting bomb carrier with ties to the DEA and the CIA. Showings of the film in Britain were canceled under threat of law suits, venues burglarized or attacked by arsonists. When Channel 4 agreed to show the film, the Scottish Crown Office and the U.S. Embassy in London sent press packs to the media, labeling the film "blatant propaganda" and attacking some of the film's interviewees, including Juval Aviv the head of Interfor.[31]

Aviv paid a price for his report and his outspokenness. Over a period of time, his New York office suffered a series of break-ins, the FBI visited his clients, his polygrapher was harassed, as mentioned above, and a contrived commercial fraud charge was brought against him. Even though Aviv eventually was cleared in court, it was a long, expensive, and painful ordeal.[32]

Francovich also stated that he had learned that five CIA operatives had been sent to London and Cyprus to discredit the film while it was being made, that his office phones were tapped, that staff cars were sabotaged, and that one of his researchers narrowly escaped an attempt to force his vehicle into the path of an oncoming truck.[33]

Government officials examining the Lockerbie bombing went so far as to ask the FBI to investigate the film. The Bureau later issued a highly derogatory opinion of it.[34]

The film's detractors made much of the fact that the film was initially funded jointly by a UK company (two-thirds) and a Libyan government investment arm (one-third). Francovich said that he was fully aware of this and had taken pains to negotiate a guarantee of independence from any interference.

On April 17, 1997, Allan Francovich suddenly died of a heart attack at age 56, upon arrival at Houston Airport.[35] His film has had virtually no showings in the United States.

## Abu Talb

The DEA sting operation and Interfor's baggage-handler hypothesis both predicate the bomb suitcase being placed aboard the plane in Frankfurt without going through the normal security checks. In either case, it eliminates the need for the questionable triple-unaccompanied baggage scenario that supposedly started in Malta. With either scenario the clothing could still have been purchased in Malta, but in any event we don't need the Libyans for that.

Mohammed Abu Talb fits that and perhaps other pieces of the puzzle. The Palestinian had close ties to PFLP-GC cells in Germany which were making Toshiba radio-cassette bombs, similar, if not identical, to what was used to bring down 103. In October 1988, two months before Lockerbie, the German police raided these cells, finding several such bombs. In May 1989, Talb was arrested in Sweden, where he lived, and was later convicted of taking part in several bombings of the offices of American airline companies in Scandinavia. In his Swedish flat, police found large quantities of clothing made in Malta.

Police investigation of Talb disclosed that during October 1988 he had been to Cyprus and Malta, at least once in the company of Hafez Dalkamoni, the leader of the German PFLP-GC, who was arrested in the raid. The men met with PFLP-GC members who lived in Malta. Talb was also in Malta on November 23, which was originally reported as the date of the clothing purchase before the indictment of the Libyans, as mentioned earlier.

After his arrest, Talb told investigators that between October and December 1988 he had retrieved and passed to another person a bomb that had been hidden in a building used by the PFLP-GC in Germany. Officials declined to identify the person to whom Talb said he had passed the bomb. A month later, however, he recanted his confession.

Talb was reported to have possessed a brown Samsonite suitcase, which US and UK investigators had identified as the piece of luggage carrying the bomb, and to have circled December 21 in a diary seized in his Swedish flat; this was the day in 1988 the bombing took place. After the raid upon his flat, his wife was heard to telephone Palestinian friends and say: "Get rid of the clothes."

In December 1989, Scottish police, in papers filed with Swedish legal officials, made Talb the only publicly identified suspect "in the murder or participation in the murder of 270 people"; the Palestinian subsequently became another of the several individuals to be identified by the Maltese shopkeeper from a photo as the clothing purchaser.[36] Since that time, the world has scarcely heard of Abu Talb, who was sentenced to life in prison in Sweden, but never charged with anything to do with Lockerbie.

In Allan Francovich's film, members of Khalid Jaafar's family—which long had ties to the drug trade in Lebanon's notorious Bekaa Valley—are interviewed. In either halting English or translated Arabic, or paraphrased by the film's narrator, they drop many bits of information, but which are difficult to put together into a coherent whole. Amongst the bits...Khalid had told his parents that he'd met Talb in Sweden and had been given Maltese clothing...someone had given Khalid a tape recorder, or put one into his bag...he was told to go to Germany to friends of PFLP-GC leader Ahmed Jabril who would help him earn some money...he arrived in Germany with two kilos of heroin..."He didn't know it was a bomb. They gave him the drugs to take to Germany. He didn't know. Who wants to die?" ...

It can not be stated with certainty what happened at Frankfurt airport on that fateful day, if, as seems most likely, that is the place where the bomb was placed into the system. Jaafar, as a DEA courier, could have arrived with his suitcase of heroin and bomb and been escorted through security by the proper authorities. Or this was a day he was a courier for Manzer al-Kassar, and the baggage handlers did their usual switch.

Or perhaps we'll never know for sure what happened. On February 16, 1990, a group of British relatives of Lockerbie victims went to the American Embassy in London for a meeting with members of the President's Commission on Aviation Security and Terrorism. After the meeting, Britisher Martin Cadman was chatting with two of the commission members. He later reported what one of them had said to him: "Your government and our government know exactly what happened at

Lockerbie. But they are not going to tell you."[37]

## Comments about the Hague Court verdict

"The judges nearly agreed with the defense. In their verdict, they tossed out much of the prosecution witnesses' evidence as false or questionable and said the prosecution had failed to prove crucial elements, including the route that the bomb suitcase took."—*New York Times* analysis[38]

"It sure does look like they bent over backwards to find a way to convict, and you have to assume the political context of the case influenced them."—Michael Scharf, professor, New England School of Law.[39]

"I thought this was a very, very weak circumstantial case. I am absolutely astounded, astonished. I was extremely reluctant to believe that any Scottish judge would convict anyone, even a Libyan, on the basis of such evidence."—Robert Black, Scottish law professor who was the architect of the Hague trial.[40]

"A general pattern of the trial consisted in the fact that virtually all people presented by the prosecution as key witnesses were proven to lack credibility to a very high extent, in certain cases even having openly lied to the court."

"While the first accused was found 'guilty,' the second accused was found 'not guilty.'...This is totally incomprehensible for any rational observer when one considers that the indictment in its very essence was based on the joint action of the two accused in Malta."

"As to the undersigned's knowledge, there is not a single piece of material evidence linking the two accused to the crime. In such a context, the guilty verdict in regard to the first accused appears to be arbitrary, even irrational.... This leads the undersigned to the suspicion that political considerations may have been overriding a strictly judicial evaluation of the case...Regrettably, through the conduct of the Court, disservice has been done to the important cause of international criminal justice."—Hans Koechler, appointed as an international observer of the Lockerbie Trial by UN Secretary-General Kofi Annan.[41]

So, let's hope that Abdelbaset Ali Mohmed al Megrahi is really guilty. It would be a terrible shame if he spends the rest of his life in prison because back in 1990 Washington's hegemonic plans for the Middle East needed a convenient enemy, which just happened to be his country.

---

For later developments in the PanAm 103 case see chapter 1, sections for March 10, 2004 and December 23, 2003.

## CHAPTER ELEVEN

# Interventions
## The Unending List

$M$ore than 20 years ago, when I set out to catalogue American interventions into foreign countries since World War II, I had a magazine article in mind, hoping to chronicle the 10 or 12 cases which were the most famous, and pretty much all I knew of. But as I began to research the subject I soon realized that there was more to this than I had imagined, a lot more. My government, I discovered, had easily been the intervention king of all history, a serial intervener.

There was scarcely any place in the known world where the CIA, the State Department, and/or the US military had not been doing their dirty work. This was not a magazine article, I decided, this was a book (which turned out eventually to be *Killing Hope*). But even so, I could scarcely have realized that I was embarking upon a lifetime project, one that shows no sign of abating. American officials, who wouldn't dare interfere in matters of state of Kansas, never hesitate to do so in the affairs of other nations. The interventions proceed on a continual basis whether a Republican or a Democrat is in the White House, liberal or conservative or centrist, Cold War or no Cold War, following a terrorist attack or a period of calm, in prosperous times or times of recession...as long as a government or a movement or an individual leader appears on the world scene and makes it evident they would be resistant to becoming a sufficiently obedient client of the American empire and the international financial institutions/neo-liberalism nexus.

In my books *Killing Hope* and *Rogue State* numerous of these interventions are documented. Presented here to add to the historical record is a brief survey of some of the interventions of the Bush administration. Iraq, Afghanistan, and Haiti are touched upon elsewhere in this book.

It will be noticed that one thing revealed by each of the interventions below is Washington's profound lack of respect for free and fair elections.

## Eastern Europe, an ongoing intervention

It has been observed that there was a very good reason for the much-publicized comment by US Secretary of War Donald Rumsfeld that France and Germany are "old Europe," and that the "center of gravity is shifting to the east." The reason is that the United States is already winning the battle for influence in the "new Europe."[1]

Since the demise of the Soviet Union, the United States has laid claim to Moscow's former republics and satellites. Apart from its 1999 bombings and other military operations in the former Yugoslavia, Washington has used the weapons of political and economic subversion for its interventions into Eastern Europe.

The standard operating procedure in a particular country has been to send in teams of specialists from US government agencies, non-governmental organizations (NGOs), American labor unions, or private organizations funded by American corporations and foundations; leading examples are the National Endowment for Democracy (NED), Agency for International Development (AID), and the Open Society organizations of George Soros, American citizen and billionaire. These teams go in with as much financial resources as needed and numerous carrots and sticks to wield; they hold conferences and seminars, hand out tons of papers, manuals and CDs, and fund new NGOs, newspapers and other media, all to educate government employees and other selected portions of the population on the advantages and joys of privatizing and deregulating the economy, teaching them how to run a capitalist society, how to remake the country so that it's appealing to foreign investors.

The American teams have been creating a new class of managers to manage a new market economy, as well as providing the capital and good ol' American know-how for winning elections against the non-believers. In the process, they pass information and experience from one country to another; thus the Soros organization—which has offices throughout the former Soviet Union—had people from Serbia, who had been involved in the successful campaign to oust Slobodan Milosevic in 2000, share their experiences with people in Georgia who were seeking to oust Eduard Shevardnadze in 2003, and were likewise successful. This transfer of techniques, including an acclaimed video shown on Georgian independent television, was cited by participants in Georgia as playing a vital role in their toppling of Shevardnadze.[2]

In Russia and in the other countries, the "success" of such globalization programs has typically resulted in the mass of the population being left in great want, much worse off than they were under communism, while a wealthy elite class is created and the country is gradually thrown open to foreign investment and control.

The reduction in the standard of living of the people in the region since 1990 can scarcely be exaggerated. The European Children's Trust reported in October 2000 that based on key indicators—such as infant mortality, life expectancy, tuberculosis, and Gross Domestic Product per capita—conditions in Central and Eastern Europe and the former Soviet Union were worse or no better than those in many so-called developing countries.[3] From Bulgaria to Poland, from Slovenia to Lithuania, the citizens have left their homes to become the guest workers, the illegal workers, the migrants, the refugees, and the prostitutes of Western Europe.

However, these countries are now honored members of NATO, proud possessors of a couple of billion dollars worth of useless military hardware they were obliged to buy from multinationals, they have the right to send their youth to the killing fields of Iraq and Afghanistan to support US wars, the American flag flies over American military bases in their lands, globalized free enterprise is king, and the wealthy elite have a lot more in common with the likes of Dick Cheney than with the great majority of their countrymen. Some prominent ex-communist apparatchiks across the region repeat oaths of fealty to America as once they parroted the Brezhnev line. Poland's president, Aleksander Kwasniewski, who was a Communist minister in the 1980s, now declares: "If it is President Bush's vision, it is mine."[4]

The Eastern European mentality implied by the above was burgeoning even before the end of the Soviet Union and the Cold War. The intellectual equation that was arrived at, consciously or unconsciously, was that if the Soviet Union was "bad", it must be "all bad". And therefore, the Soviet's principal foe must be "all good". Thus, if the Soviet command economy had multiple shortcomings, the market economy is guaranteed to bring prosperity and justice. How many Eastern Europeans, to this day, know that most of what they may see as Western benefits flowing *automatically* from the market's "invisible hand", in actuality had to be wrested from capitalism by social movements and labor unions with much attendant suffering?

All in all, NATO-occupied Eastern Europe, until recently the home of "socialist republics," has become a much more congenial place for royalty. Bulgaria's King Simeon (now prime minister), came back to reclaim his domain, as did Romania's King Michael, Yugoslavia's King Presumptive Alexander, and Albania's King Leka (son of Hitler's and Mussolini's ally, King Zog).

## Slovakia 2002

Vladimir Meciar is not a true believer in globalization. He had been a marked man in Washington since 1994 when he became prime minister as the head of the Movement for a Democratic Slovakia (MDS), the main party in a coalition that won the election on a strong anti-capitalist platform. After being unseated in the 1998 elections by Mikulás Dzurinda, a man much more comfortable with opening up the country to foreign capital, Meciar was again a candidate in 2002.

Elections were scheduled for September, but Washington began its anti-Meciar campaign in February when the American ambassador, Ronald Weiser, issued a warning to the people of Slovakia that electing Meciar once again would hurt their chances of entry into the European Union and NATO. "If the situation repeats itself, there will not be an invitation," warned the ambassador.[5]

In March, Nicholas Burns, the U.S. ambassador to NATO, arrived in Bratislavia, the Slovak Capital, and issued his own warning, reminding Slovakians that the United States had blocked Slovakia's entry into NATO in 1997 because of Meciar and could do it again. Washington still viewed Mr. Meciar as an authoritarian anti-West leader, he said. "The former government, we believe, did not demonstrate a commitment to democracy and the rule of law."[6]

To put Burns' remarks in perspective, we should keep in mind that when the United States does not want to support a particular government because that government is not receptive to the forces of globalization and/or other objectives of US foreign policy, it can always find reasons for not doing so stated in terms of democracy and freedom; conversely, Washington can find justification for supporting an ideologically-compatible regime no matter how oppressive or corrupt it may be or how much its elections may be of dubious purity; Indonesia, Mexico, Pakistan, and Peru are some examples of this in the several years preceding this period.

The Washington-based National Endowment for Democracy (NED)—the long-time front for the CIA—was also present in Slovakia, expending some $417,000 in the 12 months leading up to the election on media, electoral, youth and other projects. NED typically paints such projects in generalized, non-ideological, non-partisan colors; in Slovakia, its programs were referred to by terms such as "election-related political and organizational skills"; "voter education and mobilization activities"; and producing and distributing "a series of get-out-the-vote materials."[7] Such programs sound straight out of an American high-school textbook on civics, but they're carefully designed to aid Washington's chosen organizations, parties and individuals. The National Democratic Institute (NDI), one of NED's four principal arms, admitted that it excluded Meciar's Movement for a Democratic Slovakia from those political parties receiving aid. NDI maintained that MDS lacked "internal democracy" and "threaten(s) the participatory and representative nature of democracy."[8]

According to NED's annual report, NDI oversaw training in Slovakia that "targeted young party members, women and Roma [Gypsies]; three participants in its 'Youth in Politics' program were elected to Parliament."[9]

The main English-language newspaper in Slovakia, *The Slovak Spectator*, which was opposed to Meciar, nonetheless contended that the NED aid was a violation of Slovakian law aimed at keeping foreign influences out of elections. "Slovakia's law on political parties forbids foreign citizens or foreign legal entities, with the exception of foreign foundations and partner political parties, from supporting domestic political parties."[10]

This kind of prohibition would of course apply to NED activities in almost every country they're active in, but, inasmuch as they're backed by the US government—indeed, they *are* the US government—it's rare that any complaint against their activities gets anywhere.

Ambassador Weiser also advised some Slovak political parties not to cooperate with another political party in the event the latter got enough votes to win seats in the legislature. When questioned about this after the election, Weiser was reluctant to discuss his initiative, saying he felt it was a dead issue given that the party in question did not get into parliament.[11]

In the end, Dzurinda kept power. Although Meciar's party won the most votes, no other political party would form a coalition with them.[12] One does not have to be terribly cynical to surmise that fear of antagonizing Washington lay behind this.

After the election, *The Washington Post* reported: "Politicians and analysts here said the campaign to increase voter participation improved turnout, which in turn probably improved the vote for Dzurinda and his allies."[13]

Two months later, in November, Slovakia declared that its airspace would be open to over-flights by US aircraft in the event of an attack on Iraq,[14] and in February 2003, the government agreed to assist any US operation against Iraq and to join any US military operation.[15]

## Latin America
## Nicaragua 2001

As Sandinista presidential candidate Daniel Ortega was doing well in the polls for the November election, the Bush administration was setting out to campaign against him.

In June, US Acting Assistant Secretary of State Lino Gutiérrez, the State Department's No. 2 diplomat for Latin America, made it clear in a talk in Managua that the United States would not look kindly upon the return to power of the socialist-oriented Sandinistas. He blasted Ortega's ties to people such as Fidel Castro of Cuba and Libyan leader Moammar Gadhafi.[16] Subsequently, State Department spokeswoman Eliza Koch criticized the Sandinistas for alleged contact with Iraq, the FARC rebels in Colombia, and the ETA separatist movement in Spain.

This last accusation was made less than two months after the September 11 attacks, when any association at all with "terrorists" was being promoted by Washington as the ultimate sin.

Koch further singled out the continuing presence in the Sandinista inner circle of three so-called "hardliners"—Tomas Borge, Lenin Cerna and Alvaro Baltodano. All three, she said, "have long histories of grossly violating civil and human rights and suppressing democratic activities."[17] Another State Department official, John Keane, added to the invective by asserting that the Sandinistas still had in their fold hard-liners who were responsible for "abominations" of human and civil rights.[18] These remarks were coming from the government that ran the infamous army of thugs known as the Contras, which plagued the people of Nicaragua with genuine abominations throughout the 1980s.[19] Apart from being shameless interference in Nicaraguan politics, the State Department remarks are further testimony that the US government can say anything it cares to about Officially Designated Enemies (ODE) without ever being called to back up their charges.

There was also US Ambassador Oliver Garza, who went around handing out bags of rice with Enrique Bolaños, Ortega's main opponent, at his side. The *Miami Herald* reported that "Garza shrugged off reporters' suggestions that the two were out stumping together—even though it was a publicity-generating event held during the home stretch of a heated campaign season and Garza took the opportunity to call the opposing Sandinistas 'robbers'."[20]

Frederick Denton, senior analyst in Nicaragua for pollsters CID-Gallup was moved to declare: "Never in my whole life have I seen a sitting ambassador get publicly involved in a sovereign country's electoral process, nor have I ever heard of it."[21]

Former US president Jimmy Carter was of a like mind. He headed an international delegation of electoral observers and criticized the strong statements coming from Washington. "I personally disapprove of statements or actions by any country that might tend to influence the vote of people in another sovereign nation," he said.[22]

The US also exerted relentless pressure on the Conservative Party and succeeded in making them withdraw from the election so as to avoid splitting the conservative vote against the Sandinistas, Gutierrez personally visiting the country to make this appeal.[23]

Six days before the election, a full-page advertisement appeared in *La Prensa*, Nicaragua's leading newspaper, signed by First Brother Jeb Bush, governor of Florida; it was laid out thusly: In small blue letters: "The Brother of the President of the United States"...then a super large headline in blaring red: "GEORGE W. BUSH SUPPORTS ENRIQUE BOLAÑOS". This was all on white background, and the whole page was bordered in red, white and blue. The effect was to give the impression that the ad was inserted by the US president himself. Among other things, the ad said "Ortega has a relationship of more than thirty years with states and individuals who shelter and condone international terrorism."[24]

At the close of the campaign, Bolaños announced: "If Ortega comes to power, that would provoke a closing of aid and investment, difficulties with exports, visas and family remittances. I'm not just saying this. The United States says this, too. We cannot close our eyes and risk our well-being and work. Say yes to Nicaragua, say no to terrorism."[25]

In the end, the Sandinistas lost the election by about ten percentage points after steadily leading in the polls during much of the campaign.

For many Nicaraguans, it was a painful reminder of the 1990 election in which Washington had also engaged in serious interference, leading then, too, to a Sandinista defeat. In both elections, the impoverished people of Nicaragua were warned that a Sandinista victory would mean severe economic hostility from Washington; in 1990 they were also warned that it would mean a resumption of US military hostility as well.

It is worth observing that Nicaragua and Haiti are the nations in the Western Hemisphere that the United States has intervened in the most in the 20th and 21st centuries, including long occupations. And they are today the poorest in the hemisphere, wretchedly so.

## Bolivia 2002

Running for the Bolivian presidency on an anti-neoliberal, anti-big business, and anti-coca eradication campaign, for a party called Movement Toward Socialism (MTS), former member of Congress Evo Morales was clearly not the kind of Third Worlder the United States takes to its heart. Before the June 30 first round election, US Ambassador Manuel Rocha stated: "The Bolivian electorate must consider the consequences of choosing leaders somehow connected with drug trafficking and terrorism."[26] As seen above, since September 11, 2001, painting Officially Designated Enemies with the terrorist brush was de rigueur US foreign policy rhetoric.

After the first round—in which Morales came in second to Gonzalo Sanchez de Lozada and thus made it to the congressional runoff vote August 3—US Assistant Secretary of State for Western Hemisphere Affairs Otto Reich warned that American aid to the country would be in danger if Mr. Morales was chosen.[27] Then Ambassador Rocha and other US officials met with key figures from Bolivia's main political parties in an effort to shore up support for Sanchez de Lozada.[28] Morales lost the vote.

It should be noted that Bolivia, with 60 percent of its population living in poverty, was not anxious to adhere to the desires of Washington, whose supply-side war on drugs had failed to benefit Bolivian peasants, to whom coca is important both economically and culturally.

## Venezuela 2002

Jacobo Arbenz, Cheddi Jagan, Fidel Castro, João Goulart, Juan Bosch, Salvador Allende, Michael Manley, Maurice Bishop,

Daniel Ortega, Jean-Bertrand Aristide, Hugo Chávez...all Latin American leaders of the past half century, all progressive, all condemned to suffer the torments of hell for their beliefs by the unrelenting animosity of the United States.

Chávez had been elected president by a wide margin in 1998, breaking a lock on power by the two establishment parties that had dominated Venezuelan politics for decades. He repeated the strong electoral showing in 2000. But in the eyes of Washington officials, Chávez was no more than a man guilty of the following offenses:

He branded the post-September 11 US attacks on Afghanistan as "fighting terrorism with terrorism," demanding an end to "the slaughter of innocents"; holding up photographs of children said to have been killed in the American bombing attacks, he said their deaths had "no justification, just as the attacks in New York did not, either." In response, the Bush Administration temporarily withdrew its ambassador.[29] When she returned to Venezuela, she had what one US official called a "very difficult meeting" with Chávez, in which she told him "to keep his mouth shut on these important issues."[30]

He was very friendly with Fidel Castro and sold oil to Cuba at discount rates or in exchange for medical and other services. Chávez called for an end to the US embargo against Cuba.

His defense minister asked the permanent US military mission in Venezuela to vacate its offices in the military head-quarters in Caracas, saying its presence was an anachronism from the Cold War.[31]

Chávez did not cooperate to Washington's satisfaction with the US war against the Colombian guerrillas.[32]

He denied Venezuelan airspace to US counter-drug flights.[33]

He refused to provide US intelligence agencies with information on the country's large Arab community.[34]

He promoted a regional free-trade bloc and united Latin

American petroleum operations as ways to break free from US economic dominance.[35]

Chávez also opposed the Free Trade Area of the Americas, a globalization program high on Washington's agenda.

He visited Saddam Hussein in Iraq and Moammar Gaddafi in Libya. Secretary of State Colin Powell testified to Congress that Chávez visits "some of the strangest countries," referring to the Venezuelan's visits to Iran, Iraq and Cuba—all on the US list of alleged state sponsors of terrorism. Chávez supporters noted that Libya, Iran and Iraq are members with Venezuela of the Organization of Petroleum Exporting Countries (OPEC), in which Chávez has played a leading role.[36]

And more in the same vein, which the Washington aristocracy is unaccustomed to encountering from the servant class. Uncle Sam has been inspired to topple numerous governments which displayed considerably less disrespect for him than Venezuela did.

Chávez, moreover, had been trying to institute all manner of reforms to relieve the suffering of the poor (who comprise about 80 percent of the population), a program not likely to win favor with a class-conscious, privatization-minded US government and Venezuelan upper and middle classes: restructuring the state-owned oil company, which he regarded as having become a state-within-a-state, to achieve greater national control over oil resources; reinforcing a consitutional ban on the privatization of the oil company; changing the agreements with foreign oil companies that were excessively generous to the companies; establishing a new progressive constitution; numerous ecological community development projects; enrolling over one million students in school who were previously excluded; increasing the minimum wage and public sector salaries; halting the previous government's initiative to privatize Venezuela's social security system; reducing unemployment; introducing a credit program for women and the poor; reforming the tax system to spare the poor; making health care much more available;

lowering infant mortality; greatly expanding literacy courses; land redistribution in a society where two percent of the population controlled 60 percent of the land.[37]

## The coup

On April 11, a military coup toppled Chávez, who was taken to a remote location. Pedro Carmona, the chairman of Venezuela's largest chamber of commerce, was installed as president. He proceeded to dissolve the legislature, the Supreme Court, the attorney general's office, the national electoral commission, and the state governorships. Carmona then decreed that the 1999 constitution, which had been written by a constitutional assembly and ratified by a wide majority of voters, following the procedures outlined in the previous constitution, was to be suspended. On top of all this, the new regime raided the homes of various Chávez supporters.[38]

And what was the reaction of the US government to this sharp slap in the face of democracy, civil liberties and law, that fits the textbook definition of dictatorship?

The Bush administration did not call it a coup. The White House term of choice was "a change of government." They blamed Chávez for what had taken place, maintaining that his ouster was prompted by peaceful protests and justified by the Venezuelan leader's own actions. It occurred, said White House spokesman Ari Fleischer, "as a result of the message of the Venezuelan people."[39]

The State Department also expressed its support for the coup, declaring that "undemocratic actions committed or encouraged by the Chávez administration provoked yesterday's crisis in Venezuela."[40]

And the US ambassador to the Organization of American States (OAS), Roger Noreiga, declared that "The people of Venezuela, loyal to their republican tradition and their fight for independence, peace and liberty, will not accept any regime, legislation or authority which contradict values, principles and democratic guarantees."[41]

But Noriega was ignoring the fact that the previous September the OAS had adopted the Inter-American Democratic Charter, which expressly condemns the overthrow of democratically elected governments among its member states and requires specific actions by all members when this occurs.

The *New York Times* penned its own love note to the new government. In an editorial, the paper stated: "Venezuelan democracy is no longer threatened by a would-be dictator...[because] the military intervened and handed power to a respected business leader."[42]

Veritable grass-roots democracy the coup was.

## Reversal of the coup

The coupmakers had bitten off more than they could chew by seriously underestimating the opposition to the coup and to the instant totalitarianism which followed; they had believed their own propaganda about Chávez lacking support—huge rallies in his favor erupted—an illusion on their own part no doubt prompted by the heavy concentration of the media in the hands of the opposition, which regularly blacked out news favorable to Chávez. The post-coup support for Chávez induced elements of the military, including some who had taken part in the coup, to step in, retrieve Chávez, and bring him back triumphant to Caracas. He had been gone about 48 hours.

"Decisions to toss out the constitution and hunt down allies of Chávez," wrote the *Washington Post*, "reinforced lingering fears held by many Venezuelans, including members of the military, that what had occurred was not a popular revolt but a coup by the business elite."[43]

The Bush administration voiced no misgivings about its support of the coup. National Security Advisor Condoleezza Rice quickly declared: "We do hope that Chávez recognizes that the whole world is watching and that he takes advantage of this opportunity to right his own ship, which has been moving, frankly, in the wrong direction for quite a long time." She added that Chávez "needs to respect constitutional processes."[44]

Or as Monty Python legend, Terry Jones, put it: Chávez was ousted in "a free and fair democratic coup, only to be returned to office two days later on what seems to have been little more than the whim of the people."

## Prelude to the coup

Immediately after the coup, members of the military and of the new government said that the decision to force Chávez from power had been made six months earlier by a group of dissident officers in the Venezuelan navy and air force.[45]

As the coup was being hatched, the United States met with all the key players, either in Venezuela or in Washington: Pedro Carmona, who became president; Vice Admiral Carlos Molina, Air Force Col. Pedro Soto, and several others who in February had publicly demanded Chávez's removal; opposition legislators, and others. A US diplomat revealed that Molina and Soto had each received $100,000 from a Miami bank account for denouncing Chávez.[46]

"We felt we were acting with U.S. support," Molina said of the coup. "We agree that we can't permit a communist government here. The U.S. has not let us down yet. This fight is still going on because the government is illegal."[47]

The officers who took part in the overthrow of Chávez "understood the U.S. State Department's repeated statements of concern over the Chávez administration as a tacit endorsement of their plans to remove him from office if the opportunity arose." ... "The State Department had always expressed its preoccupation with Chávez," retired military officer Fernando Ochoa said after the coup. "We interpreted that as" an endorsement of his removal.[48]

However, American officials endeavored to make the point afterward that they had not been encouraging a coup. The White House spokesperson said that such meetings and conversations with dissidents were "a normal part of what diplomats do."[49] And the *Washington Post* reported:

> Members of the country's diverse opposition had been visiting the U.S. embassy here in recent weeks, hoping to enlist U.S. help in toppling Chávez. The visitors included active and retired members of the military, media leaders and opposition politicians. "The opposition has been coming in with an assortment of 'what ifs,'" said a U.S. official familiar with the effort. "What if this happened? What if that happened? What if you held it up and looked at it sideways? To every scenario we say no. We know what a coup looks like, and we won't support it.[50]

Of course, if the United States had been against the coup it would have informed the Venezuelan government of what was being planned and who was doing the planning and that would have been the end of it. Inasmuch as Washington normally equates democracy with free elections, here was a chance to strike a blow on behalf of democracy by saving a government that came to power through free elections on two separate occasions.

And Washington would not have financed the plotters.

## Financing the coup

The National Endowment for Democracy was on the scene, as it has been for so many other Washington destabilization operations. In their reporting year ending September 30, 2000, in a clear attempt to weaken Chávez's federal power, NED gave, amongst other Venezuelan grants, $50,000 to PRODEL, a Venezuelan organization, "To promote and defend decentralization in Venezuela. PRODEL will establish and train a network of national and state legislators and mayors to monitor government decentralization activities, advocate for the rights and responsibilities of state and local government in Venezuela, and analyze and debate pending legislation affecting local government."[51]

The following year, announcing that it was expanding its program in Venezuela in response to "a process of profound political change" embarked on by Chávez,[52] NED channeled more than $877,000 in grants to American and Venezuelan groups, none of whom supported Chávez, including $339,998 to provide training in political party and coalition building, and $154,377 to the Confederation of Venezuelan Workers (CTV)[53]

The CTV, long an anti-leftist, Cold War asset of US foreign policy through the AFL-CIO, is run by old-guard, corrupt labor leaders, angered by Chávez's attempt to reform them. The organization was a key force in the work stoppages and protest demonstrations which galvanized opposition to Chávez. As in Chile in 1973, before the overthrow of Salvador Allende, large crowds of civilians were used to create the feeling of chaos, and to establish a false picture of Chávez as a dictator, providing some of the rationale and incitement for the military to then make a coup "for the sake of the country."[54]

As Mr. Chávez's reform programs clashed with various business, labor and media groups, the Endowment stepped up its assistance, providing some $1,100,000 for the year ending September 30, 2002, including $232,526 to the CTV.[55]

CTV leader, Carlos Oretga, worked closely with Pedro Carmona in challenging the government and was invited by a NED affiliate to Washington in February where he met with Otto Reich, assistant secretary of state for Western Hemispheric Affairs, who was likely one of the masterminds of the move to topple Chávez.[56]

Inasmuch as Venezuela is the fifth largest oil producer in the world, and the third largest supplier to the United States, it

appears plausible to conclude that oil must be a significant factor in the US drive to effect regime change in the country. Yet
Washington has opposed governments and movements
throughout Latin America and elsewhere in the world with
equal determination, without oil or any other resource being a
factor. Hugo Chávez is against the excesses of US foreign policy and globalization and has let the world know this, which
makes it plain to Washington that he's not of suitable client
material. For the empire to let him get away with this would be
to set a very bad example for other non-believers.

## Postscript

Since the debacle of 2002, Chávez's natural enemies at
home and in Washington have not relaxed their crusade against
him. Opponents have been trying to unseat him through a
recall referendum, a drive that is funded in part, if not in full,
by, yes, the National Endowment for Democracy. NED gave a
grant of $53,400 to an organization called Súmate, which
appears to be running the referendum campaign. The NED
grant document, after castigating Chávez for polarizing
Venezuelan society, specifies that Súmate will "Develop a net of
volunteers and [apartidistas] trained to work in elections and in
a referendum...[and] promote popular support for the referendum."[57]

Imagine if during the recent referendum in California it
was disclosed that the Venezuelan government was funding the
movement to recall the governor.

A few weeks before the recall was to take place on August
15, 2004, former president Carlos Andres Perez, a leading member of the old guard, said in a newspaper interview that "the referendum would fail and that violence was the only way for the
opposition to get rid of Chávez."[58]

# El Salvador 2004

The March 21 election for the presidency had on one side Schafik Handal, candidate of the FMLN, the leftist former guerrilla group, which the previous year had won the largest bloc in Congress with 31 of the 84 seats and held nearly half the offices of mayor in the country. His opponent was Tony Saca of the incumbent Arena Party, a pro-US, pro-free market organization of the extreme right, which in the bloody civil war days had featured death squads and the infamous assassination of Archbishop Oscar Romero.

Handal said he would withdraw El Salvador's 380 troops from Iraq as well as reviewing other pro-US policies; he would also take another look at the privatizations of Salvadoran industries, and would reinstate diplomatic relations with Cuba.[59]

If all this wasn't reason enough for the United States to intervene in the election, there was the FMLN's announced opposition to the proposed Central American Free Trade Agreement, that Washington hoped to see become a reality in 2004.[60]

During a February visit to the country, Roger Noriega, the US Assistant Secretary of State for Western Hemisphere Affairs, met all the presidential candidates except Handal.[61] He warned of possible repercussions in US-Salvadoran relations if Handal were elected. Three Republican congressmen threatened to block the renewal of annual work visas for some 300,000 Salvadorans in the United States if El Salvador opted for the FMLN.[62] And Congressman Thomas Tancredo of Colorado stated that if the FMLN won, "it could mean a radical change" in US policy on remittances to El Salvador.[63]

Washington's attitude was exploited by Arena and the generally conservative Salvadoran press, and it became widely believed that a Handal victory could result in mass deportations of Salvadorans from the United States and a drop in remittances. At a rally, Saca asked the crowd to imagine what would happen to their remittances if Handal were to win. "Remittances! Dollars!" he bellowed to the crowd. "The administration that assures tranquility for our brothers in the United States is Arena and Tony Saca, because we have good relations with the United States."[64]

The statistics are remarkable: As many as two million Salvadorans live in the United States, sending home between $1.7 and two billion a year, a significant portion of the country's economy.

"In a political advertisement on Salvadoran television, an elderly woman reads a letter from her son who lives in the United States. He tells her he might not be able to send her more money. The camera focuses tightly on her left cheek. A single tear slowly succumbs to gravity. The son says that if leftist candidate Schafik Handal is elected president on Sunday, Salvadorans living in the United States could lose their work visas."[65]

The scare campaign included warnings that the FMLN would abolish "democracy", institute "communism", and would turn El Salvador into "another Cuba."[66] It was as if the civil war and the Cold War had never ended.

Saca updated the campaign of threats by accusing his rival of links to Islamic terrorists, repeating the story that demonstrators allegedly aligned with the FMLN had burned a US flag and chanted slogans in support of Osama bin Laden just after the September 11 attacks.[67]

Arena won the election with about 57 percent of the vote to some 36 percent for the FMLN.

After the election, the US ambassador, Hugh Douglas Barclay, declared that Washington's policies concerning immigration and remittances had nothing to do with any election in El Salvador. There appears to be no record of such a statement being made in public *before* the election when it might have had a profound positive effect for the FMLN. Although Barclay said that the embassy had in fact made such a statement before the election, he offered no details,[68] and may have been referring to a comment he made to at least one American journalist whose articles were not published in El Salvador.[69]

* * *

Mr. Castro, once, just once, show that
you're unafraid of a real election.
—George W. Bush[70]

# THE COLD WAR

# Before There Were Terrorists, There Were Communists and the Wonderful World of Anti-Communism

Under the charming aegis of the George W. Bush administration, lying has become one of the few growth industries in Washington. But it should not be forgotten that during the long winter of the Cold War as well, one had to constantly read between the li(n)es. The big lie, the big huge lie they drummed into our collective heads from childhood on was that there was a conspiracy out there, something out there called The International Communist Conspiracy, headquarters in Moscow, and active in every country of the world, looking to undermine everything that was decent and holy, looking to enslave us all. That's what they taught us, in our schoolbooks, in our church sermons, on radio and television, in our daily newspapers, in our comic books—The Communist Menace, the Red Menace, more dangerous than Saddam Hussein or Osama bin Laden were presented to a later generation; for one thing, this menace really had weapons of mass destruction.

Almost every American took this message to heart, unquestioningly. I was a good, loyal anti-communist until I was past the age of 30. Indeed, in the 1960s I was working at the State Department planning on becoming a foreign service officer, eager to join the battle against communism, until a thing called Vietnam came along and dramatically altered my thinking.

But it was all a con game. There was never any such animal as The International Communist Conspiracy. What there was, was people all over the Third World struggling for economic and political changes that didn't coincide with the needs of the American power elite, and so the US moved to crush those governments and movements even though the Soviet Union was playing hardly any role at all in these scenarios. (It is remarkable the number of those who make fun of conspiracy theories but who accepted without question the existence of an International Communist Conspiracy.)

Washington officials of course couldn't say that they were intervening to block economic or political change, so they called it fighting communism, fighting a communist conspiracy, and of course fighting for freedom and democracy. Just as now the White House can't say that it invaded Iraq to expand the empire, or for the oil, or to open the doors to multinational corporations, and such; they can't say that so they call it fighting terrorism.

Lest we forget, presented here are some of the great moments from that wonderful world of Cold-War anti-communism, a sample of the stories they told us, and what they *didn't* tell us, or played down; the myths, the lies, the half-truths fed us to justify the unceasing American interventions and the swollen military budget; the stupidities of word and deed that marked Washington's crusade; the spread of the anti-communist mentality worldwide under the knowing direction and inspiration of America's superpower information and propaganda machines; the less-than-noble nature of those who donned the mantle of anti- communism and championed the cause at home and abroad. This listing could serve to provoke laughter at the absurdity of it all if not for the extensive pain and suffering and ruined lives the crusade gave birth to. To keep it within manageable boundaries, it begins in the 1940s, although it could as well start in 1918, shortly after the Russian Revolution, when the United States and a number of other countries invaded the infant socialist nation; the Cold War can be dated from that point, or at least from 1920 when the foreign armies were gone.

> How can we account for our present situation unless we believe that men high in this government are concerting to deliver us to disaster? This must be the product of a great conspiracy, a conspiracy on a scale so immense as to dwarf any previous such venture in the history of man.
>
>     —Senator Joseph R. McCarthy, on the
>              floor of the Senate, 1951, on what he
>              saw as the infiltration of communists in
>                    the US government.[1]

**1940s**: Americans who had fought against fascism in the Spanish Civil War were not trusted by the US government in World War II and were given a very hard time. The Army didn't want to send them to the front, despite their battlefront experience, and prevented them from becoming officers, and after the war the FBI frequently harassed them, visiting their employers to tell them that these men had fought in Spain for the "communists." Such men have often been referred to as "premature anti-fascists."[2]

**1945**: Admiral Karl Doenitz, leader of Nazi Germany for 23 days after Hitler's death, went on Hamburg Radio to deliver his now- famous pronouncement that Hitler had died "fighting Bolshevism to his last breath."[3]

**1945**: "The iron curtain", an expression used a million times after World War II to denigrate the Soviet Union; contrary to popular belief, it was not coined by Winston Churchill, but rather by the Nazis. Propaganda chief Joseph Goebbels used it in a Nazi newspaper on February 23 (*ein eiserner Vorhang*), referring to the Soviet Union.[4] The new German foreign minister, Count Ludwig Schwerin von Krosigk, used it in a broadcast on May 2 in a bitter attack on Bolshevism. Churchill first used it on May 12 (after perhaps reading Schwerin von Krosigk's remark in *The Times* of London on May 3). Churchill's more famous use was of course on March 5, 1946 in Fulton, Missouri.

**1947**: Under President Harry Truman's loyalty program (instead of asking whether the government was loyal to the people, the people had to swear their loyalty to the government) all branches of the federal government were joined together in the hunt for communists, or "communists"; one of the program's provisions was the authorization for the attorney general to list "subversive" organizations, membership in any of which was grounds for dismissal or denial of employment; not merely membership, but "sympathetic association" could put an end to a career. The program and its oppressive atmosphere were soon picked up by many firms in the private sector. By the mid-1950s, 13.5 million workers were subject to security-loyalty checks; more than 15,000 had been dismissed or forced to resign from federal, state and local government positions, not including many teachers who were hounded out of their schools, and those dismissed by private companies.[5]

**1948**: The Scripps-Howard *Pittsburgh Press* published the names, addresses, and places of employment of about 1,000 citizens who had signed presidential-nominating petitions for former Vice President Henry Wallace, running under the Progressive Party. This, and a number of other lists of "communists", published in the mainstream media, resulted in people losing their jobs, being expelled from unions, having their children abused, being denied state welfare benefits, and suffering various other punishments.[6]

**1949**: In the quiet little town of Hobe Sound, Florida, late one night near the end of March, immediately after a fire siren had sounded, a disheveled man clad in pajamas rushed from a house and ran down the street wildly screaming: "The

Red Army has landed!" The man was James V. Forrestal, the United States Secretary of Defense. He was flown to the Naval Hospital in Bethesda, Maryland and kept under observation; two months later Forrestal jumped to his death from his 16th floor suite.[7]

**Late 1940s-early 1950s**: The House Committee on Un-American Activities was busy keeping Americans up to date about the Red Menace. They published a series of pamphlets, which included:

> 100 Things You Should Know About Communism in the U.S.A.
>
> 100 Things You Should Know About Communism in Religion
>
> 100 Things You Should Know About Communism in Education
>
> 100 Things You Should Know About Communism in Labor
>
> 100 Things You Should Know About Communism in Government

A sample from the first pamphlet about what a communist takeover of the United States would mean:

> Q: What would happen to my insurance?
>
> A: It would go to the Communists.
>
> Q: Would communism give me something better than I have now?
>
> A: Not unless you are in a penitentiary serving a life sentence at hard labor.

**1949-1989**: Numerous Soviet proposals to lessen the tension and danger of war (purposeful or accidental) were routinely rebuffed by the United States as if they were deadly traps. Referring to the Russians latest "peace offensive" became a common way to scoff at and brush off such proposals. Yet the fact remains that the Soviet Union, on many occasions, called for the mutual dissolution of the Warsaw Pact and NATO; indeed, it was tantamount to a standing offer; even repeated Moscow proposals to simply establish a direct dialogue with senior NATO officials were turned down. In 1949 the Soviets were ready to join NATO when it was being set up, but were refused membership.[8]

**1930s to the present**: We've all heard the figures many times...10 million...20 million...40 million...60 million...died under Stalin. But what does the number mean, whichever number you choose? Of course many people died under Stalin, many people died under Roosevelt, and many people are still dying under Bush. Dying appears to be a natural phenomenon in every country. The question is *how* did those people die under Stalin? Did they die from the famines that plagued the USSR in the 1920s and 30s? Did the Bolsheviks deliberately create those famines? How? Why? More people certainly died in India in the 20th century from famines than in the Soviet Union, but no one accuses India of the mass murder of its own citizens. Did the millions die from disease in an age before antibiotics? In prison? From what causes? People die in prison in the United States on a regular basis. Were millions actually murdered in cold blood? If so, how? How many were criminals executed for non-political crimes? The logistics of murdering tens of millions of people is daunting.

The period of 1917 to the 1930s was one marked by the horrendous cumulative devastation and chaos of the world war, the revolution, and the civil war. The issue of how many died, and how, is hopelessly, and probably permanently, muddled, particularly because of the conscious effort, beginning in the 1930s, by the German Nazis and American anti-communists to publicize the most damaging information about the Soviet Union they could put together, or fabricate. Leading the American campaign was William Randolph Hearst, a friend of Hitler, and the media empire he commanded, which relentlessly, exaggeratedly, and fictitiously, hammered home the message for its tens of millions of readers each day.[9]

Following the Chinese Communist revolution of 1949 we find a similar campaign based on the millions or tens of millions "murdered" by the government. As evidence that such beliefs in the United States were not limited to conservative newspaper publishers or right-wing kooks, here is Clark Kerr, president of the University of California at Berkeley in a 1959 speech: "Perhaps 2 or even 20 million people have been killed in China by the new regime." One person wrote to Kerr: "I am wondering how you would judge a person who estimates the age of a passerby on the street as being 'perhaps 2 or even 20 years old.' Or what would you think of a physician who tells you to take 'perhaps 2 or even twenty teaspoonsful of a remedy'?"[10]

Here is President Nixon in 1969: "For the South Vietnamese, our precipitate withdrawal would inevitably allow the Communists to repeat the massacres which followed their takeover in the North 15 years before. They then murdered more than 50,000 people and hundreds of thousands more died in slave labor camps."[11]

And here, in 2002, is Dennis Hayes, executive vice-president of the Cuban American National Foundation in Miami, an organization long hostile to the Cuban revolution to the point of clinical hysteria: Fidel Castro "is a man who has killed tens of thousands of his own citizens."[12]

**Early 1950s**: Fear of a Soviet air attack on the United States led to thousands of observation posts being set up on rooftops, balconies, towers and mountaintops, manned by hundreds of thousands of civilian volunteers. There were also countless backyard bomb shelters and underground fallout shelters, air raid drills in schools and elsewhere, with people hiding under desks, and identification bracelets for school children to wear at all times, which would help distinguish children who were lost or killed in a nuclear explosion. In one air raid drill, the President, his Cabinet, and 15,000 other government officials evacuated to secret hideaways in the Washington region.[13]

**1950s**: Mrs. Ada White, member of the Indiana State Textbook Commission, believed that Robin Hood was a Communist and urged that books that told the Robin Hood story be banned from Indiana schools.[14]

**1950s to end of cold war**: Traffic in phoney Lenin quotes was brisk, each one passed around from one publication or speaker to another for years. Here's *U.S. News and World Report* in 1958 demonstrating communist duplicity by quoting Lenin: "Promises are like pie crusts, made to be broken." Secretary of State John Foster Dulles used it in a speech shortly afterward, one of many to do so during the cold war. Lenin actually did use a very similar line, but he explicitly stated that he was quoting an English proverb (it comes from Jonathan Swift) and his purpose was to show the unreliability of the bourgeoisie, not of communists.

"First we will take Eastern Europe, then the masses of Asia, then we will encircle the United States, which will be the last bastion of capitalism. We will not have to attack. It will fall like an overripe fruit into our hands."

This Lenin "quotation" had the usual wide circulation, even winding up in the *Congressional Record* in 1962. This was not simply a careless attribution; this was an out-and-out fabrication; an extensive search, including by the Library of Congress and the United States Information Agency failed to find its origin.

"We will find our most fertile field for infiltration of Marxism within the field of religion, because religious people are the most gullible and will accept almost anything if it is couched in religious terminology."

This was a 1960s and later staple of the many religious organizations and publications of anti-communist America. At one point Lenin actually wrote: "We are absolutely opposed to the slightest affront to these workers' religious convictions. We recruit them in order to educate them in the spirit of our programme, and not in order to carry on an active struggle against religion."[15]

**1950s-1960s**: A favorite theme of the anti-communists was that a principal force behind drug trafficking was a communist plot to demoralize the United States. Here's a small sample:

Don Keller, District Attorney for San Diego County, California in 1953: "We know that more heroin is being produced south of the border than ever before and we are beginning to hear stories of financial backing by big shot Communists operating out of Mexico City."

Norris Poulson, California congressman, 1953: "The slaves of Stalin swore to break the resistance in China by...forcing or beguiling millions of Chinese into becoming narcotics addicts."

Thomas Dodd, Connecticut Senator, 1961: China "is a government which has made a state industry out of producing opium and other narcotics and peddling these drugs to criminal elements all around the world."

Henry Giordano, Commissioner of the Federal Bureau of Narcotics, 1964, interview in the *American Legion Magazine*:

**Interviewer:** "I've been told that the communists are trying to flood our country with narcotics to weaken our moral and physical stamina. Is that true?

**Giordano:** "As far as the drugs are concerned, it's true. There's a terrific flow of drugs coming out of Yunnan Province of China....There's no question that in that particular area this is the aim of the Red Chinese. It should be apparent that if you could addict a population you would degrade a nation's moral fiber."

Patrick O'Carroll, director of the Federal Bureau of Narcotics School in Washington, 1965: "Because of the smuggling of this drug by Cuban nationals, some of whom have been determined to be Castro sympathizers, we now find considerable quantities of cocaine in the United States."

Fulton Lewis, Jr., prominent conservative radio broadcaster and newspaper columnist, 1965: "Narcotics of Cuban origin—marijuana, cocaine, opium, and heroin—are now peddled in big cities and tiny hamlets throughout this country. Several Cubans arrested by the Los Angeles police have boasted they are communists."[16]

And we were told that along with drugs another tool of the commies to undermine America's spirit was fluoridation of the water.

**1951**: Mickey Spillane was one of the most successful writers of the 1950s, selling millions of his anticommunist thriller mysteries. Here is his hero, Mike Hammer, in "One Lonely Night", boasting of his delight in the grisly murders he commits, all in the name of destroying a communist plot to steal atomic secrets. After a night of carnage, the triumphant Hammer gloats, "I shot them in cold blood and enjoyed every minute of it. I pumped slugs into in the nastiest bunch of bastards you ever saw....They were Commies....Pretty soon what's left of Russia and the slime that breeds there won't be worth mentioning and I'm glad because I had a part in the killing. God, but it was fun!"[17]

And here is real life, the 1983 American invasion of Grenada...the home of the Cuban ambassador is damaged and looted by American soldiers; on one wall is written "AA", symbol of the 82nd Airborne Division; beside it the message: "Eat shit, commie faggot."... "I want to fuck communism out of this little island," says a marine, "and fuck it right back to Moscow."[18]

**1952**: A campaign against the United Nations Educational, Scientific and Cultural Organization because it was tainted with "atheism and communism", and was "subversive" because it preached internationalism—any attempt to introduce an international point of view in the schools was seen as undermining patriotism and loyalty to the United States. A bill in the US Senate, clearly aimed at UNESCO, called for a ban on the funding of "any international agency that directly or indirectly promoted one-world government or world citizenship." There was also opposition to UNESCO's association with the UN Declaration of Human Rights on the grounds that it was trying to replace the American Bill of Rights with a less liberty-giving covenant of human rights.[19]

**1953**: Several hundred books by more than 40 authors were removed from US libraries abroad at the request of the State Department. One of the main criteria in the selection was the author's refusal to tell Federal investigators about Communist affiliation. At the same time, with particular reference to periodicals, the State Department ordered the withdrawal of "any individual issues containing any material detrimental to United States objectives." Amongst the book authors who were specifically listed were: William Mandel, Philip Foner, Agnes Smedley, Edgar Snow, Dashiell Hammett, Howard Fast (later a semi-hysterical anti-communist), Alan Barth, Lillian Hellman, and Walter White.[20]

**1955**: A US Army 6-page pamphlet, "How to Spot a Communist", informed us that a communist could be spotted by his predisposition to discuss civil rights, racial and religious discrimination, the immigration laws, anti-subversive legislation, curbs on unions, and peace. Good Americans were advised to keep their ears stretched for such give-away terms as "chauvinism", "book-burning", "colonialism", "demagogy", "witch hunt", "reactionary", "progressive", and "exploitation". Another "distinguishing mark" of "Communist language" was a "preference for long sentences." After some ridicule, the Army quickly rescinded the pamphlet.[21]

Before the year was over, a Senate subcommittee issued "A Handbook for Americans", which informed the public that the inequalities in the American social system were not the cause of Americans becoming Communists. Rather, it said that Communists are likely to be "mission-minded intellectuals...psychologically maladjusted individuals...neurotics ...", and that the party was "a vehicle for anyone with an axe to grind...and an attraction for adventurous spirits who thrive on the conspiratorial atmosphere of the party."[22]

**1956**: The most famous line in the anti-communist lexicon was Soviet leader Nikita Khrushchev's "We shall bury you." But the *New York Times* reported: "in commentating on coexistence last night Mr. Khrushchev said communism did not have to resort to war to defeat capitalism. 'Whether you like it or not, history is on our side,' he said. 'We shall bury you'."[23] The Russian term used by Khrushchev literally means: We will be there at your funeral; idiomatically: We will outlive you, or our system will outlive yours. Khrushchev himself publicly explained this on several occasions in response to the unending use of his words incorrectly to indicate a Soviet plan to invade, kill and bury Americans. But unreconstructed anti-communists can still be found using the expression in the 21st century.

**1956**: Tom Dooley was an American hero, he was all over the media, his book "Deliver Us From Evil" was a runaway best seller, a *Reader's Digest* excerpt from it filled 27 pages. Dooley was an American doctor in Indochina and his writings gave Americans their first glimpse of Vietnam. He wrote of Vietnamese fleeing from the communist North to Washington's ally in the South—"What do you do for children," he wrote, "who have had chopsticks driven into their inner ears? Or for old women whose collarbones have been shattered by rifle butts? Or for kids whose ears have been torn off with pincers?" Dooley, who became known as Dr. America after his book came out, added that these atrocities "were linked to the refugees' belief in God."

But these and other Dooley stories in his compelling catalogue of communist horrors were all propaganda, a part of a CIA disinformation campaign which helped lay the groundwork for US intervention in Vietnam and gain the support of American and world public opinion. The fleeing of refugees from north to south itself owed a lot to CIA disinformation and psychological warfare.

By 1961, Tom Dooley ranked third on the Gallup poll's list of the 10 men most admired by Americans, behind President Dwight Eisenhower and the Pope.[24]

**1958**: The noted sportscaster Bill Stern (one of the heroes of my youth) observed on the radio that the lack of interest in "big time" football at New York University, City College of New York, Chicago, and Harvard "is due to the widespread acceptance of Communism at the universities."[25]

**1960**: US General Thomas Power speaking about nuclear war or a first strike by the US: "The whole idea is to *kill* the bastards! At the end of the war, if there are two Americans and one Russian, we win!" The response from one of those present was: "Well, you'd better make sure that they're a man and a woman."[26]

**1966**: The Boys Club of America is of course wholesome and patriotic. Imagine their horror when they were confused with the Dubois Clubs. When the Justice Department required the DuBois Clubs to register as a Communist front group, good loyal Americans knew what to do. They called up the Boys Club to announce that they would no longer contribute any money, or to threaten violence against them; and sure enough an explosion damaged the national headquarters of the youth group in San Francisco. Then former Vice President Richard Nixon, who was national board chairman of the Boys Club, declared: "This is an almost classic example of Communist deception and duplicity. The 'DuBois Clubs' are not unaware of the confusion they are causing among our supporters and among many other good citizens."[27]

**1966**: *Rhythm, Riots and Revolution: An Analysis of the Communist Use of Music, The Communist Master Music Plan*, by David A. Noebel, published by Christian Crusade Publications, 352 pages (expanded version of 1965 pamphlet: *Communism, Hypnotism and the Beatles*). Some chapters from the book:

Communist Use of Mind Warfare
Power of Music for Good or Evil
Communist Use of Hypnotism
Nature of Red Record Companies
Analysis of Red Records
Beatles' Religious Philosophy
Destructive Nature of Beatle Music
Communist Subversion of Folk Music
Folk Music and the Negro Revolution
Folk Music and the College Revolution

**1968**: William Calley, US Army Lieutenant, charged with overseeing the massacre of more than 100 Vietnamese civilians in My Lai in 1968, said some years later: "In all my years in the Army I was never taught that communists were human beings. We were there to kill ideology carried by—I don't know—pawns, blobs, pieces of flesh. I was there to destroy communism. We never conceived of old people, men, women, children, babies."[28]

**1968**: American-controlled Guatemala: One of the death squads, *Mano Blanca* (White Hand), sent a death warning to a student leader. Former American Maryknoll priest Blase Bonpane later wrote:

> I went alone to visit the head of the Mano Blanca and asked him why he was going to kill this lad. At first he denied sending the letter, but after a bit of discussion with him and his first assistant, the assistant said, "Well, I know he's a Communist and so we're going to kill him."
> "How do you know?" I asked.
> He said, "I know he's a Communist because I heard him say he would give his life for the poor."[29]

**1977**: Three years earlier, scientists had theorized that the earth's protective ozone layer was being damaged by synthetic chemicals called chlorofluorocarbons. The manufacturers and users of CFCs were not happy. They made life difficult for the lead scientist. In August, 1977, the president of one aerosol manufacturing firm suggested that criticism of CFCs was "orchestrated by the Ministry of Disinformation of the KGB."[30]

**1978**: Life inside a California youth camp of the ultra anti-communist John Birch Society: Five hours each day of lectures on communism, Americanism and "The Conspiracy"; campers learned that the Soviet government had created a famine and spread a virus to kill a large number of citizens and make the rest of them more manageable; the famine led starving adults to eat their children; communist guerrillas in Southeast Asia jammed chopsticks into children's ears, piercing their eardrums (see Tom Dooley above); "(American) movies are all under the control of the Communists. The theme is always that capitalism is no better than communism...You can't find a dictionary now that isn't under communist influence....The communists are also taking over the Bibles."[31]

**1980**: Former Rhodesian Prime Minister Ian Smith urged a group of white farmers to consider supporting Joshua Nkomo, a hated symbol of guerrilla war to whites, to keep Marxist Robert Mugabe out of power. Said Smith: "Tell your workers that the Marxists will take everything they have: their cattle, goats and chickens. Tell them they will also take away their children."[32]

**1980**: The Soviets' invasion of Afghanistan in December 1979 set off a series of actions in the Carter administration to punish them. The Commerce Department barred scientists from communist countries from an international scientific meeting in California and tried to make other foreign delegates sign a pledge that they would not talk about the meeting with colleagues from communist countries.[33] The United States withdrew from participation in the Olympics scheduled for Moscow. Liquor stores removed Russian vodka from their shelves.[34] Sales of grain to the Soviet Union were prohibited. And on and on. And we now know that the Soviet invasion was specifically provoked by the Carter administration to give the Soviets a taste of their "own Vietnam".

After the United States invaded Grenada in 1983—with less justification than the Russians had for invading Afghanistan—the Olympics were held in Los Angeles in 1984. No country withdrew its participation to protest the invasion and no government announced any other measure to punish the US.

**1980s:** When Pope John Paul II was wounded in St. Peter's Square in a 1981 assassination attempt by a right-wing Turkish Muslim, the anti-communists in Italy, the United States and elsewhere saw a golden opportunity to blame it on the Soviet Union and/or its Bulgarian ally. The American side was led by professional disinformationists Paul Henze, long-time CIA officer, Michael Ledeen and others at the Center for Strategic and International Studies, and Claire Sterling, who wrote an article on the shooting for *Reader's Digest* in 1982. In 1985, William Casey, CIA director under Ronald Reagan, urged senior Agency official Robert Gates to make a greater effort to lay the assassination attempt at the door of the Soviet KGB. Gates tried his best, even disregarding several contrary opinions by Agency analysts, and the fact, as evidenced by the result of a trial in Rome in 1986, that there was not a communist connection. Gates later became the CIA's director.[35]

**1980s:** The Reagan administration declared that the Russians were spraying toxic chemicals over Laos, Cambodia and Afghanistan—the so-called "yellow rain"—and had caused more than ten thousand deaths by 1982 alone, (including, in Afghanistan, 3,042 deaths attributed to 47 separate incidents between the summer of 1979 and the summer of 1981, so precise was the information). Secretary of State Alexander Haig was a prime dispenser of such stories, and President Reagan himself denounced the Soviet Union thusly more than 15 times in documents and speeches.[36] The "yellow rain", it turned out, was pollen-laden feces dropped by huge swarms of honeybees flying far overhead.[37]

**1981**: Training for the prospect of total war with the Soviet Union, 4,500 Army Reservists and National Guardsmen gathered in Monterey County, California for the largest combat medical exercise in the United States since World War II. Sporting realistic, bloody, make-believe wounds, hundreds lay in Army tent hospitals for four days, feigning awful injuries and practicing for the unthinkable.[38]

**1982**: In commenting about sexual harassment in the Army, General John Crosby stated that the Army doesn't care about soldiers' social lives—"The basic purpose of the United States Army is to kill Russians," he said.[39]

**1982**: The CIA estimated that about four million Soviet citizens were being compelled to undertake some kind of "forced labor". Defense Secretary Caspar Weinberger declared that the Soviet Union was using "slave labor". A closer reading of the story revealed that the laborers were prison inmates, or on probation and working in lieu of going to prison, or those paroled from confinement and obliged to perform certain work for the remainder of their terms.[40]

**1980s**: Senator Jesse Helms of North Carolina was an anti-communist *par excellence*, supporting noted commie-killers like the brutal military rulers Augusto Pinochet in Chile, Raoul Cedras in Haiti, and Roberto D'Aubuisson in El Salvador. Confronted with evidence that D'Aubuisson directed death squads to murder civilians, Helms replied: "All I know is that D'Aubuisson is a free enterprise man and deeply religious."

When a Witness for Peace delegation went to Helms' office and told the Senator's staff what they'd seen and heard in Nicaragua about the contras killing doctors and nurses and children, their response was, "Well, they're just Communists—they deserve to die."[41]

**1984**: During a sound check just before his weekly broadcast, President Reagan spoke these words into the microphone: "My fellow Americans, I am pleased to tell you I have signed legislation to outlaw Russia, forever. We begin bombing in five minutes." His words were picked up by at least two radio networks.[42]

**1985**: October 29 BBC interview with Ronald Reagan: asked about the differences he saw between the US and Russia, the president replied: "I'm no linguist, but I've been told that in the Russian language there isn't even a word for freedom."

**1986**: Soviet artists and cultural officials criticized Rambo-like American films as an expression of "anti-Russian phobia even more pathological than in the days of McCarthyism". Russian film-maker Stanislav Rostofsky claimed that on one visit to an American school "a young girl had trembled with fury when she heard I was from the Soviet Union, and said she hated Russians."[43]

**1986**: Swedish Prime Minister Olof Palme, progressive peace and nuclear disarmament campaigner, was assassinated in Stockholm. The father of the man accused of the murder said of his son: "They said in the news that he has a Communist phobia—but we all have."[44]

**1986**: During a performance by a Russian dance company at the Metropolitan Opera House in New York, a teargas canister exploded in the audience forcing 4,000 people to flee; at least 30 were injured.[45]

**1986**: Roy Cohn, who achieved considerable fame and notoriety in the 1950s as an assistant to the communist-witch-hunting Senator Joseph McCarthy, died, reportedly of AIDS. Cohn, though homosexual, had denied that he was and had denounced such rumors as communist smears.[46]

**1986**: After American journalist Nicholas Daniloff was arrested in Moscow for "spying" and held in custody for two weeks, New York Mayor Edward Koch sent a group of 10 visiting Soviet students storming out of City Hall in fury. "The Soviet government is the pits," said Koch, visibly shocking the students, ranging in age from 10 to 18 years. One 14-year-old student was so outraged he declared: "I don't want to stay in this house. I want to go to the bus and go far away from this place. The mayor is very rude. We never had a worse welcome anywhere."[47] As matters turned out, it appeared that Daniloff had not been completely pure when it came to intelligence gathering.[48]

**1987**: In a talk, President Reagan warned of the red menace in Central America. Just remember the words of Vladimir Lenin, he said: "The road to America leads through Mexico." The next day, the spokesman for the Russian Foreign Ministry pointed to a pile of the works of Lenin on a table and said he would eat his hat if anyone could find the quote Reagan had cited. "Lenin spoke of Mexico several times, but he said the road to Mexico goes through America." He added that Reagan had misquoted Lenin several times. "I doubt that (Reagan) ever read Lenin's works."[49]

**1989**: After the infamous Chinese crackdown on dissenters in Tiananmen Square in June, the US news media was replete with reports that the governments of Nicaragua, Vietnam and Cuba had expressed their support of the Chinese leadership. Said the *Wall Street Journal*: "Nicaragua, with Cuba and Vietnam, constituted the only countries in the world to approve the Chinese Communists' slaughter of the students in Tiananmen Square." But it was all someone's fabrication; no such support had been expressed by any of the three governments.[50] At that time, there were few, if any, organizations other than the CIA which could manipulate major media in such a manner.

**Cold War period**: If American visitors to the Soviet Union found churches that were full, this was evidence that the people were escaping from communism; if they found the churches empty, this indicated suppression of religion. If consumer goods were scarce this was interpreted as a failure of communism; if consumer goods were more plentiful, this meant that the authorities at that time were buying off the citizenry for some reason.

**Cold War period**: One of the many myths we were all taught was that science and inventiveness can't flourish under dictatorships, that science needs freedom to succeed. We were taught this of course simply to malign the Soviet Union. Yet, along with other accomplishments, the Soviets were amongst world leaders in solid-state chemistry, seismology, climate research, mathematics and plasmaphysics; Soviet physicists received five Nobel prizes; and Russia was the first country to send a satellite in orbit around the earth, one of its several historic accomplishments in outer space.[51]

**1993**: It was revealed that the Federal Emergency Management Agency (FEMA), responsible for providing aid during natural disasters, had spent most of its money on a secret program to enable the government to survive a nuclear attack, presumably from the Soviet Union. For every dollar FEMA spent on responding to disasters in the United States, almost $12 was spent on the secret program, which was built around a vast communications network that included a fleet of 300 vehicles in five mobile units scattered around the country.[52]

**2001**: A plaque honoring the dozen New Hampshire men who fought against fascism in the Spanish Civil War was installed in the Statehouse in Concord, but was removed hours later because of political opposition. In the best tradition of anti-communist propaganda, one local newspaper columnist who opposed the plaque wrote: "What is less widely known is the reign of terror unloosed upon Catholics by the Republican government in Spain. The installation of that government was followed by the burning of convents in Madrid and elsewhere." A state legislator declared that the fact that America fought fascism later does not validate the defiance of those who fought in Spain—"These people were fighting fascism at the wrong time." Others argued that the men shouldn't be honored because they had defied a US ban on travel to Spain at the time (part of the US campaign to help the fascist anti-communists).[53]

**2004**: A Victims of Communism Memorial in Washington, DC, established by an act of Congress, and an online Victims of Communism Museum are both nearing fruition this year. What can we expect from the memorial and the museum in the way of honest, non-Cold War-type history? Here's a sample from the website of the committee behind the projects: "While the horrors of Nazism are well known, who knows that the Soviet Union murdered 20 million people? Who knows that China's dictators have slaughtered an estimated 60 million? Who knows that the Communist holocaust has exacted a death toll surpassing that of all of the wars of the 20th century combined?"[54]

Who will build the Victims of Anti-Communism Memorial and Museum? For it must be understood that the worst consequences of anti-communism are not those discussed above. The worst consequences, the criminal consequences, are the abominable death, destruction, and violation of human rights that we know under various names: Vietnam, Chile, Korea, Guatemala, Cambodia, Indonesia, Brazil, Greece, Afghanistan, Iraq, Nicaragua, El Salvador, and numerous others.

## CHAPTER THIRTEEN

# Hiroshima
## Needless Slaughter, Useful Terror

[This essay first appeared in *CovertAction Quarterly*, Summer 1995]

Does winning World War II and the Cold War mean never having to say you're sorry? The Germans have apologized to the Jews and to the Poles. The Japanese have apologized to the Chinese and the Koreans, and to the United States for failing to break off diplomatic relations before attacking Pearl Harbor. The Russians have apologized to the Poles for atrocities committed against civilians, and to the Japanese for abuse of prisoners. The Soviet Communist Party even apologized for foreign policy errors that "heightened tension with the West."[1]

Is there any reason for the United States to apologize to Japan for atomizing Hiroshima and Nagasaki?

Those on opposing sides of this question are lining up in battle formation for the 50th anniversary of the dropping of the atom bombs on August 6 and 9, 1945. During last year's heated controversy surrounding the Smithsonian Institution's exhibit on the Enola Gay, the B-29 that dropped the atom bomb on Hiroshima, US veterans went ballistic. They condemned the emphasis on the ghastly deaths caused by the bomb and the lingering aftereffects of radiation, and took offense at the portrayal of Japanese civilians as blameless victims. An Air Force group said vets were "feeling nuked."[2]

In Japan, too, the anniversary has rekindled controversy. The mayors of the two Japanese cities in question spoke out about a wide "perception gap" between the two countries.[3] Nagasaki Mayor Hitoshi Motoshima, surmounting a cultural distaste for offending, called the bombings "one of the two great crimes against humanity in the 20th Century, along with the Holocaust".[4]

Defenders of the US action counter that the bomb actually saved lives: It ended the war sooner and obviated the need for a land invasion. Estimates of the hypothetical saved-body count, however, which range from 20,000 to 1.2 million, owe more to political agendas than to objective projections.[5]

But in any event, defining the issue as a choice between the A-bomb and a land invasion is an irrelevant and wholly false dichotomy. By 1945, Japan's entire military and industrial machine was grinding to a halt as the resources needed to wage war were all but eradicated. The navy and air force had been destroyed ship by ship, plane by plane, with no possibility of replacement. When, in the spring of 1945, the island nation's lifeline to oil was severed, the war was over except for the fighting. By June, Gen. Curtis LeMay, in charge of the air attacks, was complaining that after months of terrible firebombing, there was nothing left of Japanese cities for his bombers but "garbage can targets". By July, US planes could fly over Japan without resistance and bomb as much and as long as they pleased. Japan could no longer defend itself.[6]

After the war, the world learned what US leaders had known by early 1945: Japan was militarily defeated long before Hiroshima. It had been trying for months, if not for years, to surrender; and the US had consistently ignored these overtures. A May 5 cable, intercepted and decoded by the US, dispelled any possible doubt that the Japanese were eager to sue for peace. Sent to Berlin by the German ambassador in Tokyo, after he talked to a ranking Japanese naval officer, it read:

> Since the situation is clearly recognized to be hopeless, large sections of the Japanese armed forces would not regard with disfavor an American request for capitulation even if the terms were hard.[7]

As far as is known, Washington did nothing to pursue this

opening. Later that month, Secretary of War Henry L. Stimson almost capriciously dismissed three separate high-level recommendations from within the Truman (Roosevelt had just died) administration to activate peace negotiations. The proposals advocated signaling Japan that the US was willing to consider the all-important retention of the emperor system; i.e., the US would not insist upon "unconditional surrender."[8]

Stimson, like other high US officials, did not really care in principle whether or not the emperor was retained. The term "unconditional surrender" was always a propaganda measure; wars are always ended with some kind of conditions. To some extent the insistence was a domestic consideration—not wanting to appear to "appease" the Japanese. More important, however, it reflected a desire that the Japanese not surrender before the bomb could be used. One of the few people who had been aware of the Manhattan Project from the beginning, Stimson had come to think of it as his bomb—"my secret", as he called it in his diary.[9] On June 6, he told President Truman he was "fearful" that before the A-bombs were ready to be delivered, the Air Force would have Japan so "bombed out" that the new weapon "would not have a fair background to show its strength."[10] In his later memoirs, Stimson admitted that "no effort was made, and none was seriously considered, to achieve surrender merely in order not to have to use the bomb."[11]

## Meeting at Potsdam

And to be successful, that effort could have been minimal. In July, before the leaders of the US, Great Britain, and the Soviet Union met at Potsdam, the Japanese government sent several radio messages to its ambassador, Naotake Sato, in Moscow, asking him to request Soviet help in mediating a peace settlement. "His Majesty is extremely anxious to terminate the war as soon as possible", said one communication. "Should, however, the United States and Great Britain insist on unconditional surrender, Japan would be forced to fight to the bitter end."[12]

On July 25, while the Potsdam meeting was taking place, Japan instructed Sato to keep meeting with Russian Foreign Minister Molotov to impress the Russians "with the sincerity of our desire to end the war [and] have them understand that we are trying to end hostilities by asking for very reasonable terms in order to secure and maintain our national existence and honor" (a reference to retention of Emperor Hirohito).[13]

Having broken the Japanese code years earlier, Washington did not have to wait to be informed by the Soviets of these peace overtures; it knew immediately, and did nothing. Indeed, the National Archives in Washington contains US government documents reporting similarly ill-fated Japanese peace overtures as far back as 1943.[14]

Thus, it was with full knowledge that Japan was frantically trying to end the war, that President Truman and his hardline Secretary of State, James Byrnes, included the term "unconditional surrender" in the July 26 Potsdam Declaration. This "final warning" and expression of surrender terms to Japan was in any case a charade. The day before it was issued, Harry Truman had approved the order to release a 15 kiloton atomic bomb over the city of Hiroshima.[15]

Many US military officials were less than enthusiastic about the demand for unconditional surrender or use of the atomic bomb. At the time of Potsdam, Gen. Hap Arnold asserted that conventional bombing could end the war. Adm. Ernest King believed a naval blockade alone would starve the Japanese into submission. Gen. Douglas MacArthur, convinced that retaining the emperor was vital to an orderly transition to peace, was appalled at the demand for unconditional surrender. Adm. William Leahy concurred. Refusal to keep the emperor "would result only in making the Japanese desperate and thereby increase our casualty lists," he argued, adding that a nearly defeated Japan might stop fighting if unconditional surrender were dropped as a demand. At a loss for a military explanation for use of the bomb, Leahy believed that the decision "was clearly a political one", reached perhaps "because of the vast sums that had been spent on the project."[16] Finally, we have Gen. Dwight Eisenhower's account of a conversation with Stimson in which he told the secretary of war that:

> Japan was already defeated and that dropping the bomb was completely unnecessary....I thought our country should avoid shocking world opinion by the use of a weapon whose employment was, I thought, no longer mandatory as a measure to save American lives. It was my belief that Japan was, at that very moment, seeking some way to surrender with a minimum loss of "face". The secretary was deeply perturbed by my attitude, almost angrily refuting the reasons I gave for my quick conclusions.[17]

If, as appears to be the case, the US decision to drop the A-bombs was based on neither the pursuit of the earliest possible peace nor it being the only way to avoid a land invasion, we must look elsewhere for the explanation.

## Target Soviet Union

It has been asserted that dropping of the atomic bombs was not so much the last military act of the Second World War as the first act of the Cold War. Although Japan was targeted, the weapons were aimed straight to the red heart of the USSR. For more than 70 years, the determining element of US foreign policy, virtually its *sine qua non*, has been "the communist factor". World War II and a battlefield alliance with the Soviet Union did not bring about an ideological change in the anti-communists who owned and ran America. It merely provided a partial breather in a struggle that had begun with the US invasion of Russia in 1918.[18] It is hardly surprising then, that 25 years later, as the Soviets were sustaining the highest casualties of any nation in World War II, the US systematically kept them in the dark about the A-bomb project, while sharing information with the British.

According to Manhattan Project scientist Leo Szilard, Secretary of State Byrnes had said that the bomb's biggest benefit was not its effect on Japan but its power to "make Russia more manageable in Europe."[19]

General Leslie Groves, Director of the Manhattan Project, testified in 1954: "There was never, from about two weeks from the time I took charge of this Project, any illusion on my part but that Russia was our enemy, and that the Project was conducted on that basis."[20]

The United States was thinking post-war. A Venezuelan diplomat reported to his government after a May 1945 meeting that Assistant Secretary of State Nelson Rockefeller "communicated to us the anxiety of the United States Government about the Russian attitude". US officials, he said, were "beginning to speak of Communism as they once spoke of Nazism and are invoking continental solidarity and hemispheric defense against it."[21]

Churchill, who had known about the weapon before Truman, understood its use: "Here then was a speedy end to the Second World War," he said about the bomb, and added, thinking of Russian advances into Europe, "and perhaps to much else besides....We now had something in our hands which would redress the balance with the Russians."[22]

Referring to the immediate aftermath of Nagasaki, Stimson wrote of what came to be known as "atomic diplomacy":

> In the State Department there developed a tendency to think of the bomb as a diplomatic weapon. Outraged by constant evidence of Russian perfidy, some of the men in charge of foreign policy were eager to carry the bomb for a while as their ace-in-the-hole....American statesmen were eager for their country to browbeat the Russians with the bomb held rather ostentatiously on our hip.[23]

"The psychological effect on Stalin [of the bombs] was twofold," observed historian Charles L. Mee, Jr. "The Americans had not only used a doomsday machine; they had used it when, as Stalin knew, it was not militarily necessary. It was this last chilling fact that doubtless made the greatest impression on the Russians."[24]

After the Enola Gay released its cargo on Hiroshima on August 6, common sense—common decency wouldn't apply here—would have dictated a pause long enough to allow Japanese officials to travel to the city, confirm the extent of the destruction, and respond before the US dropped a second bomb.

At 11 o'clock in the morning of August 9, Prime Minister Kintaro Suzuki addressed the Japanese Cabinet: "Under the present circumstances I have concluded that our only alternative is to accept the Potsdam Proclamation and terminate the war." Moments later, the second bomb fell on Nagasaki.[25] Some hundreds of thousands of Japanese civilians died in the two attacks; many more suffered terrible injury and permanent genetic damage.

After the war, His Majesty the Emperor still sat on his throne, and the gentlemen who ran the United States had absolutely no problem with this. They never had.

The United States Strategic Bombing Survey of 1946 concluded:

> It seems clear that, even without the atomic bombing attacks, air supremacy over Japan could have exerted sufficient pressure to bring about unconditional surrender and obviate the need for invasion. Based on a detailed investigation of all the facts, and supported by the testimony of the surviving Japanese leaders involved, it is the Survey's opinion that certainly prior to 31 December 1945, and in all probability prior to 1 November 1945, Japan would have surrendered even if the atomic bombs had not been dropped, even if Russia had not entered the

war, and even if no invasion had been planned or contemplated.[26]

It has been argued, to the present day, that it wouldn't have mattered if the United States had responded to the Japanese peace overtures because the emperor was merely a puppet of the military, and the military would never have surrendered without the use of the A-bombs. However, "the emperor as puppet" thesis was a creation out of whole cloth by General MacArthur, the military governor of Japan, to justify his personal wish that the emperor not be tried as a war criminal along with many other Japanese officials.[27]

In any event, this does not, and can not, excuse the United States government for not at least trying what was, from humanity's point of view, the clearly preferable option, replying seriously to the Japanese peace overtures. No matter how much power the military leaders had, the civil forces plainly had the power to put forth the overtures and their position could only have been enhanced by a positive American response.

## CHAPTER FOURTEEN

# Will Humans Ever Fly?

## Smashing Socialism
## in the 20th Century

[This essay was part of a longer paper which appeared in *Peace Review: A Transnational Quarterly* (San Francisco), March 1997]

Imagine that the Wright brothers' first experiments with flying machines all failed because the automobile interests sabotaged each and every test flight. And then the good and god-fearing folk of the world looked upon this, took notice of the consequences, nodded their collective heads wisely, and intoned solemnly: Humans shall never fly.

Fact: Virtually every socialist experiment of any significance in the twentieth century has been either crushed, overthrown, invaded, or bombed...corrupted, perverted, subverted, or destabilized, or otherwise had life made impossible for it, by the United States. Not one of these socialist governments or movements—from the Russian Revolution to Fidel Castro in Cuba, from Communist China to the Sandinistas in Nicaragua—not one was permitted to rise or fall solely on its own merits; not one was left secure enough to drop its guard against the all-powerful enemy abroad and freely and fully relax control at home.

It has become commonplace amongst politicians, economists, industrialists and media that the answer to the question—Is socialism dead?—is not only "yes", but is *self evidently* so. They seem to accept *a priori* the curious equation that if the Soviet Union is dead, so must socialism be dead, if not all things progressive. And many on the left seem to be buying into this oddity. This equation not only ignores the past described above, but ignores the present reality as well, for since "the end of communism/socialism", communists and socialists have been elected to the highest offices in the land and/or won control of parliament in more than 20 countries, including many in the former Soviet Union and its Eastern European bloc. Consider the following sample:

## Hungary

In May 1994, four years after being voted into near oblivion, Hungary's former Communists swept back into power. Under their new name of the Socialist Party, they won 209 seats in the 386-seat parliament. "The strong showing of the Socialists," said the *New York Times*, "was attributed to widespread discontent with Hungary's first efforts at a market economy."[1]

## Poland

In September 1993, the Democratic Left Alliance (DLA)—composed of the former Communist Party and other socialist groups—won the parliamentary election and formed a new government.

In March 1995, former Communist Party official Josef Olesky became the Prime Minister.

In November of the same year, Aleksander Kwasniewski of the DLA, and a former minister in the Communist regime, defeated Lech Walesa for the presidency.

## Bulgaria

In June 1990, the former Communist Party, renamed the Bulgarian Socialist Party, won control of Parliament and filled the offices of president and prime minister. Before the year was over, the BSP was ousted in what amounted to a coup, engineered and financed by the CIA front, the National

Endowment for Democracy.[2] The party then won re-election in December 1994, with a former Communist Party official becoming prime-minister.

## Albania

March 1991, a Communist government won national elections overwhelmingly, but, as in Bulgaria, a general strike and widespread unrest, financed again by the National Endowment for Democracy, brought on the government's collapse.[3]

The current ruling party, the anti-communist Democratic Party, stays in power and keeps the Socialist Party (the former Communists) out only through elections so fraudulent that even the Clinton administration has been obliged to express its regrets about the "numerous irregularities" which "marred these elections."[4]

## Italy

In April 1996, a Left-Center coalition, composed of the Democratic Party of the Left (the former Communist Party) and the Communist Refoundation Party, won a majority of seats in both houses of parliament. The Democratic Party of the Left holds the majority of cabinet seats as well.

## Romania

Ion Iliescu, a former Communist who led Romania since the fall of dictator Nicolae Ceausescu, to whom he was a close adviser, has won election to the presidency continuously since 1990.

## Slovakia

Vladimir Meciar is the Prime Minister and the head of the Movement for a Democratic Slovakia, the main party in the ruling coalition. His party won power in 1994 on a strong anti-capitalist platform, winning 34% of the vote, more than three times that of the second place party.

## Lithuania

Algirdas-Mykolas Brazauskas, former First Secretary of the Central Committee of the Lithuanian Communist Party, was elected President in February 1993. His party, the Lithuanian Democratic Labor Party, the successor to the Communist Party, has won a majority of seats in the parliament.

## Czech Republic

The left-wing Czech Social Democratic Party came in a close second in parliamentary elections held May 31/June 1, 1996. The ruling conservatives need the support of the Social Democrats to govern. The parliament elected the leader of the Social Democrats as its new chairman.

## Portugal

In October 1995, The Socialist Party won the general election. The following January, the SP candidate, Jorge Sampaio, won election as President—the first time both the government and the president have been of the same political party since democracy was restored in 1974.

## Tajikistan

In November 1994, Imomali Rakhmonov, former Communist, was elected president and is still in office.

## Estonia

In March 1995, the voters decisively ousted the pro-market ruling coalition in favor of a coalition advocating greater commitment to social protection and vowing to rein in "cowboy capitalism". This coalition is still in power, but it has not abided by the voters' mandate, ruling more from a center-right perspective.

## Russia

Despite numerous highly questionable practices of Boris Yeltsin and his media (plus the best efforts of the United States), the Russian Communist Party, during the period of 1994-96, was the largest single bloc in the lower chamber of parliament. One of its members was the speaker. Former Soviet Communist Party Politburo member, Yegor Stroyer, was chosen chairman of the upper house of parliament. The party's leader, Gennady Zyuganov, came in a close second in national elections in 1996.

## Cyprus

In May 1996 parliamentary elections, the Communist Party won 33 percent of the vote, coming in second to the 34.5 percent won by the governing center-right coalition.

## Sri Lanka

August 1994: A Socialist alliance (People's Alliance Party) was the top vote getter in parliamentary elections.

## India

A coalition, variously described as leftist and center-left, came to power in May 1996 elections. Leading Communist Party officials were picked to head the powerful Home Ministry and the Agriculture Ministry, the first Communists to be part of an Indian government since independence in 1947.

## Nepal

In November 1994, the King appointed as Prime Minister, Man Mohan Adhikary of the Communist Party of Nepal-United Marxist-Leninist, after the party won a plurality of seats.

## Ecuador

In July 1996, a populist candidate, with strong support among the poor and disenfranchised, Abdala Bucaram, won the presidency with some 54 percent of the vote. [His regime turned out to be not progressive at all.]

## Iceland

In June 1996, left-wing politician Olafur Ragnar Grimsson was elected president with 41 percent of the vote, to his right-wing opponent's 29 percent.

## Postscript

The electoral trend described above in the former Soviet republics and Eastern European satellites, reflecting broad dissatisfaction with the newly-introduced capitalist way of life, was not permitted by the United States to blossom into progressive social change or simply to go where it might go. Washington intervened in these countries in the many ways Washington is expertly practiced at. [See chapter 11]

## CHAPTER FIFTEEN

# Overthrowing Other People's Governments

Instances of the United States overthrowing, or attempting to overthrow, a foreign government since the Second World War.

China 1949, 1950s
Albania 1949-53
East Germany 1950s
Iran 1953 *
Guatemala 1954 *
Costa Rica mid-1950s
Syria 1956-7
Egypt 1957
Indonesia 1957-8
British Guiana 1953-64 *
Iraq 1963 *
North Vietnam 1945-73
Cambodia 1955-70 *
Laos 1958 *, 1959 *, 1960 *
Ecuador 1960-63 *
Congo 1960 *
France 1965
Brazil 1962-64 *
Dominican Republic 1963 *
Cuba 1959 to present
Bolivia 1964 *
Indonesia 1965 *
Ghana 1966 *
Chile 1964-73 *

*successful ouster of a government.

Greece 1967 *
Costa Rica 1970-71
Bolivia 1971 *
Australia 1973-75 *
Angola 1975, 1980s
Zaire 1975
Portugal 1974-76 *
Jamaica 1976-80 *
Seychelles 1979-81
Chad 1981-82 *
Grenada 1983 *
South Yemen 1982-84
Suriname 1982-84
Fiji 1987 *
Libya 1980s
Nicaragua 1981-90 *
Panama 1989 *
Bulgaria 1990 *
Albania 1991 *
Iraq 1991
Afghanistan 1980s *
Somalia 1993
Yugoslavia 1999-2000 *
Ecuador 2000 *
Afghanistan 2001 *
Venezuela 2002 *
Iraq 2003 *
Haiti 2004 *

Q: Why will there never be a coup d'état in Washington?
A: Because there's no American embassy there.

# THE EMPIRE AT HOME

## CHAPTER SIXTEEN

# Conversations (sort of) with Americans

One of the joys of being an author, of being interviewed and having many essays floating around the Internet, is that it brings me into contact with a lot of swell folks I wouldn't otherwise be in touch with: morons, Jesus freaks, NewAgers babbling about "the pure rhythm of the essence of the universal life force", those whose idea of intellectualism is turning off the TV for an hour, those who have swallowed the American Dream and the American Empire whole without even spitting out the pits, those who believe that any foreigner with half a brain would rather be an American...the whole primitive underbelly of this supposedly rational society. In sum total, a group that represents one of the 12 signs that the world is ending.

My contact with these charmers arises when they call in questions during radio interviews, or sometimes it's the person who's actually interviewing me. They also pop up in audiences I speak before, but mostly it's via email that I have the pleasure of encountering their fine minds.

I'm waiting to receive my first e-mail with anthrax in it. Well, there are viruses in e-mail, why not bacteria?

When *New York Times* columnist Thomas Friedman called the anti-globalization demonstrators in Seattle "a Noah's ark of flat-earth advocates", Noam Chomsky observed: "From his point of view that's probably correct. From the point of view of slave owners, people opposed to slavery probably looked that way."

And that's the way that people like me and Noam look to my interrogators. Honed to an unusual deadness of perception by years of Monday night football, Fox News Channel, the local tabloid, and Rush Limbaugh, they are scarcely aware that large numbers of people simply do not think the way they do, that there's an alternative universe of facts and opinions out there. Inasmuch as their core political and social beliefs reflect the dominant ideology in the United States, they are not challenged as often as those on the left are. They thus tend to take their beliefs for granted and are not used to defending them as much as the left is, are not as practiced at it. I think the hostile manner in which they first engage me stems partly from the shock that such people like me even exist and are actually speaking to them over one of their favorite radio programs, or that words written by such a person have found their way to their Internet mailbox. To them, I've just stepped off the number 36 bus from Mars. And I'm upsetting their tranquillity. I may even appear scary.

I present here several fragments of my conversations with these lovely creatures as well as some typical questions from other types.

Q. Why do you hate America so much?

A: What do you mean by "hating America"? Are you asking me if I hate every building in America, every park, every person, every baseball team? Just what do you mean? What I hate, actually, is American foreign policy, what the United States does to the world.

Q. If you don't like the United States why don't you leave?

A. Because I'm committed to fighting US foreign policy, the greatest threat to peace and happiness in the world, and being in the United States is the best place for carrying out the battle. This is the belly of the beast, and I try to be an ulcer inside of it.

Q. What other country is better than the United States?

A. In what respect?

Q. In any respect.

A. Well, let's start with education. In much of Western Europe university education is free or considerably more affordable than here; even in poor Cuba it's free. Then's there's health care ...

[Note: I think that the people who ask this question truly believe that there's no good answer to their challenge; my response invariably marks the end of the dialogue.]

Q. Do you regard yourself as patriotic?

A. Well, I guess you're speaking of some kind of blind patriotism, but even if you have a more balanced view of it, what you're thinking about me would still be correct. I'm not patriotic. In fact, I don't want to be patriotic. I'd go so far as to say that I'm patriotically challenged. Many people on the left, now as in the 1960s, do not want to concede the issue of patriotism to the conservatives. The left insists that they are the real patriots because of demanding that the United States lives up to its professed principles. That's all well and good, but I'm not one of those leftists. I don't think that patriotism is one of the more noble sides of mankind. George Bernard Shaw wrote that patriotism is the conviction that your country is superior to all others because you were born in it.

Q. Do you think the United States has ever done anything good in the world? How about World War Two? Would you have fought in that war?

A. Okay, get ready to scream now. If I had been old enough, and knowing what I know now, I would have been glad to fight against fascism, but I would not have been enthused about fighting *for* the United States, or for the United States government to be more precise. Our leaders bore a great responsibility for the outbreak of the world war by abandoning the Spanish republic in the civil war. Hitler, Mussolini and the Spanish fascists under Franco all combined to overthrow the republican government, while the United States, Great Britain, France and the rest of the world, except the Soviet Union and a couple of others, stood by; worse than standing by, American corporations, like the oil companies and General Motors, were aiding the fascist side.

At the same time, the US and Britain refused the

entreaties of the Soviet Union to enter into some sort of mutual defense pact. The Russians knew that Hitler would eventually invade them, but that was fine with the Western powers who were nudging Adolf eastward at Munich. (It was collusion, not appeasement.) This finally forced the Soviets into their pact with Hitler, to be able to stall for time while they built up their defenses. Hitler derived an important lesson from all this. He saw that for the West, the real enemy was not fascism, it was communism and socialism, so he proceeded accordingly. Stalin got the same message. Hitler was in power for nine years before the United States went to war with him—hardly a principled stand against fascism—and then it was because Germany declared war on the United States, not the other way around.

[When the subject is Iraq and the questioner has no other argument left to defend US policy there, at least at the moment, I may be asked:]

Q. Just tell me one thing, are you glad that Saddam Hussein is out of power?

A. No.

Q. No?

A. No. Tell me, if you went into surgery to correct a knee problem and the surgeon mistakenly amputated your entire leg, what would you think if someone then asked you: Are you glad that you no longer have a knee problem? Of course you wouldn't be glad. The cost to you would not be worth it. It's the same with the Iraqi people, the cost of the bombing, invasion, occupation, and daily violence and humiliation has been a terrible price to pay for the removal of Hussein, whom many Iraqis actually supported anyhow.

Q. Don't you realize that the wars you criticize give you the freedom to say all the crap that comes out of your mouth?

A. Oh that's just a conservative cliché. Our wars are not fought for any American's freedom. There's been no threat to our freedom of speech from abroad, only at home, like the Red

Scare, McCarthyism, Cointelpro, and The Patriot Act.

Q. Why do you put down the establishment media so much when you cite them so often as your source?

A. The main shortcoming of the establishment media lies in errors of omission, much more than errors of commission. It's not that they tell bald lies so much as it is that they leave out parts of stories or entire stories, or historical reminders, which if included might put the issue in a whole new light, in a way not compatible with their political biases. Or they may include all the facts, leading to an obvious interpretation, but leave out suggesting an alternative interpretation of the same facts which stands the first interpretation on its head. But the information they do report is often quite usable for my purposes.

Q. You make no distinctions among US presidents since World War Two. Do you put Truman in the same category as Reagan?

A. There have been all kinds of differences in the political views of the administrations from Truman to Bush, Jr. but virtually all the significant differences concerned domestic issues. In foreign policy, they were all habitually interventionist, brutal, fanatically anti-communist, concerned mainly with making the world safe for US multinational corporations, and unconcerned about human rights (although they all paid a great deal of lip service to the concept). Truman was a major architect of the Cold War. Clinton's bombing of Yugoslavia was just as illegal, immoral and based on lies as Bush, Jr's bombings of Afghanistan and Iraq.

Q. So much of what you say just builds a wall between people, blaming one side for everything. Don't you think that we all share the blame and that you should stop thinking in simplistic terms of US and THEM?

A. I've been an activist since Vietnam, and you can't blame me or people like me for Vietnam, any more than you can blame us for Iraq, or all the other bloody American interventions in between. WE have been protesting what THEY have been doing for decades. THEY make their decisions and Congress is in bed with them and WE have virtually nothing to say in the matter. And don't tell me to elect different people to Congress unless you're prepared to provide a billion dollars to change the many state laws making it so difficult for third parties to get on the ballot; and that would be only a tiny first step.

For your further reading entertainment, here are a couple of email exchanges in full without any alterations made to them except for the removal of the senders' names and the correction of obvious typos.

From: ____@yahoo.com, March 2, 2004

President George W. Bush should go on world wide television and make the following statement..... "The United States of America from this moment on will rule the planet. We will decide who is to live and who is to die..If you do not do as we say your children will die horrible deaths at the dropping of our bombs..both conventional and nuclear. We will decide who is to be fed and who will starve. Thank you and have a nice evening." It would be great to bomb France and Germany back into the Stone Age. I am perfectly serious here. We have the power to rule the world..we should do it. And by the way..the USA does not make mistakes sir. If we killed tens of thousands of people in Iraq and elsewhere it was for a Godly cause. Go to hell you unAmerican

all love in christ
JHC

[my response]
JHC

You're beautiful. You've restored my faith in Christianity as the way to a more compassionate and peaceful world. May God bless you, and your children, and your children's children, but not the children of the devil who dwell in France and Germany. Hallelujah, I've been saved. Amen. Bill Blum

From: _____@bigpond.com, April 2, 2003

you're one very angry man; stop projecting it onto others. Reading your work I'm beginning to FEEL that the more radical and left you go you reach the far far right and become apologists for Hitler, Stalin, Pol Pot.

Listen a bit more carefully to the voices of Iraqis in exile, those that have defected and those refugees with the courage to speak out. Don't you think that their voice counts??? They want the monster Saddam out. They want to stop being terrorised. Do you really think that the average American or Australian live in a state of terror too frightened to speak out or stand up to their leaders. Give me a fucking break

AG

[my response]

I've gotten several emails lately from Iraqis living in exile, taking me to task because of my opposition to a war against their country. Each one went into great detail about how horrible a person Saddam Hussein is and how much they hate him. How can I not want to overthrow him? they demanded to know. I replied that if the only thing that was involved in the war was the removal of Saddam Hussein, with no harm done to the people or the land, I wouldn't object to it too much. I also asked each of the Iraqis if they would be willing to be in Iraq when the bombs begin to fall. Would they be willing to see their family killed, their home demolished, and their school and their mosque and their job all wiped out? Would they be willing to ingest particles of depleted uranium, which would remain in their body radiating forever? Or see their child lose a leg to a cluster bomb land mine? I also said that I despise George W. Bush at least as much as they despise Saddam Hussein, that Bush is at least as evil as Hussein—he's just killed a few thousand people in Afghanistan and is planning the same for Iraq; how many has Hussein killed lately? But my loathing of Bush, I told them, doesn't mean that I would like to see some foreign power bomb Washington; and I'd object to that not simply because I happen to live in Washington.

[from AG]

Would you have been willing for the reign of terror in Iraq to continue year after year? For thousands more innocent civilians including children & mothers tortured, maimed, killed merely for speaking out against Saddam. Children's eyes gouged out to elicit confessions from a parent; people having their tongues cut out and then left to bleed to death on streets; live bodies thrown into large mince machines.

This is all well-documented. A report of the UN in 1995 stated that human rights abuses of Saddam's regime are the worst of any country since World War 11.

It is not the intention of the 'coalition of the willing' to deliberately harm civilians. Saddam was given the opportunity to seek exile; that he did not means he is also responsible for the small number of civilian casualties that have resulted so far. However it was the intention of the Sept 11 terrorists to hurt as many innocent civilians as possible. I suggest you read 'Saddam's Bombmaker' by nuclear physicist Khidir Hamza and others who have defected. Hamza was head of Saddam's nuclear weapons project pre and post the Gulf War of 1991. General Wafiq al-Samarrai who was the head of Iraq's intelligence service, the Mukhabarat, until he defected in 1994 and Hussein Kamel (Saddam's son-in-law) who escaped but was enticed back (his entire family was then killed) both corroborated what Hamza revealed to the CIA. You surely can't argue that such a state of terror exists in the USA???? You would have had your tongue cut out for speaking out against Bush! Bush is not responsible for past mistakes, blunders, atrocities committed by previous US governments especially Kissinger who in my opinion should be tried as a war criminal.

[my response]

"Children's eyes gouged out to elicit confessions from a parent; people having their tongues cut out and then left to bleed to death on streets; live bodies thrown into large mince machines."

I challenge you to offer any proof of any of the above. Have you no ability at all to recognize propaganda? Is there anything the US government tells you about foreign policy that you don't believe?

[from AG]

Unbelievable. You are paranoid. Propaganda, you say. I'm wasting my time talking to such a person with such a narrow closed mind that he cannot respond to suffering. Proof. There's plenty but you are too frightened to find it. Go out on the street and talk to an Iraqi refugee. Web sites of Amnesty International, Red Cross, UN...I laughed yesterday when I got your e-mail but today I feel sick Go and get some therapy.

[my response]

English translation—You have no proof at all to offer. Just what I thought.

[AG then sent me an Amnesty International report dealing with events in Iraq during 2001]

[my response]

I challenged you on these words of yours: <<Children's eyes gouged out to elicit confessions from a parent; people having their tongues cut out and then left to bleed to death on streets; live bodies thrown into large mince machines.>>

I see nothing about these things in the Amnesty report.

## CHAPTER SEVENTEEN

# Cuban Political Prisoners...in the United States

[This essay first appeared in Z *Magazine*, September 2002]

The Florida Association of Criminal Defense Lawyers gave the defense team its "Against All Odds" award, established in honor of a deceased public defender who championed hopeless causes.[1]

Defending pro-Castro Cubans in Miami, in a criminal case utterly suffused with political overtones, with the US government wholly determined to nail a bunch of commies, is a task on a par with conducting a ground war against Russia in the wintertime. Even in the absence of known anti-Castro Cuban exiles on the jury, the huge influence the exiles have on the rest of the community is an inescapable fact of life in Miami, a place where the sound of the word "pro-Castro" does what the word "bomb" does at an airport.

President Bush has assured the world repeatedly that he will not heed the many calls to lift the Cuban trade embargo unless Fidel Castro releases what Washington calls "political prisoners". Bush tells us this while ten Cubans sit in US prisons, guilty essentially of not being the kind of Cubans George W. loves. If a political prisoner can be defined as one kept in custody who, if not for his or her political beliefs and/or associations would be a free person, then the ten Cubans can be regarded as political prisoners.

It all began in September 1998 when the Justice Department accused 14 Cubans in southern Florida of "conspiracy to gather and deliver defense information to aid a foreign government, that is, the Republic of Cuba" and failing to register as agents of a foreign government.[2] Four of the accused were never apprehended and are believed to be living in Cuba. Five of the 10 arrested, having less than true-believer faith in the American judicial system, copped plea bargains to avoid harsher penalties and were sentenced to between three and seven years in prison.

The US Attorney said the actions of the accused—who had been under surveillance since 1995—were an attempt "to strike at the very heart of our national security system and our very democratic process."[3] Their actions, added a judge, "place this nation and its inhabitants in great peril."[4]

Such language would appear more suitable for describing the attacks of September 11, 2001 than the wholly innocuous behavior of the accused. To add further to the level of melodrama: in the Criminal Complaint, in the Indictment, in public statements, and in the courtroom, the federal government continuously squeezed out as much mileage as it could from the fact that the Cubans had gone to meetings and taken part in activities of anti-Castro organizations—"duplicitous participation in and manipulation of" these organizations is how it was put.[5] But this was all for the benefit of media and jury, for there is obviously no law against taking part in an organization you are unsympathetic with; and in the end, after all the propaganda hoopla, the arrestees were never charged with any such offense.

The Cubans did not deny their activities. Their mission in the United States was to act as an early warning system for their homeland because over the years anti-Castro Cuban exiles in the US have carried out literally hundreds of terrorist actions against the island nation, including as recently as 1997 when they planted bombs in Havana hotels. One of the exile groups, Omega 7, headquartered in Union City, New Jersey, was characterized by the FBI in 1980 as "the most dangerous terrorist organization in the United States."[6]

Some exiles were subpoenaed to testify at the trial, which began in December 2000, and defense attorneys threw questions at them about their activities. One witness told of attempts to assassinate Fidel Castro and of setting Cuban buses and vans on fire. Based on their answers, federal prosecutors threatened to bring organized crime charges against any group whose members gave incriminating testimony and the Assistant US Attorney warned that if additional evidence emerged against members of Alpha 66, considered a paramilitary organization, the group would be prosecuted for a "long-standing pattern of attacks on the Cuban government."[7] Cuba has complained for many years that US authorities ignore information Havana makes available about those in the US it claims are financing and plotting violence.[8] None of the exiles who testified at the trial about terrorist actions were in fact prosecuted; nor were the groups they belonged to. The prosecution's threats were perhaps made because it would have been too embarrassing to let what was being admitted in open court pass without comment. But in the end, this was, after all, Miami.

The arrested Cubans were involved in anti-terrorist activities—so cherished by the government of the United States we are told—but were acting against the wrong kind of terrorists. Some of what they uncovered about possible terrorist and drug activities of Cuban exiles—including information concerning the 1997 hotel bombings—they actually passed to the FBI, usually delivered via diplomats in Havana. This presumably is what lay behind the statement in the Criminal Complaint that the defendants "attempted manipulation of United States political institutions and government entities through disinformation and pretended cooperation."[9] This language could be categorized as putting every action of the Cuban defendants in the worst possible light.

One of the Cubans, Antonio Guerrero, was employed as a manual laborer at the US naval base in Boca Chica, Florida, near Key West. The prosecution stated that Guerrero had been ordered by Cuba to track the comings and goings of military air-craft in order to detect "unusual exercises, maneuvers, and other activity related to combat readiness."[10] Guerrero's attorney, to emphasize the non-secret nature of such information, pointed out that anyone sitting in a car on US 1 could easily see planes flying in and out of the base.[11]

This particular operation of the Cuban agents is difficult to comprehend, for it is hard to say which was the more improb-able: that the US government would undertake another attack against Cuba, or that these Cubans could get timely wind of it in this manner.

The FBI admitted that the Cubans had not penetrated any military bases and that activities at the bases were "never com-promised". "They had no successes," declared an FBI spokesper-son. The Pentagon added that "there are no indications that they had access to classified information or access to sensitive areas."[12]

These statements of course did not rise from a desire to aid the Cubans' defense, but rather to assure one and all that the various security systems were impenetrable. But, in short, the government was admitting that nothing that could be termed "espionage" had been committed. Nevertheless, three of the defendants were charged with communicating to Cuba "infor-mation relating to the national defense of the United States...intending and having reason to believe that the same would be used to the injury of the United States."[13]

The FBI agents who closely surveilled the Cubans for sev-eral years did not seem worried about the reports the "espionage agents" were sending to Havana and made no attempt to thwart their transmission. Indeed, the FBI reportedly arrested the Cubans only because they feared that the group would flee the country following the theft of a computer and disks used by one of them, which contained information about their activities, and that all the FBI surveillance would then have been for naught.[14]

Somewhat more plausibly, those arrested were each charged with "acting as an unregistered agent of a foreign government, Cuba." Yet, in at least the previous five years, no one in the United States had been charged with any such offense,[15] although, given the broad definition in the law of "foreign agent", the Justice Department could have undoubtedly done so with numerous individuals if it had had a political motivation as in this case.

In addition to the unregistered foreign agent charge, which was imposed against all five defendants, there was the ritual laundry list of other charges that is usually facile for a prosecutor to come up with: passport fraud, false passport application, fraudulent identification, conspiracy to defraud the United States, aiding and abetting one or more of the other defendants (sic), conspiracy to commit espionage, and furthermore tacked onto all five—*conspiracy* to act as an unregistered foreign agent.

There was one serious charge, which was levied eight months after the arrests against the alleged leader of the Cuban group, Gerardo Hernández: conspiring to commit murder, a reference to the February 24, 1996 shootdown by a Cuban warplane of two planes (of a total of three), which took the lives of four Miami-based civilian pilots, members of Brothers to the Rescue (BTTR). In actuality, the Cuban government may have done no more than any other government in the world would have done under the same circumstances. The planes were determined to be within Cuban airspace, of serious hostile intent, and Cuban authorities gave the pilots explicit warning: "You are taking a risk." Indeed, both Cuban and US authorities had for some time been giving BTTR—which patrolled the sea between Florida and Cuba looking for refugees—similar warnings about intruding into Cuban airspace.[16]

Jose Basulto, the head of BTTR, and the pilot of the plane that got away, testified at the trial that he had received warnings that Cuba would shoot down planes violating its airspace.[17]

In 1995, he had taken an NBC cameraman on a rooftop-level flight over downtown Havana and rained propaganda and religious medals on the streets below,[18] the medals being capable of injuring people they struck. Basulto—a long-time CIA collaborator who once fired powerful cannonballs into a Cuban hotel filled with people[19]—described one BTTR flight over Havana as "an act of civil disobedience."[20] His organization's planes had gone into Cuban territory on nine occasions during the previous two years with the pilots being warned repeatedly by Cuba not to return, that they would be shot down if they persisted in carrying out "provocative" flights. A former US federal aviation investigator testified at the trial that in the 1996 incident the planes had ignored warnings and entered an area that was activated as a "danger area."[21]

Also testifying was a retired US Air Force colonel and former regional commander of the North American Air Defense Command (NORAD), George Buchner. Citing National Security Agency transcripts of conversations between a Cuban battle commander on the ground and the Cuban MiG pilots in the air, he stated that the two planes were "well within Cuban airspace" and that a Cuban pilot "showed restraint" by breaking off his pursuit of the third plane as the chase headed toward international airspace.

Buchner's conclusion was at odds with earlier analyses conducted by the United States and the International Civil Aviation Organization (which relied heavily on intelligence data provided by the US). However, he added that the three planes were acting as one and that Cuba was within its sovereign rights to attack them—even in international airspace—because the plane that got away had entered Cuban airspace, a fact not disputed by the prosecution or other investigators.

"The trigger," said Buchner, "was when the first aircraft crossed the 12-mile territorial limit. That allowed the government of Cuba to exercise their sovereign right to protect its airspace." He stated, moreover, that the BTTR planes had given up their civilian status because they still carried the markings of the US Air Force and had been used to drop leaflets condemning the Cuban government.[22]

Two days after the incident, the *New York Times* reported that "United States intelligence officials said that at least one of the American aircraft—the lead plane, which returned safely to Florida—and perhaps all three had violated Cuban airspace." United States officials agreed with the Cuban government that "the pilots had ignored a direct warning from the air traffic control tower in Havana."[23]

Hernández was charged with murder for allegedly giving Cuban authorities the flight plan of the planes flown by Brothers to the Rescue.[24] Even if true, the claim appears to be rather meaningless, for the Federal Aviation Administration (FAA) stated after the incident that after BTTR had filed its flight plan with their agency, it was then transmitted electronically to the air tower in Havana.[25] In any event, on that fateful day in February, when the three planes crossed the 24th parallel—the beginning of the area before entering Cuba's 12-mile territorial limit, which the Cuban government, like other governments, defines as an air-defense identification zone—Basulto radioed his presence to the Havana Air Control Center and his intention to continue further south. Havana, which was already monitoring the planes' flight, replied: "We inform you that the area north of Havana is activated [air defense readied]. You are taking a risk by flying south of twenty-four."[26]

Hernández was also accused of informing Havana, in response to a request, that none of the Cuban agents would be aboard the BTTR planes during the time period in question; one of them had flown with BTTR earlier. This too was equated in the indictment with "knowingly...to perpetrate murder, that is, the unlawful killing of human beings with malice aforethought."[27]

In the final analysis, the planes were shot down for entering Cuban airspace, for purposes hostile, after ignoring many warnings from two governments. After a January 13, 1996 BTTR overflight, Castro had issued orders to his Air Force to shoot down any plane that entered Cuban airspace illegally.[28] And just two weeks prior to the shootdown, a delegation of retired US officials had returned from Havana warning that Cuba seemed prepared to blow the Brothers' Cessnas out of the sky.[29] Gerardo Hernández was not responsible for any of this, and there was, moreover, a long history of planes departing from the United States for Cuba to carry out bombing, strafing, invasion, assassination, subversion, weapon drops, agricultural and industrial sabotage, and other belligerent missions.[30] According to a former member of BTTR—who redefected to Cuba and may have been a Cuban agent all along—Basulto discussed with him ways to bring explosives into Cuba to blow up high tension wires critical to the country's electrical system and plans to smuggle weapons into Cuba to use in attacks against leaders, including Fidel Castro.[31] At the time of the shootdown, Cuba had been under a 37-year state of siege and could never be sure what such enemy pilots intended to do.

Yet Hernández was sentenced to spend the rest of his life in prison. Ramón Labañino and Antonio Guerrero, the manual worker at the US naval base, were also sentenced to life terms; they and Hernández were all found guilty of conspiracy to commit espionage. Fernando González was put away for 19 1/2 years, and René González received 15 years. All five were convicted of acting as an unregistered agent of a foreign government as well as *conspiracy*—that great redundancy tool that is the lifeblood of American prosecutors—to do the same. All but one had the laundry list of identification frauds thrown at them.

For most of their detention since being arrested, the five men have been kept in solitary confinement. After their convictions, they were placed in five different prisons spread around the country—Pennsylvania, California, Texas, Wisconsin and Colorado—making it difficult for supporters and attorneys to visit more than one. The wife and five-year-old daughter of René González were denied visas to enter the United States from Cuba to visit him. Hernández's wife was already at the Houston airport with all her papers in hand when she was turned back, although not before undergoing several hours of FBI humiliation.

The United States is currently engaged in a world-wide, open-ended, supra-legal campaign to nullify the rights of any individuals who—on the most questionable of evidence or literally none at all—might conceivably represent any kind of terrorist threat.

But if the Cubans—with a much longer history of serious terrorist attacks against them by well known perpetrators—take the most reasonable steps to protect themselves from further attacks, they find that Washington has forbidden them from taking part in the War Against Terrorism. This is particularly ironic given that the same anti-Castro exile groups who have attacked Cuba have committed numerous terrorist acts in the United States itself.

## CHAPTER EIGHTEEN

# Treason

## None Dare Call It Nothing

[This essay first appeared in *CovertAction Quarterly*, Winter 1999]

> "He betrayed his country"—yes, perhaps he did, but who among us has not committed treason to something or someone more important than a country? In Philby's own eyes he was working for a shape of things to come from which his country would benefit.
>
> —Graham Greene,
> on Kim Philby[1]

At an unheralded, yet historic, moment after World War Two, the American Republic was replaced by a National Security State. There thus began a subtle process in government hitherto known only in civil law—"the exception that swallows the rule." Lawyers use the phrase to describe some anomaly in the law, an exception to a general rule or norm, that becomes so large or so widely used as virtually to nullify the rule itself. This principle had not previously been thought to apply to the requirements of the U.S. Constitution. Slowly but surely, however, "national security" has become such an exception.

"Persons shall be secure in their persons, houses, papers, and effects, against unreasonable searches and seizures," except in cases of national security.

"The accused shall enjoy the right to be informed of the nature and cause of the accusation," except in cases of national security.

"Cruel and unusual punishments shall not be inflicted," except in cases of national security.[2]

The case of the United States vs. Theresa Squillacote and her husband Kurt Stand ended on October 23, 1998 in Alexandria, Virginia, with the jury finding the Washington, D.C. political activist couple guilty of "conspiracy to commit espionage," "attempted espionage," and related charges having to do with classified documents. They were sentenced to 22 years and 19 years in prison although they were not found guilty of—nor were they even charged with—doing harm to a single creature on the face of the earth.

The American government excels at these charades, leaving scarcely anything to chance. Under William J. Clinton we have seen a steady drumbeat of legislation designed to give the FBI and other law enforcement agencies greater and still greater powers to climb deep inside the lives of individuals in the United States.

As it invariably does, the super-secret court created by the Foreign Intelligence Surveillance Act (FISA)[3] gave the FBI all the go-aheads it asked for in this case, thus making it all nice and "legal." The court was created in 1978 to authorize electronic searches for counterintelligence purposes, with its powers expanded in 1995 to authorize physical searches as well, all free from Fourth Amendment requirements of warrants and upon "probable cause."

The FBI carried out an investigation and surveillance of Stand and Squillacote for more than two years, most of that period spent in listening in round the clock on the phone conversations of the couple...conversations between the husband and wife, between the wife and her psychiatrist, between the husband and the wife's psychiatrist, between them and everyone, about everything; with Terry crying uncontrollably during one of her attacks of depression, and Kurt repeatedly trying to comfort her; played in the courtroom, on FBI tape, forever.

During this time the FBI secretly entered the couple's home on several occasions, planting listening devices throughout, picking up all human sound. And while in the house, they pored through every drawer, every closet, every book, every photo, every piece of paper; downloading the computer's entire store of personal files. While on the outside, their trash was picked through, and there was surveillance, whenever feasible, including videos.

And what had inspired such an indecent violation of the couple's privacy in the first place? After the unification of Germany, Squillacote's and Stand's name had been found on cards of the defunct East German intelligence service, the Stasi, cards purchased, along with vast amounts of other material, by the CIA, and still kept by the United States despite repeated requests from the German government for their return.[4] There were code names and real names, but no indication of any actual acts performed by either of them.

Stand, 43, a "red-diaper baby", had worked in the American labor movement and the Democratic Socialists of America for many years. Squillacote, 40, active in the Committees of Correspondence (an offshoot of the fragmented U.S. Communist Party), is an attorney, who had held several government positions, the last one with the Pentagon in the Office of Acquisition Reform, dealing with the laws and regulations concerning Defense Department purchases. She had a Secret security clearance at the time she resigned in January 1997.

The couple lived in the integrated Northeast Washington neighborhood of Brookland with their two children, aged 14 and 12, Karl and Rosa (after Karl Liebknecht and Rosa Luxemburg, the noted German socialist revolutionaries murdered by the state in 1919).

After their extraordinarily prolonged and intimate investigation of the two, the FBI still had nothing to pin on them. It is highly questionable that the investigation should legally have been undertaken in the first place. The FISA law is written in the present tense, clearly referring to a current "foreign power or an agent of a foreign power" as the target of the proposed surveillance. Inasmuch as the foreign power in question, East Germany, ceased to exist five years before the application to surveil Stand and Squillacote was made, the FBI application to the FISA court ought to have been held invalid at its inception. As the Washington Post has noted, the FISA wiretaps "are intended under the law to respond to imminent threats, not to collect evidence for criminal cases."[5]

The indictment states that after the dissolution of East Germany, the defendants' German contact established an espionage relationship with the USSR and then Russia, and "one or more of the defendants planned" to meet with a Russian in 1992. Whether this was secretly told the FISA court to "satisfy" the requirement of a current foreign power as the target; i.e. Russia, in order to get the court's approval, will never be known. But in any event, the alleged planned meeting never took place and this "plan" constituted the entirety of the evidence supporting a "current" espionage operation. Inasmuch as the FBI application for the FISA warrant was made three years after the planned meeting, the use of the Russian connection to create a "current threat" would appear to carry no weight.

A motion on these grounds to exclude the evidence collected by the FBI was turned down by US District Court Judge Claude Hilton, who declared that it was not his job to "second guess" the FISA court. With the rarest of exceptions, when an American judge hears the mantra of "national security" invoked, his years in law school become but a dim memory.

## The South African connection

The FBI's search of the couple's computer had turned up a letter Squillacote had written to Ronnie Kasrils, South African deputy defense minister, who is also a leader of the South African Communist Party. The letter to Kasrils, written after reading his political memoir, was, except for brief opening and closing remarks, a duplicate of a paper she had written and passed around in a study group she belonged to in Washington. It was an analysis of the world political situation and the prospects for building socialism.

The FBI also found, stuck in a book, a Christmas card that Kasrils had sent in reply, with a short note of thanks for her letter. Neither the letter nor the card even remotely hinted at any kind of espionage. Indeed, inasmuch as Squillacote had used a pseudonym and a Post Office Box and had made no mention of her position at the Pentagon, Kasrils could have no idea of who she was or what she might have access to.

The FBI decided that the evidence they couldn't uncover would have to be created. From the voluminous detailed information compiled on Terry Squillacote, of the most intimate nature, the Bureau's team of psychologists put together a Behavioral Analysis Program (BAP), outlining her weaknesses and vulnerabilities. Now part of the permanent public record are comments like: She "has an intense dislike of her stepmother...she is unkempt and has body odor...ignores and neglects her children...suffers from cramps and depression...her mother was prone to depression; her sister committed suicide; and her brother is taking anti-depressants...totally self-centered and impulsive. She has no concern for applying logic to thought or argument about long-term issues such as ethics, loyalty or most other moral reasoning."

The BAP concluded that "it is most likely that she will be easily persuaded if an approach is made to her that plays more to her emotions." A scenario was developed "designed to exploit her narcissistic and histrionic characteristics." The report added that "She will likely grieve for about one year for her lost (former) East German contact [with whom she had had a romantic relationship]. This is an important time period in which it is possible to take advantage of her emotional vulnerability."[6]

It appears to have worked as the FBI envisioned. A letter was sent to Terry supposedly from Kasrils offering a meeting between her and a member of "one of our special components" (read: intelligence service). Before long she passed this undercover FBI agent four documents: Defense Planning Guidance (FY 1996-2001) (Draft); Defense Planning Guidance (FY 1997-2001); Defense Planning Guidance Scenario Appendix (FY 1998-2003); and International Arms Trade Report September-October 1994.

In court, defense attorneys endeavored valiantly to show that the bulk of the significant information in these documents was already in the public record—congressional hearings, the *New York Times*, Jane's Defence Weekly, and elsewhere. One of the documents had actually been declassified before the trial began.

The prosecution, for its part, presented two "experts": William H. McNair of the CIA, and Admiral Dennis Blair of the Pentagon, formerly the Associate Director of Central Intelligence for Military Support. The two men were straight out of Central Casting—so arrogant, tightly-wound and doctrinaire as to make Captain Queeg look like a stoned flower child. Both insisted repeatedly that the fact that "secret" information was in the public domain did not change the fact that it was still a "secret"; that the "authoritative" version locked in a Pentagon file was more valuable to a potential enemy than what appeared in the media, even if the two versions were entirely identical.

During one exchange, McNair was asked to read a passage aloud to show the similarity between the "secret" and public versions of one of the documents. He refused, on the grounds of...yes, national security. At another point, Blair said that the release of the documents had caused serious damage. He was not challenged by the defense attorneys to explain in any way the nature of this damage. Except for a rare moment or two, the attorneys treated the two men with considerable deference, frequently apologizing to them for any possible misunderstanding, or imagined offense.

Again and again, when they were obliged to give an

answer that they thought might benefit the defense case, the two government witnesses quickly editorialized how this was not necessarily what it appeared to be. Neither the defense attorneys nor the judge ever cautioned either witness to limit himself to answering the question at hand.

The two men testified under a legal doctrine that says such witnesses, if appropriately qualified, are "expert witnesses", and that what they declare in court is to be regarded as "expert evidence" or "expert testimony", due to their special knowledge, skill or experience in the subject about which they are to testify. And the opposing side—in this case the defense — when it knows it will lose a motion to disqualify the witnesses, states that it is in agreement as to their expertise. The fact that such witnesses can be—and in this case were—terminally biased seems to be completely lost in the process. If either of the "expert witnesses" had been part of the jury panel, the defense would undoubtedly have challenged their selection without a moment's hesitation.

## Romantic Revolutionary

It remains obscure why Theresa Squillacote thought that such documents could be of any help to the government of South Africa, or to Cuba or Vietnam (she asked the FBI agent whether South Africa passed such information to those countries, and was assured that it did). It may also seem puzzling that she would accept unquestioningly that anyone from South African intelligence, or any intelligence service, would be politically progressive, simply because he told her an appropriate story about government oppression of his parents.[7] But she has pointed out that her thinking was influenced by her experience with the East German intelligence personnel. Some of them, she feels, were truly anti-fascist, socialist reformers, and internationalists.

From this and other testimony at the trial, it appears that

Squillacote had a highly romanticized view of revolution and her role in it. She had long fancied herself as an adventurous spy, with close ties to the East Germans during the 1980s, including the romantic connection. Part of her saw her job at the Pentagon, 1991-97, as a means to somehow further the cause, yet she received "highest outstanding performance" ratings on her job during three of those years, and a "reinventing government" award in 1996.

Another apparent contradiction lies in the fact that after exchanging the totally innocuous letter and card with Kasrils, and then receiving his supposed letter to arrange a meeting with a South African intelligence agent, she was taped telling her brother, with great excitement: "I did it! I did it!" And then telling the undercover FBI agent: "I was kind of hoping he [Kasrils] would read between the lines and he did read between the lines. And that's why we're here." These gushingly juvenile remarks undoubtedly hurt her entrapment defense seriously.

There is no evidence, however, that she ever passed the Stasi any classified documents during the life of that organization; indeed, during that period she never held a position which gave her access to such material. She and her husband did, however, pass unclassified material to the East Germans, things they came across in the public domain that they thought would be of interest to them, including items on Jesse Jackson's presidential campaign and the 1984 re-election of Ronald Reagan.

Kurt Stand, whose ties to East Germany went back to his German father, never had access to classified documents. The only overt acts he was charged with were having made photocopies of the Pentagon documents his wife obtained and having whited out the word "secret" from them.

Why, the prosecution kept asking, would the two defendants have undertaken secret travel to meet their German handlers, received special espionage paraphernalia and training, used code names, etc., if all they were passing to the Stasi was unclassified material?

Could the defense make the jury understand that during the Cold War an American could not have open contact with East Germany without risking heavy-handed scrutiny and harassment from U.S. authorities? In the 1950s, Kurt's father, a refugee from Naziism, had been fired or blacklisted from several jobs in the United States because of his politics, and after the FBI informed at least one of his employers that he supported leftist causes.

In her meetings with the phony South African, Terry appeared to be offering more of the same non-secret material. At their first meeting, in fact, she gave him an unclassified Defense Department document on the subject of "DOD Interaction with the Republic of South Africa."

From numerous phone taps, and from things said by Terry to the agent, it was evident that she was looking to leave her Pentagon position in the very near future. The FBI knew that it had to make her take the fatal step as soon as possible. While she was of a mind to offer political analysis/policy material, the agent made it clear to her that he wanted more "practical" material, "information not otherwise available to the public"; "scoops" is a word he used. Thus it was that she took copies of the four documents from the Pentagon. In five previous years at that job, she had not done any such thing. And six months had elapsed since she had received the card from Kasrils and had not written back to him. The FBI had built a crime where none had existed before. Her lawyer called it "entrapment." The prosecution said that she was clearly "predisposed" to commit such an act.

## The Third Man

There had been a third person arrested in October 1997—James Clark, 50, who had in fact passed classified documents to the East Germans and had blabbed about it to an FBI agent pretending, in his case, to be a Russian intelligence agent. He entered into a plea agreement before the trial began. Clark had obtained the documents from two friends who worked at the State Department, telling them he needed such material about the Soviet Union and Eastern Europe for a graduate class he was taking. After Clark's plea agreement, his attorney stated that "We have spent hundreds of hours investigating...and I've not spoken to one person who indicated that Jim did anything to harm the national defense."[8]

Clark's sentencing was delayed until he testified for the prosecution at the Squillacote/Stand trial. The three of them had met at the University of Wisconsin at Milwaukee in the early 1970s. Clark testified with full knowledge that the degree of severity of his sentence would be influenced by his testimony. Yet he stated that he had never conspired with them for any espionage purpose and knew of no classified material that either one had ever passed to the East Germans. In December, Clark was sentenced to 12 years and seven months, the shortest prison term recommended under federal guidelines.

Those in the national security establishment who play "the secrets game" for a living are usually much more upset by the act of—the very idea of—someone not taking the game seriously than in the disclosure of the secrets themselves, which, in their moments of reflection, they must know to be trifling matters in the larger world of realpolitik. During the Cold War, can it be imagined that there were secrets which, if known by the Soviet Union or the United States, could have tipped the balance of power and terror to any significant degree at all? Most of foreign policy secrecy is maintained only to avoid embarrassment over the exposure of unethical actions or public disinformation, not because of any danger to national security.

And the harshness of the punishment for "treason" is proportional to the loathing of the act by those who play the secrets game professionally.

The two individuals who passed the documents to Clark have not been charged with a crime. One lost his security clearance and job, the other is on leave with pay. It's very difficult to explain the gulf between the government's treatment of these two and the treatment of Clark, Stand and Squillacote, except that the latter three are all self-described "communists".

In the end, the defense had to contend with America's state religion: patriotism, a phenomenon which has convinced many of the citizenry that "treason" is morally worse than murder or rape, even if it's a victimless crime. The jury lived in Northern Virginia, home of the CIA, the Pentagon, and a host of other national security institutions. Several of them had had, or still had, a security clearance. Almost certainly, the same held for people close to them. The chief prosecutor, in his opening remarks, made it a point to tell the jury that Terry and Kurt "hated the United States. They were dedicated communists."

It was absolutely vital—*sine qua non*—for the defense attorneys to pierce this American frame of mind that comes with mother's milk, that penetrates every ganglion of the American nervous system. Patriotism, like religion, meets people's need for something greater to which their individual lives can be anchored. But the lawyers—from a liberal corporate law firm, acting largely pro bono—were not up to the task. It was a radical task—nothing that law school prepares one for very well—and they were not radicals. Instead of challenging the jury's mind set, they catered to it.

Their unquestioning deference to the CIA and Pentagon witnesses, referred to above, is a case in point. Moreover, on at least two occasions, one of the defense attorneys, in citing a document, made it apologetically clear that he wasn't going to mention certain information in it, like numbers. He was thus reinforcing the mystique of "classified information", and "national security". And instead of flaunting their clients' social and political idealism—their fighting for a better world—as a wonderful thing, they apologized for it, telling the jury things like: "You may think they've acted stupid or foolish, and we may think so too, but it's not illegal to act stupid or foolish."

And no mention that in a world of murderers, rapists, torturers, and robbers, Theresa Squillacote and Kurt Stand hadn't hurt anyone. The United States government has made sure that they will pay dearly for that.

As will their young children, bringing to mind the plight of the Rosenberg children. Ironically, the children of Stand and Squillacote have received some aid from the Rosenberg Fund for Children, set up by Robert Meeropol, one of the sons of Julius and Ethel Rosenberg, to help the children of progressive parents who have been imprisoned or otherwise persecuted because of their politics.

## CHAPTER NINETEEN

# If John Kerry
# is the Answer,
# What is the Question?

[written March 1, 2004]

Of all the issues that the presidential campaign will revolve around, none is more important to me than foreign policy. I say this not because that is my area of specialty, but because the bombings, invasions, coups d'état, depleted uranium, and other horrors that are built into United States foreign policy regularly bring to the people of the world much more suffering and despair than any American domestic policy does at home. I do not yearn for "anybody but Bush." I yearn for a president who will put an end to Washington's interminable indecent interventions against humanity. This is, moreover, the only way to end the decades-long hatred that has spawned so many anti-American terrorists.

So desperate am I to have the chance to vote for someone like that, that a few days ago I allowed myself to feel a bit buoyed when John Kerry, in response to a question about the situation in Haiti, said that the Bush administration "has a theological and ideological hatred for Aristide" which has led to the administration "empowering" the rebels.[1] To me that remark revealed a significant nuance of understanding of the world of US foreign policy that rarely makes it to the lips of an American politician. Could it be, I wondered, that Kerry is actually a cut or two above prevailing wisdom and rhetoric on such matters? (I must point out that, holding little expectation, I seldom closely follow who's who amongst establishment politicians, so until very recently I knew almost nothing specific about Kerry; in fact, I only just learned to distinguish him from Bob Kerrey, former senator from Nebraska.)

As it happens, the next day Kerry delivered a talk entirely about his views on foreign policy, particularly about the war on terrorism.[2] And my heart lost its buoyancy.

He called for an increase of "40,000 active-duty Army troops"—not exactly the kind of relief our shell-shocked world hungers for.

"But nothing else will matter unless we win the war of ideas," Kerry said. "We need a major initiative in public diplomacy to bridge the divide between Islam and the rest of the world. For the education of the next generation of Islamic youth, we need an international effort to compete with radical Madrassas."—This is the stuff of public relations, improving "image," ignoring the reasons for anti-Americanism. The problem, however, ain't a misunderstanding and it ain't due to poverty. It's the interventions, stupid; it's the harm we do to those people.

"We have seen what happens when Palestinian youth have been fed a diet of anti-Israel propaganda," Kerry added. Again, no weight given to anything Israel has done to the Palestinians; it's all just a matter of propaganda; Palestinians are becoming suicide bombers because of something someone said, not because of the Israeli devastation of their lives.

In fact, the US has done remarkably well in "the war of ideas". As noted in chapter 2: In June, 2003 the Pew Research Center released the results of polling in 20 Muslim countries and the Palestinian territories which revealed that while people interviewed had much more "confidence" in Osama bin Laden than in George W. Bush, "the survey suggested little correlation between support for bin Laden and hostility to American ideas and cultural products. People who expressed a favorable opinion of bin Laden were just as likely to appreciate American technology and cultural products as people opposed to bin

Laden. Pro-and anti-bin Laden respondents also differed little in their views on the workability of Western-style democracy in the Arab world."[3]

Kerry actually refers to this poll in his talk, but he mentions only the support of bin Laden, not the apparent contradictions found in the rest of the results.

"I will strengthen the capacity of intelligence and law enforcement at home and forge stronger international coalitions to provide better information and the best chance to target and capture terrorists even before they act."—As if the United States was not already wiring, tapping, bugging and surveilling every institution in the known world and every creature that moves across the earth, and summarily imprisoning them by the thousands. It sounds like a remark Kerry threw in, as with many of his other remarks, hoping to demonstrate a nonexistent difference between his foreign-policy views and those of the Bush administration.

"I will not hesitate to order direct military action when needed to capture and destroy terrorist groups and their leaders."—As *The Washington Post* observed, "Kerry appeared to outline his own preemptive doctrine in the speech."[4]

Kerry faulted Bush for providing insufficient funding for the National Endowment for Democracy. He probably thought he was on safe ground here; the word "democracy" always sells well. But this is his most depressing comment of all. He's calling for more money for an organization that was set up to be a front for the CIA, literally, and that for 20 years has been destabilizing governments, progressive movements, labor unions, and anyone else on Washington's hit list.[5] Which would be a worse mark against Kerry, that he doesn't know this about NED, or that he does know it? It sounds like another throwaway to imply a divide between him and George W.

So, what do we have here? Not a single word about the tens of thousands killed by US military actions in Afghanistan and Iraq; not a word about anything the United States has ever done anywhere in the world that could conceivably lead to anyone ever harboring justified resentment against the United States and seeking retaliation.

Not a word about ending, or even lessening, interventions.

It does not require total cynicism to point out that at most, at best, John Kerry's beef with the Bush administration over foreign policy—to the extent that he really has any—is a very minor difference of opinion between technocrats, Kerry offering a few tiny adjustments, a tweaking here or there. Most of his policy suggestions concerned things already being done by the Bush administration.

In sum total, nothing at all threatening, or even challenging, to business as usual for American foreign policy. What relief from the bully's outrages can the world expect from a John Kerry administration? What relief from the outrages done in our name can we Americans expect?

I think I can go back to ignoring establishment politicians.

## CHAPTER TWENTY

# Winning Hearts and Mindless

*[The Ecologist* (London), September 2003]

Since the United States thumbed its nose at the world by invading Iraq, the burning question among the ranks of the anti- war movement here as well as elsewhere has been: How do we stop the monster before it kills again?

In the absence of European and Arab governments showing a lot more courage to stand up to the empire, it's the American people we have to look to, for no one has the potential leverage over the monster than the monster's own children have. And that's the problem, for the American people are...well...how can one put this delicately?...like one in every 50 adult Americans claims a UFO abduction experience; a National Science Board survey found that 27 percent of adults believe the sun revolves around the earth; according to a Gallup poll 68 percent believe in the devil (12 percent are unsure); and most Americans believe God created evolution.

There are all kinds of intelligence in this world: musical, scientific, mathematical, artistic, academic, literary, and so on. Then there's political intelligence, which might be defined as the ability to see through the bullshit which every society, past, present and future, feeds its citizens from birth on to assure the continuance of the prevailing ideology.

Polls conducted in June showed that 42% of Americans believed that Iraq had a direct involvement in what happened on 11 September, most of them being certain that Iraqis were among the 19 hijackers; 55% believed that Saddam Hussein had close ties to al Qaeda; 34% were convinced that weapons of mass destruction had recently been found in Iraq (7% were not sure); 24% believed that Iraq had used chemical or biological weapons against American forces in the war (14% were unsure).

"If Iraq had no significant WMD and no strong link to Al Qaeda, do you think we were misled by the government?" Only half said yes.

"Given the intensive news coverage and high levels of public attention [to the events in Iraq]," said one pollster, "this level of misinformation suggests some Americans may be avoiding having an experience of cognitive dissonance." That is, having the facts conflict with their beliefs.

One can only wonder what, besides a crowbar, it would take to pry such people away from their total support of what The Empire does to the world. Perhaps if the government came to their homes, seized their first born, and took them away screaming? Well, probably not if the government claimed that the adored first born had played soccer with someone from Pakistan who had a friend who had gone to the same mosque as someone from Afghanistan who had a picture of Taliban leader Mohammed Omar on his wall.

We're speaking here of people who get virtually all their news from the shock-and-awe tabloid weeklies, AM-radio talk shows, and television news programs which, because of marketplace pressure, aim low in order to reach the widest possible audience, resulting in short programs with lots of commercials, weather, sports, and entertainment. These news sources don't necessarily have to explicitly state the above falsehoods to produce such distorted views; they need only channel to their audience a continuous stream of statements from the government and conservative "experts" justifying the war and demonizing Saddam Hussein as if they were neutral observers; ignore contrary views except when an expert is on hand to ridicule them and label them "conspiracy theories"; and never put it all together in a coherent enlightening manner. This constant drip-drip of one- sided information, from sources who can be described as stenographers for the powers-that-be, can produce any benighted variety of the human species.

One company, Clear Channel, owns 1,200 US radio stations and sponsored "Rallies for America" which promoted the White House plan to attack Iraq.

Many Americans, whether consciously or unconsciously, actually pride themselves on their ignorance. It reflects their break with the overly complicated intellectual tradition of "old Europe". It's also a source of satisfaction that they have a president who's no smarter than they are. They could be happy under totalitarianism, might well come to prefer it, and may be helping to advance it in the United States even as you read this.

This, then, is a significant segment of the target audience of the American anti-war movement, which has the unenviable task of winning hearts and mindless.

"Mit der Dummheit kämpfen Götter selbst vergebens," wrote Friedrich Schiller. "With stupidity even the gods struggle in vain."

## CHAPTER TWENTY-ONE

# *Being There* with Alan Greenspan and Ayn Rand

. [*The Ecologist* (London), October 2003]

He can pass for none other than Chauncey Gardener, the main character of the book and film "Being There". Gardener, brought to life by Peter Sellers, was a simple man with very simple thoughts and behaviour, who might well have been considered to be borderline "retarded", but fortuitous circumstances and the deference toward him by those of insufficient intellect and/or courage resulted in him being thought brilliant by people in high positions.

Alan Greenspan is the head of the Federal Reserve Bank, an institution which influences the American banking system in various significant ways, the most well-known of which is to lower or raise the prime interest rate. During the past few years Greenspan has ordered the rate lowered about a dozen consecutive times, each time supposedly to give a boost to a sluggish economy. The fact that he's had to repeat the exact same step a dozen times in a row can give you an idea of how effective his policy has been. But even as the economy continues its downward spiral, it's rare indeed that anyone in the media or the halls of government dares to criticize Greenspan; the man has achieved sanctity, like dear old Chauncey.

Thus it was both remarkable and welcome that a member of Congress had the nerve to publicly take Greenspan to task. In July, Rep. Bernie Sanders of Vermont, the only "independent" in the House of Representatives (meaning not officially a

Democrat or a Republican), faced Greenspan across the table at a congressional hearing and said:

"Mr. Greenspan, I have long been concerned that you are way out of touch with the needs of the middle class and working families of our country, that you see your major function and your position as the need to represent the wealthy and large corporations. I think you just don't know what's going on in the real world." Country clubs, cocktail parties, millionaires and billionaires are not the real world, Sanders said. The real world is where America lost 3 million jobs in two years, where the national debt is ballooning, where people are losing health care and seniors can't pay for prescription drugs, where bankruptcies are on the rise and CEOs make 500 times what their workers make, where the manufacturing sector is shrinking and American workers are losing out to workers overseas. "Do you give one whit of concern," asked Sanders, "for the middle class and working families of this country?"

Greenspan—a friend and devoted follower of Ayn Rand, the selfishness guru, who turned the emulation of two-year olds into a philosophy of life—replied: "Congressman, we have the highest standard of living in the world."

"Wrong," said Sanders, "Scandinavia has a higher standard of living."

Unaccustomed to having to defend any of his profundities, Greenspan could do no better than to counter with: "We have the highest standard of living for a country of our size."

This was quite a comedown from "in the world", and inasmuch as the only countries of equal or larger population are China and India, and Indonesia is the fourth largest, Greenspan's point is rather difficult to evaluate.

The idea that the United States has the highest standard of living in the world is one that is actually believed by numerous grownups in America, and most of them believe that this highest standard applies across the board. They're only minimally conscious of the fact that whereas they've made extremely painful sacrifices to send a child to university, and they often simply can't come up with enough money, and even if they can the child will be very heavily in debt for years afterward, in much of Western Europe university education is either free or eminently affordable; as it is in Cuba and was in Iraq under Saddam Hussein.

The same lack of awareness about superior conditions in other countries extends to health care, working hours, vacation time, maternity leave, unemployment insurance, and a host of other social and economic benefits.

In short, amongst the developed nations, the United States is the worst place to be a worker, or sick, or seeking a university education; or, in the land of the two million incarcerated, to be a defendant.

To which the Chauncey Gardeners of America, including the one sitting in the Federal Reserve and the one sitting in the Oval Office, would say: "Duh! Whaddaya mean?"

## CHAPTER TWENTY-TWO

# If in Doubt, Call the FBI

*[The Ecologist* (London), May 2002]

"Always strive to have empathy. Understand that from a policeman's point of view, a police state is a good thing."

—Paul Krassner (prominent American humorist)

During the cold war, one of the numerous dastardly things we in the West were taught about communist states was that people there were instigated to spy on their neighbors, to watch them and listen in on them and report any signs of unorthodox beliefs to the authorities.

In the *weltanschauung* of present day America, The Evil Empire has been replaced by the Evil Axis and "unorthodox beliefs" by "suspicious behaviour". What constitutes the latter may well be limited only by the imagination of a good citizen.

National Neighborhood Watch, which until recently was a folksy community program concerned with burglars, muggers and drug traffickers, has now been enlisted in the war against international terrorism. The federal government has financed the doubling of local Neighborhood Watch groups nationwide to 15,000, the Department of Justice has published a "Citizens' Preparedness Guide", and, to make sure that no one confuses Washington *circa* 2002, with Moscow *circa* 1936, familiar and heartwarming TV personality Ed McMahon has been brought in to publicize the Watch program.

McMahon is best known as the sidekick of comedian Johnny Carson, whom he'd introduce on TV each night with

"Heeeere's Johnny!" At a March 6 unveiling of the new Watch program, he introduced Attorney General Ayatollah John Ashcroft with...yes..."Heeeere's Johnny!" McMahon had his 9-year-old granddaughter with him; she smiled and carried a teddy bear. Who can mistrust such a government? How can Osama bin Laden hope to defeat such clever infidels?

At a meeting of a local Watch program in Washington, held to kick off the new campaign, the woman in charge declared: "If we see a Ryder truck [a rental used in the two major terrorist attacks in the US prior to 11 September] and we know nobody's moving in, somebody would call the police." Decent Americans can only pray that the next would-be terrorists don't learn of any other brand of rental truck.

Those who should be reported, according to the "Citizens' Preparedness Guide", include individuals seen "suspiciously exiting a secured, non-public area near a train or bus depot, airport, tunnel, bridge, government building, or tourist attraction". The reader, unfortunately, is not advised what to do if an individual is seen doing any of these things in a laid-back, nonchalant manner.

Also cause for alarm:

> You are told of or overhear someone discussing a future plan for a terrorist act, to use a gun or other weapon in an unlawful manner, to mail or deliver a dangerous package or letter, to set off a bomb or an explosive, to release a poisonous substance into the air, water, or food supply. You hear or know of someone who has bragged or talked about killing or harming citizens in terrorist attacks or who claims membership in an organization that espouses killing innocent people.

The problem with this of course is that the average American hears such things on almost a daily basis and thus tends to dismiss them as idle chatter or good natured kidding. In the summer of 2001, as we all know, many people in New York observed 19 individuals, swarthy Middle East types all, tossing paper airplanes into buildings in the Wall Street area and yelling "BOOM!" as they doubled over in laughter. The ever-trusting New Yorkers just looked on in appreciative amusement, an attitude that the Watch campaign is determined to change.

But since 11 September, even before this new government program, the citizenry have in fact been on relatively high alert. In November, when a customer at a Chicago Post Office requested stamps "without the American flag", the Post Office called the police, who were there within minutes to interrogate the young man. Later a postal inspector did the same before the fellow was sold the stamps.

That same month, a young woman in North Carolina received a visit at home from two Secret Service agents: "Ma'am," said one of the agents, whose function is to protect the president, "we've gotten a report that you have anti-American material." This turned out to be a poster which depicted George W. Bush holding a length of rope against a backdrop of lynching victims, and reads: "We hang on your every word. George Bush: Wanted, 152 Dead", a reference to the number of people executed by the state of Texas while Bush was governor.

A 60-year-old San Francisco man, Barry Reingold by name, was working out at his gym and expressed reservations about the war on terrorism to his fellow weight lifters. They questioned his loyalty, which he refuted. Next thing he knew, the FBI was paying him a visit at his home.

I hasten to add that I have not made up any of these three stories; similar examples have piled up like autumn leaves. When asked by a reporter about the civil liberties implications of such happenings, White House press secretary Ari Fleischer had this to offer: "People have to watch what they say and what they do".

The War on Drugs had already turned the US into a police state; not the worst police state in history to be sure, not even the worst police state the world today, but a police state nonetheless. It's long been facile for "authorities" of all kinds to use possession of drugs, or planted drugs, to put an "undesirable" person out of commission. The term itself, "War on drugs", tells police that they're warriors fighting a war, and in a war, you use the tactics of war, anything goes.

At times, the War on Terrorism makes one feel as if the whole country has been turned into one large airport security checkpoint. How long before the United States is like Mexico—with everybody averting their eyes as the cops stroll by—but with better plumbing.

## CHAPTER TWENTY-THREE

# The Election Circus

[*The Ecologist* (London), December 2003]

So desperate are so many Americans to be rid of the primitive who calls himself President of the United States that they are embracing some rather questionable replacements, principally, if not solely, on the belief that the person can beat Bush in the 2004 election. The latest savior is General Wesley Clark, who only recently discovered that he's a Democrat, after publicly expressing effusive praise for Bush and the Republicans more than once in the previous two years. He has been heralded not only by the young and naive, and the old and desperate, but by some who should know a lot better, including Michael Moore, celebrated author and filmmaker, and Robert Scheer, Los Angeles Times columnist and longtime progressive writer and activist.

In Wesley Clark, as with Bush, we have a man who appears to be imbued with a degree of compassion and empathy for faraway, powerless strangers which approaches zero.

At the start of the 78-day US/NATO bombing of Serbia in 1999, which he oversaw as Supreme Allied Commander in Europe, Clark declared that unless the Serbian government gave in to the (wholly unreasonable and extortionist) demands of the Western powers, "We are going to systematically and progressively attack, disrupt, degrade, devastate and ultimately destroy these forces and their facilities and support."

During the bombing, Clark was among 68 leaders charged with war crimes by a group of international-law professionals from Canada, the United Kingdom, Greece, and the American Association of Jurists. The group filed its well-documented complaints with the International Criminal Tribunal for the Former Yugoslavia in The Hague, Netherlands, charging leaders of NATO countries and officials of NATO itself with crimes similar to those for which the Tribunal had issued indictments shortly before against Serbian leaders. Amongst the charges filed by the group were: "grave violations of international humanitarian law", including "wilful killing, wilfully causing great suffering and serious injury to body and health, employment of poisonous weapons and other weapons to cause unnecessary suffering, wanton destruction of cities, towns and villages, unlawful attacks on civilian objects, devastation not necessitated by military objectives, attacks on undefended buildings and dwellings, destruction and wilful damage done to institutions dedicated to religion, charity and education, the arts and sciences."

At one point in the bombing campaign it was reported that Clark "would rise out of his seat and slap the table. 'I've got to get the maximum violence out of this campaign—now!'"

It was also only recently that Clark discovered that he was against the war in Iraq, although it's still not clear when this conversion took place, nor, equally important, just why.

If I were forced to choose between Clark and Bush on election day, or if I were paid well enough to give one of them my vote, I'd give it to Bush. He is a known evil; the world and, increasingly, the American public have seen through this cartoonly awful man. There are currently at least half a dozen fervently anti-Bush books on or hovering about the best-seller lists, his continuous and reckless unconcern for the truth—enough to full up a future Bush Liebrary—being a major theme of most of them. With Clark in the White House, there would be a new and long honeymoon period and there's no telling what this lover and practitioner of violence would do with his new found power.

Before Clark came along, the most prominent Democratic candidate, very enthusiastically embraced by those looking for a knight on a white horse to slay the Dubya Dragon, was Howard Dean, former governor of Vermont. The chances of him putting an end to the empire's global atrocities can be gauged by the fact that he has stated that he would not reduce the Pentagon's budget nor withdraw American forces from Iraq. Those desperate for a dragon slayer imbue their knights with all manner of wished-for attributes, but Howard Dean isn't even a liberal. "I don't mind being characterized as 'liberal'," he said. "I just don't happen to think it's true."

Another leading contender is Senator Joseph Lieberman, whose views on foreign policy, military matters, and expansion of the empire are so indistinguishable from those of Bush that it's been said that the only reason to vote for Lieberman over Bush is that Bush isn't Jewish enough.

The only one of the nine announced Democratic candidates who is a genuine progressive is Dennis Kucinich, a Congressman from Ohio, but precisely because of that he doesn't attract support from the swollen-wealth sectors, the *sine qua non* of electoral politics in the United States, where an outright auction for the presidency would be more efficient.

None of the candidates has anywhere near the "star power" of Arnold Schwarzenegger, California Governor (sic, sick), which almost guarantees victory given the intellectual and psychic state of so many American voters. This state of mind was perhaps best captured by the case of Bill Lockyer, the Democratic Attorney General of California who announced that he had voted for Republican Schwarzenegger because he was won over by the actor's message of "hope, change, reform and optimism." "I hope I'm not being conned," Lockyer said. "The people who voted for him hope they are not being conned."

Recalling the actor who has to tell people: "I'm not really a doctor, I just play one on television," someone should inform Mr. Lockyer that Schwarzenegger is quite accustomed to reading scripts written by other people who are highly practiced in the art of manipulating an audience to produce a desired emotional effect.

## CHAPTER TWENTY-FOUR

# The Best Democracy Money Can Buy, by Greg Palast

[*The Ecologist* (London), April 2002]

It's enough to make one cynical. American elections are manipulated, British parliamentarians are bribed, scientific research is financed by companies who are interested parties, energy crises are rigged, and a score of other varieties of modern-day sleaze.

What's that? You say you're already cynical? Well, unless you're so cynical that you can't even bring yourself to utter a word in the hope of changing anything, Greg Palast's new book can be a handy tool.

*The Best Democracy Money Can Buy* is composed of dozens of essays—many of which are actually summaries of Palast's investigative journalism escapades—on the myriad ways those of power and wealth have stolen and/or perverted cherished ideas and institutions of the United States and the United Kingdom.

Palast, an American who writes for *The Guardian* and *The Observer* of London, has the uncanny knack of turning up at the wrong place at the right time. His showcase essay has to do with the 2000 US presidential election in Florida, and how Governor Jeb Bush and his team shamelessly contrived the removal of thousands of voters' names from the election rolls; voters who were in large measure black (read Democratic voters). The result was nothing less than the placing in the White House of Jeb's brother George. This is by now a well-known story, thanks to Palast, who adds a lot of details to it in the book. What I found most disturbing, albeit not terribly surprising, is that when he approached mainstream media in the US to give the story the play it deserved, their reaction was to call Jeb Bush's office for confirmation. Jeb Bush's office denied it. And that was good enough for the mainstream media. It's not easy for loyal, unquestioning Americans to embrace the idea of the US as a banana republic.

The IMF and the rest of the international financial mafia are a favorite target in the book. Palast details the onerous conditions imposed upon poor countries by the IMF. Some of the details he says derive directly from confidential IMF documents that came into his hands. I, and I'm sure many other readers, would love to see the exact wording used by IMF, to see how they rationalize their oppressive policies, and what kind of euphemisms they resort to, or if they push their policies unabashedly. Unfortunately, Palast only paraphrases the details, doesn't quote them, and doesn't show any examples of the secret pages in the book. Inexplicably, the one page he shows in this section, from the World Bank, is only the cover page of a report. Documentation is not Palast's strong point; there are scarcely any notes.

Of significance is the essay on "The Economic Miracle of Chile", the oft-repeated claim by conservatives of the supposed marvelous benefits of the Pinochet regime's laissez-faire, supply-side economic policies. Palast describes it as a case of "deregulation gone berserk", which eventually drove the country into bankruptcy and depression and needed "a large dose of socialism" to rescue it.

Palast is generally adept at making economic and other issues readable because of his breezy, personalized, iconoclastic style, although there are occasions when more unadorned language, a slower pace, and a "books for dummies" approach would have served the reader better. That's part of the problem with the essay on the California "energy crisis" of the late 1990s and 2000. I've read several accounts of that event with not one coming even close to making it understandable. Palast is an improvement over the others, but his account still left me with more questions than answers. In fairness to him, his essay was not designed to be a primer *per se* on the California energy crisis, but rather a discussion of the dangers of electricity deregulation, but it refers so much to the events in California that a fuller deconstruction of those events would seem to be in order.

Overall, the multitude of subjects and issues covered and the frequent flights from one to the next can be a bit jarring and disorienting. There is often a want of the continuity that a good book needs. But Palast's humour sometimes makes up for a shortcoming or two. An example:

"The Kyoto Protocol aimed to slash emissions of 'greenhouse gases' which would otherwise fry the planet, melt the polar caps and put Blackpool and Los Angeles under several feet of water. (It will also have negative effects.)"

Palast, it should be noted, is a native of Los Angeles.

## CHAPTER TWENTY-FIVE

# The Myth of America's "Booming Economy"

[Written 1999-2000, but can be applied to any other period during which we're assured that the US economy is robust.]

You cannot escape it. You read it and hear it everywhere. From every news medium, every politician—the economy is booming...thriving...soaring...the leading economic indicators are looking great...stock market is going through the roof..."economy showed signs of continued strength last month as Americans' personal income rose by a robust .7 percent"...prosperity everywhere...the world's richest country ...

But...but what about...what about ...

- the working poor, the millions who toil at full-time jobs, yet remain below the official poverty level (an unrealistically low figure to begin with), their real purchasing power below 1979 levels

- the husbands and wives each having to work full time so that together they manage to rise a little above the poverty level

- the millions forced to surrender 30 to 70 percent of their paycheck for rent

- those living in severely substandard housing

- the more than a million families who do not have indoor bathrooms or hot-and-cold running water

- the more than a million people who don't own a telephone

- the unemployed (the picture's even worse if we go by the real number, not the distorted figure announced to the

public which excludes those who have stopped looking for
a job, those who don't own a phone, and others)

- those who want and need a full-time job, but can only get
a part-time job, minus benefits
- those who want and need a permanent job, but can only
get a temporary job, minus benefits
- the underemployed—college graduates and those with
advanced degrees working at relatively menial jobs with
no connection to their studies
- the more than 43 million without any health insurance
- the even greater number without dental insurance
- the further millions with inadequate health insurance,
including those with Medicare and Medicaid
- the elderly who spend half their income for health care
and prescriptions
- the elderly who have to choose between prescriptions and
food; (about half the prescriptions written go unfilled
because many elderly people literally have to make this
choice)
- the elderly who purchase cat and dog food, but don't own
any pets
- the many millions with inadequate sick leave or maternity leave, or none at all
- those—the great majority of employees—who get two
weeks vacation or less, compared to the European norm of
five weeks
- those forced to choose between heat and sufficient food in
the winter
- those suffering, some dying, on sweltering summer days
because they can't afford an air conditioner or are concerned about their electricity bill
- those whose phone, gas or electricity has been turned off
for non-payment
- the homeless

- those one paycheck or one illness or one divorce away from homelessness

- those living five to ten people in a one-bedroom apartment

- the millions who go to bed hungry at least part of every month; (A January 2000 report from the Center on Hunger and Poverty at Tufts University stated that 30 million Americans worry about where they will get their next meals.)

- those frightened by the welfare reform law of 1996 into not applying for food stamps, welfare or Medicaid

- the 1.8 million souls in prisons and jails

- those who have enlisted in the military to escape dead-end poverty

- those who want to go to college but can't afford to

- those who go to college at the cost of a huge debt hanging round their neck for years

- the illegal aliens working as semi-slaves in sweatshops

- the almost 20 percent of American households who are broke, with a net worth of zero or less, more than double the number of 30 years ago

- those living on their credit cards, making only the minimum payments each month, as the exorbitant interest piles up year after year

- the more than 50,000 businesses which filed for bankruptcy last year

- the 1,500,000 individuals who filed for bankruptcy last year

- the numerous cleaning women and maids who spend four hours on a bus each day to and from their minimum-wage job

- the middle-class people who maintain their standard of living by each working 50, 60, 70 hours per week, by their choice or their employer's dictate, plus a daily two or three hour commute, returning home totally wiped out and overstressed

- those hanging on to jobs they hate—jobs making them sick—only because of the health insurance and pension
- those living only on social security
- those living only on welfare
- the more than a million Native Americans living on reservations, for whom much of the above has to be multiplied

What's booming are soup kitchens and homeless shelters. And a growing majority of those waiting in line for a meal or a bed are actually employed.

## CHAPTER TWENTY-SIX

# And Now For Something Completely Different
## A New Yorker
## trapped in Los Angeles

W hat's your sign?" he asks, as he's asked people a thousand times before.

"No parking," I reply, as I've replied a thousand times before at Los Angeles parties.

"Very funny. So what's your sign?"

"You should be able to tell me what my sign is if that stuff means anything."

"You probably didn't believe Nostradamus's predictions when you lived in the middle ages," he continues unfazed.

"Oh, so now we're into reincarnation," I say. "Perhaps I've been inflicted upon you because of your bad karma."

"I was a dog in ancient Egypt," says a woman munching on a carrot stick.

I look at her to see if she's grinning or something. She's not. There seems to be no escaping these people in La La Land. I can see the Statue of Liberty waving at me to come home where I belong, and escape the clutches of all these CMFs (California Metaphysical Fruitcakes).

"I'm not quite sure what kind of dog I was," adds the Carrot Lady. "But I've been doing research on what kinds were common back then."

Others in the group nod wisely and sympathetically, while

I resist the temptation to ask her whether she had been house-broken, or whether they had canned dog food in ancient Egypt.

"That stuff about astrology has been disproved by science time and again, honest to guru," I venture to Horoscope Man. "It's all a bunch of Taurus."

"Science can't prove or disprove anything with absolute certainty," he says. "The very act of examining a phenomenon changes it."

"We all create our own reality," a lady nursing a Perrier chimes in. "I'm creating you right now. I created the medium. I created the spirit entities. So therefore I've created everything."

I look around for a little man with a big net. When I turn back to the Perrier Lady, I suddenly realize she bears a striking resemblance to Shirley MacLaine.

At this point, perhaps sensing a soul in need of saving, the Carrot Lady offers to read my palms, my tea leaves, my aura, my horoscope, and my tarot. As a wave of utter disinterest washes over me, I reflect on the fact that Los Angeles has 15 meta-physical bookstores and is the place you can get your car repaired through an "Astral Mechanix" that will do a full astro-logical profile of your car based on the time it left the manufac-turer (using the engine block number). You also get a set of instructions on psychic healing exercises for your car.

Girolamo Cardano would have been at home in L.A., he being the 16th century mathematician, doctor and astrologer, whose faith in astrology reputedly led him to commit suicide so that he might die on the very day predicted by his horoscope. Hmmm, could that possibly catch on here?

The Perrier Lady now delivers a lecture for my benefit on aromatherapy, colortherapy, ayurveda, hypnotherapy, medita-tion, sound therapy, candles, crystals, hot-sesame-oil massages, herbs, herbal steam therapy, astanga yoga, spas, yantra yoga, acupressure, tao yoga, scrying, kundalini yoga, venus kriyas, tantric yoga, goddess worship, angi yoga, numerology, boko-maru, vegetarianism, tai chi chu'an, tai chi qi gong, circle dances, Indian sweat cabins, mantras, zen sheshin, ESP, precognition, and other sacred shrines visited by spiritual hypochondriacs.

As I fade in and out of consciousness, I hear the word "oneness" five times, "unity" six times, "spiritual" eight times, "healing" and "holistic" eleven times each, and "energy" twenty-one times. I am promised that I'll unlock my inner awareness, harmonize my chakras, make the mind-body connection, open up to my higher power, heal internal organs and emotional problems, be elevated to another astral plane, and achieve Nirvana.

The Perrier Lady is smiling, the smile of a saleswoman who knows secrets that are good for you.

What did I do in my previous life to deserve this?

I am already half out the door, heading for LAX...any flight destination Big Apple, as long as the pilot doesn't believe in reincarnation.

# Notes

## Frontpiece

1  *New York Times*, March 26, 1989, p.16
2  Colin Powell with Joseph E. Persico, *My American Journey* (New York, 1995), p. 291

## Introduction

1  Frances Fitzgerald, *America Revised* (New York, 1980), pp.129, 139
2  CNN, December 27, 2001
3  Theodore Roosevelt, *Winning of the West*, volume 3, p.44 of the four-volume set (U of Nebraska Press, 1995); written in the 1890s.
4  For a detailed chronology of these events see *The Washington Post*, May 20, 2004, p.19
5  *New York Times*, November 4, 1983, p.16.
6  *New York Herald Tribune*, April 25, 1965, p.18
7  Speech delivered May 11, 1966, *Public Papers of the Presidents of the United States, Lyndon B. Johnson*, vol. 1, p.496
8  Letter to the *New York Times*, October 29, 1965, p.42
9  Said to Daniel Ellsberg; see Ellsberg's book *Secrets: A Memoir of Vietnam and the Pentagon Papers* (Penguin Books, 2002), p.184.
10  UPI, Saigon, October 31, 1967
11  *Congressional Record*, House, May 12, 1966, pp. 9977-78, reprint of an article by Morley Safer of CBS News.
12  Daniele Ganser, "*Operation Gladio: NATO's Stay-Behind Armies and Terrorism in Western Europe*", forthcoming in 2005 in English from Frank Cass Publishers (London) and in Italian from Fazi Editore (Rome). For a brief summary of Gladio, see William Blum, *Killing Hope: U.S. Military and CIA Interventions Since World War II* (Common Courage

Press, Maine, 2004), pp.63-4,106-8

13  Sam Halper, former Caribbean Bureau Chief of *Time* maga-
    zine, "The Dominican Upheaval", *The New Leader* (New
    York), May 10, 1965, p.4

14  Ovidio Diaz Espino, *How Wall Street Created a Nation: J.P.
    Morgan, Teddy Roosevelt, and the Panama Canal* (2001), p.41

15  William Fulbright, *The Arrogance of Power* (1966), p.3

16  *Morning News* (New York), December 27, 1845, cited in
    Ray Allen Billington, *The Far Western Frontier, 1830-1860*,
    vol. 2, p.149

17  Frank Freidel, "Dissent in the Spanish-American War and
    the Philippine Insurrection" in Samuel Eliot Morison, et.
    al., *Dissent in Three American Wars* (Harvard University
    Press, 1970), p.77

18  Blum, *Rogue State: A Guide to the World's Only Superpower*
    (Common Courage Press, Maine, 2000) and *Killing Hope*,
    op. cit.; the Library of Congress study appears as Appendix
    II in the latter.

19  This last expression comes from Uruguayan writer Eduardo
    Galeano, speaking of that country's dictatorship, as he told
    it to Lawrence Weschler, *A Miracle, A Universe* (New York,
    1990), p.147

20  White House press release, May 3, 2004

21  "Defense Planning Guidance for the Fiscal Years 1994-
    1999", as quoted in *New York Times*, March 8, 1992, p.14
    (emphasis added)

22  *Department of State Bulletin*, August 12, 1945

23  *The Washington Post*, June 7, 2004

## Chapter One

1  *Washington Post*, June 6, 2004

2  Peter Jenkins, *Mrs. Thatcher's Revolution* (Cambridge, MA
   1988)

3  *The Guardian* (London), September 28, 1984, p.15

4   *Washington Post*, July 1, 2004
5   "NATO bombed Chinese deliberately," *The Observer* (London), October 17, 1999; and November 28, 1999. Also see *Extra! Update* (Fairness and Accuracy in Reporting, New York), December 1999
6   Interfax News Agency, April 2, 2003
7   Hans Christian Stroebele, Green Party member of the German parliament, at the time of the publication of the torture pictures.
8   Knight Ridder newspapers, May 10, 2004
9   James Becket, *Barbarism in Greece* (New York, 1970), p.16. Becket was sent to Greece in December 1967 by Amnesty International.
10  *The Economist* (London), August 17, 1996, US Edition
11  Constitution of the International Military Tribunal, meeting at Nuremberg, Germany, 1945, Article 8
12  *Los Angeles Times*, March 16, 1991, p.8
13  For a detailed history of these propaganda campaigns, see: Morris Kominsky, *The Hoaxers: Plain Liars, Fancy Liars, and Damned Liars* (Branden Press, Boston, 1970)
14  *Washington Post*, October 28, 2003, p.1
15  *New York Times*, April 16, 2004
16  *Washington Post*, April 14, 2004
17  *The Times* (London), April 7, 2004
18  *Washington Post*, October 21, 1999, "Back Channels" column by Vernon Loeb
19  *Washington Post*, March 8,2004
20  *New York Times*, March 26, 2004
21  *Washington Post*, March 27, 2004
22  William Blum, *Rogue State: A Guide to the World's Only Superpower*, pp.3-4
23  *Los Angeles Times*, February 26, 2004
24  CBS Evening News, August 20, 2002
25  ABC Nightline, December 4, 2002
26  State Department press release, February 24, 2001

27 CNN Late Edition with Wolf Blitzer, July 29, 2001
28 White House press release, January 29, 2004, from Bush speech
29 *Washington Post*, April 1, 2004
30 Ibid., March 5, 2004
31 Ibid., March 3, 2004
32 For all: *The Guardian* (London), February 25, 2004; *Washington Post*, February 25-27
33 http://members.aol.com/bblum6/haiti2.htm, particularly the second half.
34 Ibid.
35 *Washington Post*, February 16, 2004
36 Associated Press, June 16, 2001
37 *Chicago Tribune*, January 28, 2004
38 *Washington Post*, February 7, 2004
39 http://www.suicidewall.com/SWStats.html
40 *Washington Post*, November 19, 2002
41 Ibid., February 7, 2004
42 *The Guardian* (London), September 19, 2002
43 *Washington Post*, October 21, 2002, p.A25
44 Ibid., Dec. 28, 2003
45 United Press International, March 3, 1986
46 State Department news release, August 26, 2003
47 *St Louis Post-Dispatch*, December 17, 2003
48 United Press International, April 9, 1986
49 *Washington Post*, Nov. 29, 2003
50 *New York Times*, November 6, 2003
51 Guatemala: Stephen Schlesinger and Stephen Kinzer, *Bitter Fruit: The Untold Story of the American Coup in Guatemala* (1982), p.183; Jagan: Arthur Schlesinger, *A Thousand Days* (1965), p.774-9; Bishop: Associated Press, May 29, 1983, "Leftist Government Officials Visit United States"
52 *Miami Herald*, April 29, 1996, p.1
53 *Los Angeles Times*, February 24, 1994, p.7
54 *New York Times*, April 16, 2002

55 *The Pentagon Papers* (NY Times edition, Bantam Books, 1971), pp.4, 5, 8, 26.

56 United Press International, October 16, 2003

57 *The Seattle Times*, October 15, 2003, p.A7

58 For all the details, see William Blum, *"Killing Hope: US Military and CIA Interventions Since World War II"*, chapter 45.

59 *Washington Post*, November 5, 2003, p.C3

60 Ibid., June 26, 2003, p.16

61 White House press briefing, Nov. 14, 1997, US Newswire transcript

62 *Philadelphia Inquirer*, March 2, 2003, p.A2

63 Ryan Lizza, "Where angels fear to tread", *New Republic*, July 24, 2000

64 *The Washington Post*, August 2, 1997, p.A1 and February 6, 1998, p.B1 re Tempelsman. Other speculation concerned diamond investors Jean Raymond Boulle and Robert Friedland.

65 *Washington Times*, April 11, 2003

66 *Miami Herald*, May 5, 2003

67 *New York Times*, March 18, 2003

68 *Sidney Morning Herald*, March 25, 2003

69 *Washington Post*, March 31, 2003

70 Robert Kagan, *Of Paradise and Power: America and Europe In the New World Order* (New York, 2003), p.99

71 *The Observer* (London), April 7, 2002

72 *Washington Post*, February 4, 2003, p.C3

73 Roger Morris, *Partners in Power* (New York, 1996), pp.102-4

74 Essay by Daniel Brandt, "Clinton's CIA Connection", can be found as NameBase NewsLine, No. 15, October-December 1996, on Brandt's website which houses his superlative database (NameBase) on the CIA and related matters: www.namebase.org

75 *Washington Post*, October 5, 1988, p.1

# Chapter Two

1   *Miami Herald*, September 12, 2001
2   Agence France Presse, November 19, 2002
3   *The Guardian* (London), December 19, 2001, article by Duncan Campbell
4   *Washington Post*, August 1, 2003, p.4
5   *New York Times*, August 22, 1998, p.15
6   *Washington Post*, June 23, 2004; Ibid., June 28, p.19: "there were 8,688 attacks on U.S. forces in Iraq from May 2, 2003 [after major combat operations were declared over], to about 8 p.m., June 25, 2004. That's about 20 a day, though the more recent average is closer to 40 to 50."
7   Jim Dwyer, et al., *Two Seconds Under the World* (New York, 1994), p.196; see also the statement made in court by Ramzi Ahmed Yousef, who planned the attack, *New York Times*, January 9, 1998, p.B4
8   *Washington Post*, October 3, 2002, p.6
9   Agence France Press, December 23, 2002; *Washington Post*, November 9, 2002
10  *Los Angeles Times*, November 13, 2002, p.6
11  Associated Press, November 7, 2002
12  Ibid.
13  Voice of America News, April 21, 2003
14  *Washington Post*, June 15, 2002
15  US Department of Defense, Defense Science Board 1997 Summer Study Task Force on DOD Responses to Transnational Threats, October 1997, Final Report, Vol.1 http://www.acq.osd.mil/dsb/trans.pdf, p.31
16  *New York Times*, March 26, 1989, p.16
17  Colin Powell with Joseph E. Persico, *My American Journey* (New York, 1995), p.291
18  *Boston Globe*, October 12, 2001, p.28
19  *Washington Post*, March 27, 2003
20  Ibid., June 4, 2003, p.18

21  Pentagon briefing, June 30, 2003
22  *Washington Post*, June 29, 2003
23  Ibid., July 24, 2003, p.7
24  Ibid., August 8, 2003
25  Ibid., June 17, 2004, p.14
26  Associated Press, June 19, 2004
27  *The Guardian* (London), November 1, 2002
28  *Washington Post*, November 19, 2002

## Chapter Three

1   Marc W. Herold, "Daily Casualty Count of Afghan Civilians Killed by U.S. Bombing", http://pubpages.unh.edu/~mwherold Note: This is the 2004 information, which includes the previous years as well; or see Herold's book, *Blown Away: The Myth and Reality of Precision Bombing in Afghanistan* (Common Courage Press, forthcoming in 2004)
2   David Rose, "Attackers did not know they were to die", *The Observer* (London) October 14, 2001
3   *Washington Post*, October 2, 1999
4   First quote: *The Guardian* (London), December 20, 2001, p.16; second quote: US Defense Department briefing, November 1, 2001
5   William Blum, *Rogue State: A Guide to the World's Only Superpower*, pp.76-7
6   *New York Times*, October 28, 2001, p.B1
7   *Milwaukee Journal Sentinel*, 10/31/01, p.10A
8   Fox News Channel: "Special Report with Brit Hume", November 5, 2001
9   *Washington Post*, November 12, 2001, p.C1
10  *Boston Globe*, February 18, 1968
11  *Miami Herald*, September 12, 2001, p.23
12  *Rogue State*, op. cit., chapter 9
13  *Washington Post*, December 26, 2001, p.16

14  Ibid., December 22, 2001, p.16
15  *The Independent* (London), November 14, 2001, article by Robert Fisk
16  *The Times* (London), December 27, 2001, p.1; *Washington Post*, December 28, 2001, p.8
17  *Washington Post*, December 27, 2001, p.C2

## Chapter Five

1  *New York Times*, January 28, 1998, p.19
2  Senate Commitee on Banking, Housing, and Urban Affairs, "U.S. Chemical and Biological Warfare-Related Dual Use Exports to Iraq and Their Possible Impact on the Health Consequences of the Persian Gulf War", Report of May 25, 1994, Chapter 1.
3  Ibid., p.37
4  Ibid., Report of October 7, 1994, p.3
5  Ibid., Report of May 25, 1994, p.11
6  The document is undated and does not bear Haig's name, but the facts are clearly as stated above. The document was discovered by journalist Robert Parry amongst the files left behind in the Capitol building by the House task force investigating the "October Surprise". Parry submitted a question to Haig about it, who was shocked that the document had leaked and did not deny its authenticity.
7  *New York Times*, February 7, 1998, p.8
8  *Washington Post*, February 1, 1998

## Chapter Six

1  *New York Times*, March 2, 2003, Sect.4, p.2
2  US Department of the Army, *Afghanistan, A Country Study* (Washington, DC, 1986), discusses some of the government programs to improve women's lives, pp.121, 128, 130, 136, 223

## Chapter Seven

1   Seymour Hersh, "The Missiles of August", *The New Yorker*, October 12, 1998, p.36
2   David Hirst, *The Observer* (London), August 23, 1998
3   Ed Vulliamy et al, *The Observer* (London), August 23, 1998
4   Ibid.
5   David Hirst, *The Observer* (London), August 23, 1998
6   *The Observer* (London), August 30, 1998
7   *USA Today*, August 25, 1998
8   *The Observer* (London), August 30, 1998
9   Ibid.
10  Ibid.
11  Hersh, op. cit., p.40
12  Ed Vulliamy et al, *The Observer* (London), August 23, 1998
13  Associated Press, August 24, 1998
14  *Washington Post*, July 25, 1999, p.F1

## Chapter Eight

1   *The Nation*, May 12, 1997, editorial, p.6
2   *Newsday* (New York), April 25, 1997
3   *The Observer* (London), April 27, 1997
4   *Newsday* (New York), April 25, 1997
5   *Daily News*, (New York), April 24, 1997
6   *Washington Post*, April 24, 1997
7   *Ibid.*, April 27, 1997, p.29
8   William Blum, *Killing Hope: US Military and CIA Interventions Since World War II*, p.173-4
9   *Washington Post*, May 30, 2002

## Chapter Nine

1   *Washington Post*, April 23, 1997, p.4
2   *Chicago Tribune*, February 19, 1998
3   *Baltimore Sun*, February 19, 1998

4   NBC "Today" show, February 19, 1998
5   "Democracy Now!", Pacifica Radio, February 19, 1998, interview of John Strange, who had asked Albright a question that prompted her to make the promise to meet afterward.
6   *Baltimore Sun*, February 19, 1998
7   *Washington Post*, May 5, 1997, p.20
8   Ibid., May 14, 1997
9   Ibid., Feb. 28, 1996
10  *Los Angeles Times* and *Washington Post*, both February 27, 1991, p.1
11  *Middle East International* (London), October 21, 1994, p.4
12  *New York Times*, January 1, 1997
13  *Washington Post*, March 1, 1999, p.13
14  Colin Powell with Joseph Persico, *My American Journey* (New York, 1995), p.576

## Chapter Ten

1   "Opinion of the Court", Paragraph 39
2   Mark Perry, *Eclipse: The Last Days of the CIA* (Wm. Morrow, New York, 1992), pp.342-7.
3   "Opinion of the Court", Par. 55
4   "Opinion of the Court", Par. 68
5   See, e.g., *Sunday Times* (London), November 12, 1989, p.3.
6   For a detailed discussion of this issue see, *A Special Report from Private Eye: Lockerbie the Flight from Justice*, May/June 2001, pp.20-22; *Private Eye* is a magazine published in London.
7   *Sunday Times* (London), December 17, 1989, p.14. Malta is, in fact, a major manufacturer of clothing sold throughout the world.
8   "Opinion of the Court", Par. 89
9   Ibid.
10  *The Guardian* (London), June 19, 2001

11  *New York Times*, November 15, 1991

12  *Los Angeles Times*, November 15, 1991

13  *New York Times*, April 13, 1989, p.9; David Johnston, *Lockerbie: The Tragedy of Flight 103* (New York, 1989), pp.157, 161-2.

14  *Washington Post*, May 11, 1989, p.1

15  *New York Times*, December 16, 1989, p.3.

16  Department of the Air Force—Air Intelligence Agency intelligence summary report, March 4, 1991, released under a FOIA request made by lawyers for PanAm. Reports of the intercept appeared in the press long before the above document was released; see, e.g., *New York Times*, September 27, 1989, p.11; October 31, 1989, p.8; *Sunday Times*, October 29, 1989, p.4. But it wasn't until January 1995 that the exact text became widely publicized and caused a storm in the UK, although ignored in the United States.

17  *The Times* (London), September 20, 1989, p.1

18  *New York Times*, November 21, 1991, p.14. It should be borne in mind, however, that Israel may have been influenced because of its hostility toward the PFLP-GC.

19  Reuters dispatch, datelined Tunis, February 26, 1992

20  *The Guardian*, February 24, 1995, p.7

21  Margaret Thatcher, *The Downing Street Years* (New York, 1993), pp.448-9.

22  *National Law Journal* (New York), September 25, 1995, p.A11, from papers filed in a New York court case.

23  *Barron's* (New York), December 17, 1990, pp.19, 22. A copy of the Interfor Report is in the author's possession, but he has been unable to locate a complete copy of it on the Internet.

24  *Barron's*, p.18.

25  *The Times* (London), November 1, 1990, p.3; *Washington Times*, October 31, 1990, p.3

26  Government Information, Justice, and Agriculture Subcommittee of the Committee on Government

Operations, House of Representatives, December 18, 1990, passim.

27  Ibid.

28  The film, "The Maltese Double Cross" (see below).

29  *Sunday Times* (London), April 16, 1989 (traces); Johnston, op. cit., p.79 (substantial). "The Maltese Double Cross" film mentions other reports of drugs found, by a Scottish policeman and a mountain rescue man.

30  *New York Times*, November 1, 1990

31  *Financial Times* (London), May 12, 1995, p.8, and article by John Ashton, leading 103 investigator, in *The Mail on Sunday* (London), June 9, 1996.

32  Ashton, op. cit.; *Wall Street Journal*, December 18, 1995, p.1, and December 18, 1996, p.B2

33  *The Guardian* (London), April 23, 1994, p.5

34  *Sunday Times* (London), May 7, 1995.

35  Francovich's former wife told the author that he had not had any symptoms of a heart problem before. However, the author also spoke to Dr. Cyril Wecht, of JFK "conspiracy" fame, who performed an autopsy on Francovich. Wecht stated that he found no reason to suspect foul play.

36  Re Abu Talb: (all 1989) *New York Times*, October 31, p.1; December 1, p.12; December 24, p.1; *Sunday Times* (London), November 12, p.3; December 5; *The Times* (London), December 21, p.5. Also the Associated Press, July 11, 2000

37  Cadman in "The Maltese Double Cross". Also see *The Guardian*, July 29, 1995, p.27

38  *New York Times*, February 2, 2001

39  Ibid.

40  *Electronic Telegraph UK News*, February 4, 2001

41  All quotations are from Koechler's report of February 3, 2001, easily found on the Internet

## Chapter Eleven

1   Mark Almond, *New Statesman* (London), February 3, 2003.
2   *Washington Post*, November 25, 2003, p.22; *Wall Street Journal*, November 24, 2003, p.1; Neil Clark, "Profile—George Soros," *New Statesman* (London), June 2, 2003; the "Central and Eastern Europe" section of the Annual Reports of the National Endowment for Democracy, beginning 1991, mention many of these programs, see also NED's website.
3   *The Irish Times*, October 12, 2000. For later information about conditions in Eastern Europe a Google search under [poverty children "eastern europe'] will produce many reports.
4   Last two sentences derived from an article by Mark Almond in *New Statesman* (London), February 3, 2003
5   *Washington Times*, March 1, 2002, p.16
6   Ibid.
7   National Endowment for Democracy, Annual Report 2002, pp.40-1
8   *The Slovak Spectator*, November 18, 2002
9   National Endowment for Democracy, Annual Report 2002, p.35
10  *The Slovak Spectator*, November 18, 2002
11  Ibid., November 17, 2002
12  Associated Press, November 22, 2002
13  *Washington Post*, September 23, 2002, p.15
14  *The Slovak Spectator*, November, 19, 2002
15  Interfax-Europe, February 3, 2003
16  *Miami Herald*, October 29, 2001; *The Guardian* (London), June 6, 2001
17  Both of Koch's remarks: Associated Press, October 6, 2001
18  *New York Times*, November 4, 2001, p.3
19  See Blum, *Killing Hope*, chapter 49
20  *Miami Herald*, October 29, 2001

21  Ibid.

22  *New York Times*, November 4, 2001, p.3

23  Nicaragua Network Hotline (Washington, DC), July 23, 2001, www.nicanet.org/pubs/hotline0723 2001.html; *The Guardian* (London), June 6, 2001

24  Nicaragua Network Hotline (Washington, DC), October 29, 2001; www.nicanet.org/pubs/hotline1029 2001.html; *New York Times*, November 4, 2001, p.3

25  *New York Times*, November 4, 2001, p.3

26  *The Observer* (London), July 14, 2002

27  Ibid.

28  *Washington Post*, August 5, 2002, p.9; ZNet Commentary, "Evo Morales and opposition to the US in Bolivia", by Erin Ralston in Bolivia, July 15, 2002 <www.zmag.org/ZNET.htm>

29  *New York Times*, November 3, 2001

30  *Washington Post*, February 23, 2002, p.18

31  *Financial Times* (London), September 26, 2001

32  *Washington Post*, April 3, 2002, p.1

33  Ibid. "Stratfor's Global Intelligence Update," May 27, 1999, current URL: http://www.stratfor.com/coms2/page_home

34  *Washington Post*, April 13, 2002

35  Stratfor's, op. cit.

36  *Washington Post*, April 13, 2002

37  Gregory Wilpert, "An Imminent Coup in Venezuela?", ZNet Commentary, www.zmag.org, April 11, 2002, Wilpert was a Fulbright scholar in Venezuela; Conn Hallinan, "U.S. cooking up a coup in Venezuela?", *San Francisco Examiner*, December 28, 2001

38  *Washington Post*, April 15, 2002, p.1

39  Ibid., April 13, 2002, p.17

40  State Department press statement, April 12, 2002

41  Agence France Presse, April 13, 2002

42  *New York Times*, April 13, 2002, p.16

43  *Washington Post*, April 15, 2002, p.1

44  The Associated Press, April 14, 2002

45  *Washington Post*, April 14, 2002, p.1

46  *The Times* (London), April 17, 2002; *Washington Post*, April 17, 2002, p.8, April 18, p.17 ($100,000)

47  *Washington Post*, April 21, 2002, p.1

48  Ibid., April 14, 2002, p.1

49  Ari Fleischer, White House press conference, April 16, 2001

50  *Washington Post*, April 13, 2002, p.1

51  National Endowment for Democracy, Annual Report 2002, p.55

52  Ibid., 2001, p.49

53  Ibid., 2001, p.54-5

54  Kim Scipes, "AFL-CIO in Venezuela: Déjå Vu All Over Again," *Labor Notes*, April 2004, www.labornotes.org, see archives

55  National Endowment for Democracy, Annual Report 2002, p. 61-2

56  *New York Times*, April 25, 2002; *The Observer* (London), April 21, 2002

57  See http://venezuelafoia.info to view the NED documents

58  *Washington Post*, July 26, 2004, p.16

59  *Boston Globe*, March 21, 2004; *Washington Post*, March 21, 2004

60  *Boston Globe*, March 21, 2004

61  *Christian Science Monitor*, March 19, 2004

62  *Boston Globe*, March 21, 2004

63  *Miami Herald*, March 28, 2004

64  Catherine Elton, Houston Chronicle Foreign Service, March 18, 2004

65  Ibid. The report added that "Arena denies having anything to do with the television ad, which it says was paid for by a private citizen whose name is shown in the commercial's final frame."

66  *Washington Post*, March 21, 2004

67  *Boston Globe*, March 21, 2004
68  *La Prensa*, (El Salvador) online edition, March 24, 2004. http://archive.laprensa.com.sv/20040324/nacion/nacion7.a sp
69  Catherine Elton, *Christian Science Monitor*, March 19, 2004
70  *Los Angeles Times*, May 21, 2002

## Chapter Twelve

1  *Congressional Record*, June 4, 1951, p.6602.
2  Paul Glickman, "The Adventures of a Premature Anti-Fascist", *Express* (San Francisco East Bay weekly), August 28, 1981. A Google search under "premature anti-fascists" will disclose many similar stories.
3  *San Francisco Chronicle*, December 26, 1980
4  *A Dictionary of Historical Quotations* (London 1985), quotation no. 763
5  Joel Kovel, *Red Hunting in the Promised Land: Anti-Communism and the Making of America* (New York, 1994), p.129
6  David Caute, *The Great Fear: The Anti-Communist Purge Under Truman and* Eisenhower (New York, 1978), pp.216-7
7  Albert E. Kahn, *High Treason: The Plot Against the People* (New York, 1950), p.328; the details of the incident first became public when the leading American journalist of the time, Drew Pearson, revealed them on his radio broadcast of April 10, 1949.
8  *The Guardian* (London), December 6, 1986 ("NATO rebuffs Russian approach"); *Los Angeles Times*, March 10, 1989 (op-ed by John Tirman); Ibid., October 25, 1989 ("U.S. Rejects Soviet Bid to Drop Alliances"); Ibid., October 26, 1989, p.7; TASS News Agency, March 9, 2000; Associated Press, June 16, 2001 ("Putin Cites 1954 NATO Document").
9  See Douglas Tottle, *Fraud, Famine and Fascism* (Toronto,

1987)

10  Morris Kominsky was the person. See his book, *The Hoaxers: Plain Liars, Fancy Liars, and Damned Liars* (Branden Press, Boston, 1970), pp.357, 360

11  TV speech, November 3, 1969, *Public Papers of the Presidents, Richard Nixon, 1969*, p.425

12  Cybercast News Service (www.cnsnews.com), December 30, 2002

13  *New York Times*, June 19, 1955, p.E2

14  Thorwald Esbensen, "How Far Have the Book Burners Gone?" in *School Executive*, May 1957

15  A detailed discussion of all three examples can be found in Kominsky, op. cit., pp.27-45, along with numerous other examples of anti-communist myths which went a long way toward creating an anti-Soviet atmosphere in the popular imagination.

16  Kominsky, op. cit., chapter 6

17  Elaine Tyler May, *Homeward Bound* (New York, 1988), pp.97-8

18  *The Guardian* (London), November 25, 1983; *The Observer* (London), October 30, 1983, p.9

19  *New York Times*, June 29, 1952, p.1; June 30, p.18

20  Ibid., June 22, 1953, p.1

21  Ibid., June 14, 1955, p.28; June 15, p.7; June 19, p.E2

22  Ibid., December 28, 1955; all the ellipsises are in the article.

23  Ibid., November 20, 1956, p.15

24  *Los Angeles Times Magazine*, December 15, 1991. CIA role in refugees fleeing: Bernard Fall, *The Two Vietnams* (New York, 1967, 2nd revised edition), pp.153-4; *The Pentagon Papers* (NY Times edition, 1971), Document No. 15, pp.53-66.

25  Victor Navasky, *Naming Names* (New York, 1980), p.335. Stern's broadcast was on October 6, 1958.

26  Fred Kaplan, *The Wizards of Armageddon* (1983), p.246

27  *Washington Post*, March 9, 1966, p.3

28  Cited in numerous places; e.g., Colman McCarthy's column in *The Washington Post*, May 11, 1993

29  *Washington Post*, February 4, 1968, p.B1.

30  *Los Angeles Times*, July 14, 1988

31  Erin Donahue, *San Francisco Chronicle*, October 4, 1978, p.4

32  United Press, February 1, 1980

33  *San Francisco Chronicle*, February 23, 1980, p.10

34  Associated Press, January 22, 1982

35  Edward Herman and Frank Brodhead, *The Rise and Fall of the Bulgarian Connection* (New York, 1986), passim; *Los Angeles Times*, September 15, 1991

36  *New York Times*, March 9, 1982, p.1; March 23, 1982, pp.1,14; *The Guardian* (London), November 3, 1983, March 29, 1984; *Washington Post*, May 30, 1986.

37  Julian Robinson, et al, "Yellow Rain: The Story Collapses", *Foreign Policy*, Fall 1987, pp.100-117; *New York Times*, August 31, 1987, p.14.

38  *San Francisco Chronicle*, May 28, 1981

39  Ibid., June 7, 1982

40  *International Herald Tribune*, November 8, 1982

41  Eric Bates, "What You Need to Know About Jesse Helms", *Mother Jones* magazine (San Francisco), May/June 1995

42  *The Standard* (London), August 13, 1984

43  *The Guardian* (London), January 4, 1986

44  Ibid., March 15, 1986

45  Ibid., September 4, 1986

46  Ibid., August 4, 1986

47  Ibid., September 16, 1986

48  Ibid., September 16, 1986 (column by Jill Tweedie); October 13, 1986

49  *San Francisco Chronicle*, May 7, 1987

50  *Wall Street Journal*, June 12, 1989, p.14; commentary by Alexander Cockburn, column in the *LA Weekly*, June 23-29, 1989

51  Daniel Greenberg, "The Disturbing Lesson of Soviet

Science", *Washington Post*, August 11, 1998; see also *The Guardian* (London), November 19, 1986

52  *Los Angeles Times*, February 22, 1993

53  Associated Press Online, February 17, 2001; *New Hampshire Sunday News*, February 18, 2001, column by Jack Kenny

54  http://www.victimsofcommunism.org/

## Chapter Thirteen

1  *Los Angeles Times*, June 26, 1988, p.8

2  Ibid., August 3, 1994

3  Ibid., March 16, 1995, p.1

4  Ibid.

5  In June and July 1945, Joint Chiefs of Staff committees predicted that between 20,000 and 46,000 Americans would die in the one or two invasions for which they had drawn contingency plans. While still in office, President Truman usually placed  the number at about a quarter of a million, but by 1955 had doubled it to half a million. Winston Churchill said the attacks had spared well over 1.2 million Allies. (Barton Bernstein, "The Myth of Lives Saved by A-bombs," *Los Angeles Times*, July 28, 1985, IV, p.1; Barton Bernstein, "Stimson, Conant, and Their Allies Explain the Decision to Use the Atomic Bomb," *Diplomatic History*, Winter 1993, p.48.)

6  Stewart Udall, *The Myths of August* (New York, 1994), pp.73, 75; Martin S. Quigley, *Peace Without Hiroshima* (Lanham, MD, 1991), pp.105-6; Charles L. Mee, Jr., *Meeting at Potsdam* (New York, 1975), p.76

7  Tim Weiner, "US Spied on its World War II Allies," *New York Times*, August 11, 1993, p.9

8  Udall, pp.73-79

9  Ibid., p.73. Vice President Truman was never informed about the bomb. After Roosevelt's death, when he assumed office, it was Secretary of State James Byrnes who briefed

him on the project. (Henry L. Stimson and McGeorge Bundy, *On Active Service in Peace and War* (New York, 1947). Bundy is recognized as the principal author of these Stimson memoirs.

10  Udall, p.76

11  Stimson, p.629

12  Mee, p.23

13  Ibid., pp.235-6; See also: Hearings Before the Committee on Armed Services and the Committee on Foreign Relations (US Senate), June 25, 1951, p.3113, for reference to another peace overture.

14  *Los Angeles Times*, January 9, 1995, p.5

15  Mee, p.239

16  Ibid., pp.75, 78-9; and William Manchester, *American Caesar: Douglas MacArthur 1880-1964* (Boston, 1978), p.437

17  Dwight Eisenhower, *The White House Years: Mandate for Change, 1953-1956* (New York, 1963), pp.312-3

18  In an attempt, as Churchill said, to "strangle at its birth" the infant Bolshevik state, the US launched tens of thousands of troops and sustained 5,000 casualties.

19  Mee, p.22

20  "In the Matter of J. Robert Oppenheimer", Transcript of Hearing Before Personnel Security Board, Washington, DC, April 12, 1954 to May 6, 1954 (Washington, DC 1954), p.173

21  Weiner, op. cit.

22  Weiner, op. cit.

23  Bernstein, *Diplomatic History*, pp.66-8. This passage, actually written by Bundy for "On Active Service", was deleted from that book because of pressure from State Department official George F. Kennan.

24  Mee, p.239

25  Ibid., pp.288-9

26  United States Strategic Bombing Survey (Pacific War), 1

July 1946, p.26

27  Edward Behr, *Hirohito: Beyond the Myth* (New York, 1989), chapter 24; *The Guardian* (London), June 18, 1983

## Chapter Fourteen

1   *New York Times*, May 30, 1994
2   William Blum, *Killing Hope: US Military and CIA Interventions Since World War II*, chapter 51.
3   Ibid.
4   *Christian Science Monitor*, June 10, 1996

## Chapter Seventeen

1   Associated Press (AP), May 11, 2001
2   US District Court, Southern District of Florida, case #98-3493, Criminal Complaint, September 14, 1998, "Conclusion" paragraph. Hereafter, "Criminal Complaint".
3   EFE News Service (based in Madrid, with branches in the US), March 28, 2001
4   *Miami Herald*, September 18, 1998
5   Criminal Complaint, paragraph 7
6   *New York Times*, March 3, 1980, p.1
7   EFE News Service, March 28, 2001
8   See for example *Miami Herald*, March 28, 2001, p.1B
9   Criminal Complaint, paragraph 7; see also paragraph 26.
10  Ibid., paragraph 19
11  *Miami Herald*, September 23, 1998
12  *Washington Post*, September 15, 1998, *Miami Herald*, September 16, 1998
13  US District Court, Southern District of Florida, Case No. 98-721, Second Superseding Indictment, May 7, 1999, Count 2, Section D
14  *Miami Herald*, September 16, 1998
15  Department of Justice, Bureau of Justice Statistics, reported to author by John Scalia, statistician at the bureau.

16 Associated Press, May 8, 2001

17 EFE News Service, March 28, 2001

18 Carl Nagin, "Backfire", *The New Yorker*, January 26, 1998, p.32

19 Jefferson Morley, "Shootdown", *Washington Post Magazine*, May 25, 1997, p.120

20 EFE News Service, February 1, 2001

21 Ibid., March 1, 2001

22 Associated Press, March 21, 2001, *Miami Herald*, March 22, 2001

23 *New York Times*, February 26, 1996, p.1

24 Associated Press, December 5, 2000

25 *New York Times*, February 26, 1996, p.1. It is not clear from the article whether the transmission was made by the FAA or by BTTR.

26 *The New Yorker*, op. cit., p.34

27 Second Superseding Indictment, op. cit., Count 3, Section A

28 *The New Yorker*, op. cit., p.33

29 *Newsweek*, March 11, 1996, p.48

30 Jane Franklin, *Cuba and the United States: A Chronological History* (Ocean Press, Australia, 1997), see index under "Planes used against Cuba"; William Blum, *Killing Hope: US Military and CIA Interventions Since World War II* (Common Courage Press, Maine, 1995), Cuba chapter.

31 *Washington Post*, February 27, 1996

## Chapter Eighteen

1 From the Introduction to Kim Philby, *My Silent War* (Great Britain, 1969), p.7

2 The preceding is adapted from an approach taken by Frank Mankiewicz in his book, *Perfectly Clear* (New York, 1973). The quoted words are from the Fourth, Sixth, and Eighth Amendments to the Constitution.

3   See Philip Colangelo, "The Secret FISA Court: Rubber Stamping on Rights" in *CovertAction Quarterly*, Summer 1995, #53, pp.43-9

4   *Washington Post*, Nov. 22, 1998, p.2

5   Ibid., October 31, 1998, p.8

6   FBI document, National Security Division, "Behavioral Analysis Program Team Report", June 20, 1996

7   Ironically, the FBI agent, Douglas Gregory, testified that apartheid was only "occasionally" brutal to blacks; that he believed Nelson Mandela to be a communist; and that South Africa "is a member of the Communist Bloc."

8   *Washington Post*, June 4, 1998

## Chapter Nineteen

1   *Newsday* (New York), February 27, 2004

2   Talk at UCLA, February 27, 2004; full text at: http://international.ucla.edu/article.asp?parentid=8320

3   *Washington Post*, June 4, 2003, p.18

4   Ibid., February 28, 2004

5   See William Blum's essay on NED at: http://members.aol.com/superogue/ned.htm

# Index

# About the Author

Williiam Blum left the State Department in 1967, abandoning his aspiration of becoming a Foreign Service Officer, because of his opposition to what the United States was doing in Vietnam.

He then became one of the founders and editors of the *Washington Free Press*, the first "alternative" newspaper in the capital.

Mr. Blum has been a freelance journalist in the United States, Europe and South America. His stay in Chile in 1972-3, writing about the Allende government's "socialist experiment" and its tragic overthrow in a CIA-designed coup, instilled in him a personal involvement and an even more heightened interest in what his government was doing in various parts of the world.

In the mid-1970's, he worked in London with former CIA officer Philip Agee and his associates on their project of exposing CIA personnel and their misdeeds.

His book on U.S. foreign policy, "Killing Hope: U.S. Military and CIA Interventions Since World War II", first published in 1995 and updated since, has received international acclaim. Noam Chomsky called it "Far and away the best book on the topic."

In 1999, he was one of the recipients of Project Censored's awards for "exemplary journalism" for writing one of the top ten censored stories of 1998, an article on how, in the 1980s, the United States gave Iraq the material to develop a chemical and biological warfare capability.

Blum's book "Rogue State: A Guide to the World's Only Superpower", was published in 2000. It was written in reaction to the bombing of Yugoslavia, which, we were told, was done for humanitarian purposes. The book is in effect a mini-encyclopedia of all the un-humanitarian actions of the US government during the past half century. It has been translated into a dozen languages.

In 2002, "West-Bloc Dissident: A Cold War Memoir" appeared.

During 2002-2003, Blum was a regular columnist for the magazine "The Ecologist", which is published in London and distributed globally.

In 2004, Blum was appointed as an advisor to the International Committee of the Green Party of the United States.